Praise

INCREASING

Jewish Wisdom & Gu

to Strengthen & Calm Bod

"An inspired, intelligent book that will teach you how to have a meaningful meditation practice. The YouTube meditations are a special bonus for beginners."

—**Nan Fink Gefen, PhD**, author, *Discovering Jewish Meditation: Instruction & Guidance for Learning an Ancient Spiritual Practice*

"I can tell immediately when I'm in the presence of a great teacher, one who offers wisdom with nuance and maturity rather than clichés and truisms. Elie Spitz is my teacher. Becoming whole requires a whole practice—not prayer or reflection or mindfulness or study or intuition or movement, but all of them in balance. Elie Spitz seamlessly integrates a lifetime of spiritual seeking and wisdom into this remarkable guide for wholly living."

—**Rabbi Mike Comins**, author, *Making Prayer Real: Leading Jewish Spiritual Voices on Why Prayer Is Difficult and What to Do about It*

"Offers wisdom and guidance for absolutely everyone."

—**Edith R. Brotman, PhD, RYT-500**, author, *Mussar Yoga: Blending an Ancient Jewish Spiritual Practice with Yoga to Transform Body and Soul*

"A thoroughly contemporary guide to Jewish spiritual practice, drawing on Jewish sources as well as a wide range of teachings from many traditions. An easy and plain-spoken guide to techniques of visualization and guided meditation."

—**Arthur Green**, author, *Judaism's Ten Best Ideas: A Brief Guide for Seekers*

"This inspiring work is a spiritual journey with wisdom and guidance to lead us toward a life of peace and wholeness.... A book to read and re-read, a book you will want to share with those you love."

—**Rabbi Naomi Levy**, founder and spiritual leader, Nashuva; author, *Hope Will Find You*

INCREASING
WHOLENESS

Jewish Wisdom & Guided Meditations
to Strengthen & Calm
Body, Heart, Mind & Spirit

RABBI ELIE KAPLAN SPITZ

Congregation
B'nai Israel
קהילת בני ישראל

*A Gift from Barbara and Joseph Baim with best
wishes to you for a New Year of peace both from
within and in the world.*

The Roslyn and Joseph Baim Family Foundation

Barbara and Joseph Baim

*In Loving Memories of
Roz Baim, David Marmor, and Bert Adler*
2015

Increasing Wholeness:
Jewish Wisdom and Guided Meditations to Strengthen and Calm Body, Heart, Mind and Spirit

2015 Quality Paperback Edition, First Printing
© 2015 by Elie Kaplan Spitz

Biblical and Talmudic translations are the author's, and Talmudic quotations are from the Babylonian Talmud unless otherwise indicated.

Library of Congress Cataloging-in-Publication Data

Spitz, Elie Kaplan, 1954– author.
 Increasing wholeness : Jewish wisdom and guided meditations to strengthen and calm body, heart, mind and spirit / Rabbi Elie Kaplan Spitz.
    pages cm
 ISBN 978-1-58023-823-6 (quality pbk.)—ISBN 978-1-58023-830-4 (ebook) 1. Meditation—Judaism. 2. Spiritual life—Judaism. I. Title.
 BM723.S675 2015
 296.7'2—dc23
                                                    2014048516

10 9 8 7 6 5 4 3 2 1

Manufactured in the United States of America
Cover design: Jenny Buono
Cover art: © Mamziolzi/Shutterstock
Interior design: Tim Holtz

For People of All Faiths, All Backgrounds
Jewish Lights Publishing
A Division of LongHill Partners, Inc.
Sunset Farm Offices, Route 4, P.O. Box 237
Woodstock, VT 05091
Tel: (802) 457-4000 Fax: (802) 457-4004
www.jewishlights.com

CONTENTS

WELCOME TO INCREASING WHOLENESS

"There is nothing new under the sun" (Ecclesiastes 1:9), and yet wisdom beckons with fresh insight. Marie Syrkin, a professor of English at Brandeis University, once informed me, "Only a few times a century does a person say something new. The art of speaking is to say the familiar in an unfamiliar way."

My goal is not to say something entirely new, rather it is to surprise you with ancient wisdom and imaginative insights that move you toward greater inner ease and effectiveness, offering you greater wholeness. By "wholeness" I mean a fuller sense of awareness of your inner life and greater integration and strengthening of the four dimensions of self: the physical, emotional, intellectual, and intuitive.

At our best, we may experience a taste of completeness infused with gratitude that prompts expressions of compassion and justice. At our best we are most alive: loving those around us and transcending our own personal needs, attuned to a caring, dynamic Presence intertwined with the whole of creation. The goal of this book is to enable you to live more frequently at your best, with inner peace while engaging with others.

Most people resist being told to change. And yet most of us would acknowledge that our lives are incomplete and that we live with an undertow of anxiety and reactivity. Most people would say, "Yes, I seek greater wisdom and inner peace." But change cannot be compelled from the outside. The motivation needs to emerge from within, and therefore tools for gaining greater inner wholeness are precisely those that address our inner life.

This book recognizes that we are often preoccupied jugglers, fragmented in our attention. We are challenged to discern priorities and to make time for that which is most important, especially family, friendship, faith, and personal growth and well-being. We yearn to breathe with greater ease, to become more focused, creative, loving, and at one with the world.

To achieve greater equilibrium and effectiveness, our minds utilize two complementary capacities: the analytic and the imaginative. In a scientific world, the analytic is often elevated as superior, even as "truth." Yet there are limitations to relying only on facts and logic. Imagination is needed for empathy, for creativity, and for making personal decisions, since what really matters to us is more intuitively known than calculated from a checklist. In the biblical description of Creation, God declares, "Let us make *adam* [an earthling] in our image and after our likeness" (Genesis 1:26). In the original Hebrew the roots of the two descriptive words are *tzelem* (image) and *dimyon* (likeness). Related roots are used in contemporary Hebrew for the words "camera" and "imagination." A photograph presents an object "as it is," although even then it is subject to changes in angle, light, and context. A painted portrait relies on the imagination of the artist in interpreting the subject by evoking what lies beneath the surface. A photograph and a painting of the same woman present very different perspectives—both of which contribute to an understanding of the subject. Albert Einstein, a master of the analytic, is said to have stated, "Logic will get you from A to B. Imagination will take you everywhere." We use imagination to dream, to communicate, to play, and to discern priorities. We rely on the rational mind to measure, to solve problems, to evaluate, and to validate. Both modes of understanding are necessary for wholeness.

At the beginning of that Creation story, we are told that the world was originally in a state of *tohu vavohu*, Hebrew for "chaos" or "unformed void." As the first act of Creation, God declared, "Let there be light"—and there was light (Genesis 1:3). This is not physical light, since the sun is only put into the sky on the fourth day. This light signifies awareness—thus, Creation begins with an articulated idea. After God's initial act, we are told, "And God saw that the light was good" (Genesis 1:4). Repeatedly, God surveys the unfolding of Creation and proclaims, "It is good" (Genesis 1:4, 10, 18, 21, 25, 31). Rabbi Simon Greenberg, a contemporary sage, emphasized that our sacred challenge is to appraise our world and to declare like

God, "It is good." To make such a statement is to read the daily newspaper and not to despair. To "see through God's eyes" is to pierce beneath the surface of uncertainty, stress, and even chaos. Inner peace comes with letting go of expectations that the world is perfect. With the combined light of analytic and imaginative awareness, we may perceive in the world an underlying unity and goodness.

Our worldview matters in fashioning a quiet place within. A key to quiet and contentment is the recognition that *happiness equals expectations met*. We may increase happiness by adjusting expectations. But if we set our goals too low, we fail to realize possibilities and find abiding contentment. Actualizing potential requires setting goals just beyond our immediate reach. Although stretching toward goals may cause some disappointment if we don't reach them, the alternative often results in wallowing or feeling stuck and failing to cultivate our potential. When we approach and even surpass our short- or long-term goals, we are rewarded with great satisfaction.

In this book, we will employ imaginative inner journeys to gain a greater understanding of expectations for ourselves and of others. We will simultaneously seek both inner ease and heightened awareness. These journeys will require a certain suspension of judgment, and the material that will emerge from such inner adventures is often paradoxical. We will see that when we reach inward most deeply, we become most universal, and when we reach outward most expansively, we may touch our core. The universal quest for inner peace emerges from knowing that we both long for unconditional acceptance as we are now and are willing to change. Only when a musical instrument's strings are pulled in two opposite directions simultaneously does the tautness enable a melodic sound. Likewise, imagination and analytic mind are both needed for attunement. After utilizing a guided inner journey, we will employ analytic thought to translate the insights into practical, reliable, and just action.

INTRODUCTION

A Tale of Responsibility

I write as a rabbi, a student of sacred writings and spiritual resources who has dedicated more than twenty-five years to teaching and counseling. I have found that meditation, guided imagery, prayer, and service can strengthen and calm our bodies, hearts, minds, and spirits. I write as a fellow traveler, seeking to elevate a good life toward greater wholeness and even holiness. I do not claim to live in a state of sublime enlightenment. I write this guidebook to address my own anxiety and yearning for sustained inner harmony and transcendence. I have come to accept vulnerability as a natural state. Life contains uncertainties and even danger, and we are wisely on guard. A false inner peace may entail passivity. And yet we may consciously engage in practices that enable us to truly live with greater steadiness and connection to those around us and to our core.

Many of the stories brought to me as a rabbi describe shifts throughout the day from confidence to vulnerability, from contentment to longing, from pessimism to optimism, and back again. We are often so busy with our immediate tasks—at home, in the community, and at work—that we are unaware of these swings and their underlying causes. While driving, preparing dinner, or falling asleep at night, we may catch ourselves trying to recall what it was that so troubled us earlier in the day. Yet whether we are attuned to the phenomenon or not, the inner shifts take a toll on our energy and on our relationships. Amid mood swings, we miss the opportunity to step back with a pause to identify what pulls us off-balance—physically, mentally, emotionally, and spiritually. We may grow impatient, overly sensitive, or overbearing as we try to impose greater control over the lives of those around us as a solution to our own instability and even chaos.

The life experience of Rabbi Simcha Bunim, a sage of nineteenth-century Ukraine, offers instruction. As a young rabbi, he sought to change the entire world. He traveled widely and preached with great intensity. When he paused, he saw that despite his passionate preaching, he had failed to make much of an impact. So he turned his attention to his hometown. Here too, his words went largely unheeded. "So be it," he thought. "I will start with my own family." He was soon exasperated. He looked at himself and concluded, "Before I try to reshape others, I need to start with myself. For the only control that we really have is over our own behavior and interpretation of events. If I am successful, I may realize my own capacity to change and model goodness for others." After he succeeded in changing himself, he saw that his family was different, his neighborhood was different, his city was different, and in a sense the entire world was different.[1]

Inner peace depends on the self-discipline to respond wisely to life's unfolding. We often cannot control what happens to us, only how we interpret those events. With willpower, we may choose the course of our subsequent action, even reshaping our habits. As stated in the *Big Book of Alcoholics Anonymous*, a text that incorporates centuries of spiritual wisdom, "We are here to sweep off our side of the street."[2] To make a positive change, we begin with recognizing the behaviors that we can control, while simultaneously reaching out lovingly to others. This book seeks to strengthen our self-awareness, willpower, and the traits that we want to define us.

Ancient Practices Across Faiths

Practical resources and everyday tools have developed across faiths and over the centuries for us to cultivate our ability to pause before reacting, to step back and gain perspective, to reach a quiet, still place in order to make wise choices. Meditation clears the mind through single-pointed concentration, promoting tranquility and clarity. Visualization engages the imagination to make more tangible and accessible what is otherwise elusive, whether a memory, qualities of character, or an image of God. Sacred texts offer narratives, prayers, and blessings that allow us to connect to a Presence beyond our individual self and that elicit our deepest insights. Although universally found, each of these spiritual practices requires personalization.

The process of acquiring sacred wisdom may be compared to preparing a cup of tea. Licking tea leaves is not particularly satisfying. To produce a tasty cup of tea requires that we add hot water to dried leaves placed in a container and patiently allow them to steep. The tea leaves are the received ideas of liturgy, Torah text, or meditation technique, whether presented as dry ink on a page or as spoken instruction. We need to bring our life experience—the hot liquid—to craft a personal, uplifting brew. We also need time for a steady focus, and a container, or specific setting, for a full-bodied experience that provides a fresh taste.

Moving toward inner wholeness involves a constancy of effort with a wisdom practice. A reward for such effort is cultivating the capacity to pause and reflect before acting. In my own life, I rely on an array of daily practices to increase my inner balance and my awareness of the present, including daily meditation, prayer, and study of sacred texts.

Treasures Close to Home

My spiritual life is quite different from that of my pious grandfather who lived in Eastern Europe before the end of the Second World War. He viewed the Torah, the Five Books of Moses, as dictated by God to Moses letter by letter. I view the Torah as written by humans within the context of history. And yet I prize the Torah as a product of inspiration, of humans reaching to see the world as if from God's point of view, composing a text that is infused with a Consciousness that transcends place and time. I experience the Torah as both a love letter from God and as morally troubling. There are passages that reflect the views of society in ancient times, such as the acceptance of slavery or the secondary status of women. No sacred document remains fixed as time passes, and no one faith possesses "the Truth," exclusive access to God's revelation. In my studies, I join the conversation of Torah commentators across generations, seeing myself as a student and servant of God. In rereading scripture, I am startled by the purposefulness of each word and the layers of significance to be uncovered in each narrative and law. Torah possesses the richness of a collective dream, filled with symbolism awaiting interpretation.

Where my saintly grandfather's circle was largely composed of fellow faithful Jews, my community includes practitioners of many religions who worship, study, and serve together. Although my Jewish faith is my spiritual home, I explore and engage a broader world. I return home from travels to local houses of worship and to temples, shrines, and churches far away with precious souvenirs of insight from congregations and religious leaders that I incorporate into my own practice. And yet I usually find that the remarkable wisdom I have gleaned from others was already present in my own tradition.

What we seek in the way of wisdom may already exist right before us. I have gained guidance from great teachers of Buddhism, Hinduism, Islam, and Christianity. I have traveled around the globe to learn from religious leaders, whether at a Hindu temple on the island of Kauai or at a Christian monastery dedicated to song and silence in Burgundy, France. Spiritual growth requires the willingness to honor helpful ideas wherever they are found, the commitment to explore deeply within the tradition one knows best, and the discipline to work at a practice. World faiths share much because we as humans are more alike than different, with similar physical processes, emotional experiences, thinking patterns, and spiritual questions. Differing faiths are analogous to streams emerging from a common water source, each distinctive and yet, at their best, each offering a taste of divine wisdom. We access spiritual insight through studies of the words of sages, whether of our chosen faith tradition or others, and by addressing our personal fears. We deepen those insights and move toward wholeness through humbly and steadfastly engaging with ancient spiritual practices and internalizing them as our own.

Guided Meditation

Much of the wisdom of traditional faiths is already present in the deepest recesses of our being, which is why those insights resonate for us. Guided meditation offers us a path into our inner life and the wisdom that lies at our core. Among the techniques for going inward is guided visualization in the form of wakeful dreaming. I will repeatedly offer these types of exercises with words and videos throughout this book. Visualization depends on imagination to encounter the past vividly or to conjure up entirely new experiences. It helps greatly to have a guide to direct us inward so as to let go of analytic thought and allow for spontaneous experiences.

I was privileged to participate in weekly visualizations over several years with two artists of the imagination, Colette Aboulker-Muscat of Jerusalem[3] and Marielle Fuller of Laguna Beach, California.[4] Each of these women led original imagery sessions up until just weeks before their respective deaths at the age of ninety-three. My many experiences of guided imagination with them offered insight and greater ease in going inward. I culled from their techniques a fashioning of imageries that felt natural for me to use in aiding others.

Participating in a guided visualization is like dancing: refraining from self-consciously watching ourselves, trusting that we are doing just fine, and allowing for surprise. When we suspend judgment or analysis during guided visualization, leaving such reflection for later, riveting images and profound insights arise spontaneously.

To enable your participation in the exercises, particularly the guided meditations, this book offers videos that can be accessed by QR codes (those boxes with the squiggles). You can download a free QR code reader app onto your phone from your phone's app store. Then, using your smartphone camera, "scan" the QR code by taking a picture of it. That video will automatically appear in your smartphone browser. You can also simply use the web address listed underneath each QR code. (Please note that the web addresses are case sensitive, so you'll need to type them exactly as they appear in the text.)

http://youtu.be/
rcLYRwkVrdM

"Try It to Know If You Like It"

The tools that I will offer to increase your inner awareness and wholeness address all aspects of your full self: the physical, emotional, intellectual, and spiritual. By strengthening and integrating these four dimensions we become wiser and more attuned to our inner life, the world around us, and the Divine. By engaging with meditation, for instance, you will enhance concentration and physical calm. Of course the tools that I will share are not the only available resources to attain greater wholeness. This book simply offers a variety of complementary experiences with the hope that you will find a few that particularly resonate for you and are worth incorporating into your daily practice.

A literal appreciation for different tastes is an insight that has emerged with greater clarity in recent decades in the food business.[5] Prior to the mid-1980s, leaders in the food industry tended to look for the "perfect product," the product that would ideally make all its customers happy. Prego hired Dr. Howard Moskowitz, who had earned his doctorate at Harvard in clinical psychology, to investigate. He directed the preparation of forty-five different kinds of spaghetti sauce, varying in thickness, amount of garlic, tartness, salt, visible solids, and more. Each participant was asked to taste and rate ten of the sauces. Analyzing the data, Moskowitz concluded that there was no one perfect sauce but rather several appealing sauces. People's preferences fell into one of three categories: plain, spicy, and chunky. Prego soon sold the first commercial chunky spaghetti sauce and over the next decade would sell more than $600 million of it.

Moskowitz taught two things with his approach to food. The first was that "the mind does not know what the tongue wants." He succeeded by getting people to taste and respond, rather than asking about preferences in the abstract. As another example, he found that when people were asked what kind of coffee they liked, they consistently responded, "A dark, rich, hardy roast." Yet, when given different coffees to taste, only a third preferred the dark, rich, and hardy roast. Many tasters preferred a milky, weak coffee. We know what we like based on experience and not on preconceived notions.

Moskowitz's second finding was that there is no universally loved sauce or cup of coffee, but clusters of preferences. When a group of people are given only one kind of coffee, the overall rating is 60 on a scale of 100. When given a choice from several options, the average rating of the drink goes up to a score of 75. A score of 60 is a shrug; a 75 is a smile. Choice is essential to optimize success, whether with food or self-growth.

In the pages that follow, there are many different kinds of exercises. The goal is to offer you many tastes with the hope that you will find a pattern of practice that suits your disposition. When offered a "try this," please do. It is my hope that you will incorporate a variety of experiences from this book into your regular practice to deepen your self-awareness, nurture your inner wholeness, and even enable self-transcendence. Although there are differing styles and needs, you will find that certain universals, such as a focus on breath, will enable you to gain greater balance from within. The instruction to breathe out is to create a focal point. Breathing in will occur naturally.

This book offers guided meditations using breath, visualization of inner journeys, recitation of blessings of gratitude, and study of sacred texts. Read the book slowly, savor the experiences, and access your imagination. To more fully engage in the experience of going inward, I provide videos to introduce the chapters and guide you in the exercises. When you get to a link, please take the time to pause to allow the video to facilitate a described experience. Notice how your increasing calm simplifies relationships, helps resolve conflicts, and focuses you on what really matters.

The test of a spiritual teaching is whether it leads to better prayer. The test of prayer is whether it leads to action beyond the self, actions of compassion and justice. Supporting and serving those in need through small acts of kindness or ongoing commitments of time will add purpose and increase your steadiness. Increasing moments of wonder and self-transcendence will elicit awareness of a Divine Presence and perspective that is intertwined with the whole of creation and goes beyond it. A folk saying teaches, "The best time to plant a tree is twenty years ago; the second best time is now." You have the ability to choose change and to do so now. Please join me in planting and cultivating inner seeds of wisdom toward harvesting greater wholeness.

CHAPTER ONE

SEEKING GREATER WHOLENESS

A widespread "secret" is that each of us feels incomplete. It is a secret because we often mask our vulnerability in order to protect ourselves and to look more attractive. And yet we each fluctuate in the course of any day between calm and unease. Even when we enjoy life's daily satisfactions, there is also an inner gnawing over unresolved problems. To quote Helen Telushkin, mother of Rabbi Joseph Telushkin, "The only people that I know who are very happy are the people that I do not know very well." We naturally yearn for simpler times, knowing that we are surrounded by great beauty, kindness, and wonder, but we seesaw between the enjoyment of life's goodness and anxiety over its disappointments.

I turn to scripture as a sacred story to enhance perspective, offering a balcony-like view on my own experiences. Reading Genesis chapters 1 and 6 closely, we find dramatic shifts in God's appraisal of Creation, showing that our own emotional swings are quite normal.

Sacred Text Study: God's Emotional Life

In the first chapter of Genesis, after God surveys each day (except the second), God declares, "It is good." We feel God's joy. On the sixth day, the day of fashioning animals and humans, God's enthusiasm grows. On this day, God exclaims, "And it is very good." Five chapters later, Creation has gone awry; God's trust in humanity is shattered:

> The Eternal saw that human wickedness on earth was increasing and how every product of his innermost thought was only for evil all the time. And the Eternal regretted having made humanity on earth, and God was anguished to the core. The Eternal said, "I will

wipe out from the earth the earthlings that I have created—humans
together with animals, creeping crawlers, and birds of the sky—for
I regret that I made them." But Noah found favor in the eyes of the
Eternal. (Genesis 6:5–8)

What a dramatic shift from divine contentment to divine resentment!
Here in the Torah, God is learning on the job the difficulty of forging
relationships and maintaining harmony. We can identify with God's angst.
Consider the outrage that you have felt witnessing selfishness, callousness, and even intentional cruelty. Fortunately, God has the wisdom
to pause rather than hurtle forward with outrage. In that pause, God
observes Noah. The disappointment with humankind is still present, but
God's perspective shifts upon finding hope. God will enter into a covenant
with Noah, marking with the rainbow the promise never to destroy the
world again. God's attentive pause provides time and the opportunity to
consider a new perspective. In the story of Noah, God's conscious pause
leads to renewal.

Later in the Torah, before Moses ascends Mount Sinai to receive the Ten
Commandments, the biblical text quotes God as saying, "Go up to Me on
the mountain and be there" (Exodus 24:12). For the traditionally faithful,
each word of the Torah is purposeful. The phrase "and be there" seems
unnecessary.[1] Rabbi Menachem Mendel of Kotzk, teaching in Poland in the
first half of the nineteenth century, observed that God's words express to
Moses the need for more than physical presence. Atop Mount Sinai, Moses
needs full attentiveness.[2]

Learning to bring a fuller awareness moment by moment is our path
to wholeness and even divine encounter. When fully present, we are
awake to gratitude and a worldview that simultaneously acknowledges
the world's messiness and goodness. All too often we are distracted by
our fears and we only notice what we expect to see. The early Rabbis
imagined two Israelite slaves, Shimon and Levi, as they departed Egypt
for the Promised Land. As the waters of the Reed Sea parted, they moved
forward along the path of dry land with eyes cast downward. Shimon
commented, "Mud here, mud there." Levi rejoined, "Bricks here, bricks
there."[3] Neither man appreciated what had just happened or the immediate miracle of the waters gathered as walls at either side. Each saw only

the familiar mud, the source of the bricks of their daily labor. Likewise, without peripheral vision for the larger world and attentiveness for what is immediately before us, we miss encountering wonder and memorable surprises.

Cultivating the art of the attentive pause—especially when we feel disappointed, angry, or overburdened—opens possibilities. With practice, we may find that meditation, walking, chanting, singing, knitting, or dancing brings us to rest in an interior spaciousness that transcends our immediate surroundings. In inner stillness, we may experience the grace of belonging, guidance, and joy that transcend the logic of the mind. At times, I experience these deep states of awareness as encounters with an abiding Divine Presence and Mystery.

In the course of writing this book, I have explored the place of God in my life and how faith factors into a worldview. After all, I am a rabbi and am fascinated by sacred experiences and religious beliefs. Each of us may experience a relationship with the Divine differently. As the early Jewish sages commented, "God is like a mirror. The mirror never changes, but everyone who looks at it sees a different face."[4] What is sure is that we use different metaphors to describe our experience with the Divine. My belief in God emerges more from intuition than from logic. God is an abiding Consciousness to whom I express gratitude and who guides me forward toward fulfilling my potential for wholeness and love. To live spiritually is to view the world as if through the eyes of the Creator, at times with disappointment and always with a sense of awe and responsibility.

 Try This: **Identifying an Obstacle to Inner Peace**

Stand or sit in a chair, feet flat on the floor, hands relaxed. Close your eyes. Breathe out. In a moment, with your image-making talent, you will reach into your clothing above your heart and find an object that represents an impediment to your inner ease. Allow yourself to be surprised by what object emerges.

http://youtu.be/
yPmcMX13huM

Now with your mind's eye, reach in beneath your clothes above your heart and pull out an object identified with a current tension. Examine it closely using multiple senses, and become aware of what the object represents to you.

Breathe in the tension identified with the problem, and as you breathe out, spontaneously express in a word or phrase a response to the problem.

Breathe out and feel increased inner ease. Become aware of the possibility and goodness of change. In a moment you will return to wakefulness while retaining a strong memory of the object and the insight as to finding resolution.

Breathe out and open your eyes.

Breath as Life

Across faiths, breath is a vehicle for spiritual discovery and connection to something greater than the individual. With each exhalation we breathe ourselves into the world, and with each inhalation we literally breathe in our surroundings. We are each at once permeable and uniquely self-contained. For over twenty years I have begun most days with a focus on the rhythms and sensations of breathing. My practice combines the teachings of ancient sages and contemporary teachers from diverse backgrounds.

My wife was told in medical school that the first breath we inhale at birth remains in the depths of our lungs and leaves us only with our final exhalation, so that our breath is a link to our origins. The Bible goes even further, saying that our breath emerged at the dawn of time and from its very Source. And God "breathed into his nostrils the breath of life, and the earthling became a living being" (Genesis 2:7). In Hebrew, the words for "breath" and "soul" are the same word, *neshamah*. Breath is linked to consciousness. Consider the following exercise to gain awareness of the close ties between bodily breath and heart, mind, and spirit.

 Try This: **Breath, Eyes, and Mood**

Stand and extend one hand outward with your palm facing you and your arm outstretched about six inches away from your body, almost as if you were holding an open book away from your body. Breathe out. Become aware of your breath, and focus your eyes on your lowered palm. With a straight elbow, slowly

http://youtu.be/ ZCt4aKJpLus

raise your arm upward until your palm is above your head. Notice the change in your breathing as you slowly raise your hand and your eyes move upward. Repeat the exercise with the awareness that when your palm reaches a location in space just above the horizon, your chest opens up and your breathing becomes more expansive.

Now focus again on your lowered palm and place on it an image that you associate with anxiety—whether a person, an object, or a task. As you look down at your palm, notice that your breathing is relatively short and your chest constricted. Focus on the negative image, and slowly raise your outstretched hand in front of you toward the ceiling. Notice what happens. Just above eye level, the negative image falls away. It is hard to hold a negative thought when your eyes are gazing above the horizon and your breathing opens up. The slipping away of negativity is quite surprising. Try it again. Put that negative image on your palm and notice that it slides away when you start breathing more expansively, usually when your gaze is just above the horizon.

Remember Shimon and Levi, who failed to lift up their eyes and marvel at the miracle of the splitting of the Reed Sea as they fled Egypt toward freedom? The physical and emotional planes on which we live overlap and shape each other, as with breath and vision. To describe an anxious or frenzied state we say, "I could not catch my breath," and for a sad mood, "I was downcast." When calm, we exude, "I was breathing easy" and "Things were looking up."

When we are short of breath, it is hard to think straight. When we are calm, we can more readily access memories from long ago and find the answers to questions we sought during wakefulness. When we are deeply focused and relaxed on a sustained level, we may intuitively become aware of insights that have long eluded us. Although such moments of clarity may feel like a gift, they can be cultivated through dedication and practice. Alignment of the physical (body), emotional (heart), intellectual (mind), and intuitive (spirit) planes of our existence allows us to move toward the wholeness that we seek. In the coming chapters, we will explore and try to better integrate each of these four dimensions.

Components of Self

As we begin to explore the four dimensions of the inner self, it is helpful to discuss the parallels to the Jewish mystics' description of a multifaceted soul. Ideas have a history and the following words for *soul* were used with different emphases at different times.[5] Elements of the soul are nested one within the other like colorfully painted Russian *matryoshka* dolls. The mystics identify each of these realms of awareness with a concept found in the Bible. Studying this ancient insight into the four planes on which we exist informs our understanding of our complexity and our capacity to live with greater wholeness.

Nefesh—Physical Vitality

Jewish mystics largely shared their insights orally until the twelfth century, when they began to put their ideas into writing. In the *Zohar*, the influential commentary to the Torah that first appeared at the end of the thirteenth century, the physical soul is labeled as *nefesh*. In the story of Creation, both water creatures and land animals are called *nefesh chayah*, "living beings" (see Genesis 1:20–21, 24). The *nefesh* makes possible animation that is absent from a rock, serving as a life force that allows us to breathe, grow, sense, and do.

Ruach—Emotions

Our emotional aspect is referred to as *ruach*, which also means "wind." In speaking to Noah of the flood to come, God refers to living beings as *ruach chayim*, "breathers of life" (Genesis 6:17).[6] Emotions rise and fall like the wind, unseen but wielding great force. In the mystical tradition, both humans and animals possess *nefesh* and *ruach*, vitality and emotions.

Neshamah—Mind

Neshamah describes a plane of existence that is distinctive to humans, the plane associated with the mind. In the Creation story, God breathes the soul/breath of life, *nishmat chayim* (Genesis 2:7), into Adam. Onkelos, a prominent Roman nobleman in first-century Israel who converted to Judaism, was among the first translators of the Hebrew Bible. He influentially rendered *nishmat chayim* into Aramaic, the language in Israel at the time of Jesus, as *ruach memalela*, "a speaking spirit." Speech enables reflection, idea formation, and transmission of culture. In the Genesis account, as we saw earlier, God distinctly uses words as the vehicle of Creation. For example, when God says, "Let there be light"—*zap*—"there was light"

(Genesis 1:3). Our ability to speak mirrors God's capacity to reason, to create, and to establish a record that persists across time and space.

Chai—Spirit or Intuition

The fourth plane of consciousness is the intuitive. In the *Zohar*, this plane is folded into the category of *neshamah*.[7] Later mystics pulled out the intuitive dimension as a separate category. From the sixteenth century onward, Jewish thinkers used *neshamah* to refer to the analytic mind as the faculty of observation, measurement, formula making, and verification. The facet of self we think of as "intuition" was identified as a higher level of encountering the world. The mystics used the Hebrew acronym *chai* (*chet-yud*), meaning "life," to refer to two overlapping capacities: *chayah*, "aliveness," referring to spontaneous insights drawn as if from beyond the self, and *yehidah*, or "uniqueness," as the experience of floating in the expansiveness of God's presence and glimpsing the unity of life from God's point of view.

Those who went before us offer a vocabulary that points toward self-actualization by integration of a multifaceted inner life. Whether or not we see ourselves as a mystic, each of us may strengthen awareness, functioning, and connection of our four planes of self.

Taking a Bite

The value of a spiritual practice is known only through personal experience. Undertaking meditation, prayer, or sacred text study may at first feel daunting and unfamiliar. Such a defensive posture is natural with any new undertaking. The way to begin is opening to experience. Just as words alone cannot convey the taste of a lemon, we need to take a bite to engage the flavor. Likewise, reading a cookbook recipe does not reveal if you will enjoy a described dish; you have to literally smell and taste the results. In this book, I offer both stories and theory, but the emphasis is on guiding you into experiences, whether new or previously tried, so that you will draw out your own insights and further integrate the components of your inner self.

Similarly, in moving forward, your wisdom will emerge from taking calculated risks. A divorcée, for instance, shared her fears in starting to date: "How will I know the kind of person I should go out with? How will I know if I should move forward in a relationship? Which parts of my past should I shed and which should I strengthen?" Mourning the loss of her marriage took time. When she felt ready, she began to date, and in doing so she observed what made her feel valued, safe, and happy. Her questions gained clarity, if not full resolution, through the combination of action and reflection.

There is also a need to distinguish past experiences from current reality. A highly anxious father came to me recently before his daughter's back surgery to correct her scoliosis. He shared that years before, his father had entered a hospital for a heart transplant and never emerged because his organs had shut down during the surgery. The son was subsequently filled with fear upon entering a hospital. I emphasized that his teenage daughter was very different from her grandfather, who had suffered from heart disease for many years, which had compromised the health of other organs. "Your daughter is healthy—and back surgery," I said, "does not pose the dangers of a heart transplant." To aid him in making that distinction, I encouraged him to write letters to and from God, an exercise that I will describe in greater detail later. I also advised him to draw a circle for focus on an index card and to write above it, "My daughter will be fine," and to place the index card on the bathroom mirror for regular reminders of trust. When a loved one is ill, it is natural to experience fear, but this is reduced when we employ our minds to make distinctions. In advancing our own lives, we need goals and the willingness to employ self-discipline, an inquisitive mind, and risk taking.

Beware of False Promises

In seeking greater wholeness, beware of instructors who promise, "If you perform this set of exercises, you will be relieved of all anxiety and experience enduring joy." The revered mystic known as the Baal Shem Tov, who founded Hasidism, a Jewish folk-mystical tradition, in eighteenth-century Ukraine, taught, "How do you determine if 'holy men' are charlatans? Ask them if they can rid you of all your prideful thoughts. If they say 'yes,' know that they are fakes."[8] Even more dramatically, a ninth-century Zen Buddhist sage charged, "If you meet the Buddha, kill the Buddha!"[9] These warnings are intended to protect followers from charismatic personalities who claim to have all the answers for total transformation. The reality is that we will invariably encounter feelings of physical exhaustion, anxious vulnerability, racing thoughts, and spiritual quandaries. Ancient practices offer greater calm, but not an end to the physical, emotional, intellectual, and spiritual swings that come with being alive in this world.

Rabbi Alan Lew was a seasoned practitioner of meditation before he began rabbinical school at the age of thirty-eight. His return to Jewish practice is well described in his memoir *One God Clapping*.[10] Alan had a tremendous capacity for concentration. As a student, he would literally sit for hours of uninterrupted study, and he excelled. As a rabbi of a large synagogue in San Francisco, he organized a daily meditation group that met each morning for an hour before the start of the formal prayer services. Among Alan's poems is the following:

> After twenty minutes of Yoga, forty-five
> minutes of meditation, forty minutes of
> prayer, a half-hour of exercise and
> a half-hour bath, I felt
> pretty good for a few minutes.[11]

"For a few minutes" is not much—and yet it is a great deal. Rabbi Lew was modest, even self-effacing. His "few minutes" rippled into his day. His spiritual practice helped define him as a man of calm resolve and steadfast care of others. Although there are those who overpromise results, there are also teachers of integrity who convey genuine skills. Although no one spiritual technique will meet all of your needs, greater equilibrium can come from study with such teachers and commitment to regular spiritual practice.

Sacred Text Study: Mount Sinai's Action Plan

The decision to move toward wholeness may come upon us suddenly or over time, perhaps when we lose a loved one or experience a sudden change in life, or as everyday struggles with conflict and commitments reach the point of overwhelming us. As we set off on the path to change, we need both motivation and a plan. This is a teaching that is illuminated by the biblical text. Specifically, the motivational drama of Mount Sinai and the Ten Commandments contrasts with the myriad laws that immediately follow. The scene opens at the foot of Mount Sinai, where the Israelites witness a magnificent sound and light show: "There was thunder and lightning and a thick cloud upon the mount.... Now Mount Sinai was smoking because the Eternal descended upon it in fire ... and the whole mount trembled greatly" (Exodus 19:16, 18). Then God's voice is heard as if from atop Mount Sinai. God addresses the entire people (Exodus 19–20). The words of the Ten Commandments are concise and easy to remember, providing an overview of a relationship with God and foundational ethical guidelines. Mount Sinai's presentation is supremely motivational. The plan of action immediately follows, detailed in one hundred verses of ritual and ethical laws, from dealing with the theft of an ox to fair treatment of strangers in the land (Exodus 21–24).

Likewise, when we seek to move toward wholeness, we recognize the need for both a target and an action plan. Similarly, my physical therapist has given me daily exercises to alleviate shoulder pain. The idea alone of living without pain does not produce results. Change requires a full-bodied, detail-oriented set of routines.

After God delivers the laws, the Israelites respond, "All that the Eternal has spoken we will do and we will hear" (Exodus 24:7). When we commit to act and to learn, we may progress toward our goals. We are limited in time and energy and need to carefully choose where to focus our attention and what warrants a plan for the future.

In most areas of our lives, we rely on the expertise of others. For example, we may start our cars with little understanding of what takes place under the hood. Yet the areas that we care about most deeply we study intently. A connoisseur of wine, for instance, through intent study develops the capacity to distinguish nuanced smells and subtle tastes.[12] In seeking excellence in our chosen profession, we keep up with the latest technical ideas, often marked by a rarefied vocabulary. To learn ourselves well warrants close attention to specifics, too, both theoretical and practical. Personal growth entails the investment of time. There are no shortcuts that lead to substantial changes in how we see ourselves and react to life.

Achieving Resolutions

Moving toward wholeness entails setting clear and attainable goals and establishing steps to achieve those goals. The obstacle we so often encounter in achieving New Year's resolutions is that we set lofty goals, such as growing spiritually or getting fit or reading more, without a specific plan, such as practicing meditation for a week, walking thirty minutes each morning, or keeping a book in the car. The following five steps outline essential ingredients for making positive change.

1. Goals: Set specific, clear, attainable goals, simple both to explain and to execute, with benchmarks to note progress.
2. Journal: Write on a regular basis to reflect on your progress and to reinforce your purpose.
3. Partner: Converse with another person who is undertaking the same process to discuss your experiences and share advice, thereby reinforcing your motivation and feeling nourished by friendship.
4. Anticipate setbacks: Be gentle with yourself. Taking on new habits goes against the grain of ease and familiarity. When you miss a day's practice, just return to the path the following day.
5. Celebrate: On meeting a goal, such as completing a week of meditation or a chapter of this book, congratulate yourself on your progress.

✺ Try This: **Epsom Salt Bath**

An underpinning of this book is that perspective is gained with enhanced calm. Toward that end, consider taking an Epsom salt bath. In the words of Dr. Mehmet Oz, "Epsom salt is a natural exfoliant and anti-inflammation remedy that can be used to treat dry skin, sore muscles, small wounds and even to fight illness. It can also be added to any bath or foot soak to create a luxurious at-home spa experience."[13]

> Epsom salt is found in most pharmacies and usually comes in a container of four to six cups. Pour the entire container into the bath and fill with very hot water, both to ensure that the Epsom salt dissolves and to add to your relaxation. Ease into the water, because of the high temperature. Bathe for twenty minutes, rinse, and then lie down for twenty minutes. Allow yourself to relax, with no other agenda.
> Consider taking such a bath as a weekly commitment to yourself.

Seeing the Familiar in Unfamiliar Ways

Ecclesiastes declared over two millennia ago, "There is a phenomenon of which it is said, 'Look, this one is new!' but it has already occurred in ages that went long before us" (Ecclesiastes 1:10). I hope to prompt you to see the familiar in unfamiliar ways by using tried-and-true practices that will change you from within. With patience, perseverance, and practice, you can nurture your wholeness. When you encounter the inevitable everyday disappointments, the frustrations of meeting competing commitments, or the world's chaos, you will respond with greater patience, wisdom, and steadiness. Inner integration is a foundation for reaching out beyond yourself with compassion and effectiveness.

This book is structured along the lines of the Jewish daily liturgy, which moves sequentially from body to heart to mind to spirit to hand. This flow will allow you to appreciate the interconnection of your inner life with your sacred yearnings and deeds. It also emphasizes that you are multifaceted and that your unity entails recognizing and aligning yourself with the world and God. Traditional Jewish daily prayer ends with a call for peace: "May God, who makes peace in the heavens, make peace below for all of us." The yearning for peace and wholeness comes to us across the generations and points us toward an abiding aspiration.

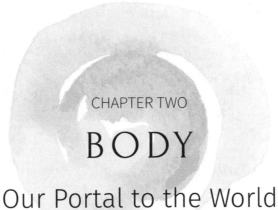

CHAPTER TWO

BODY

Our Portal to the World

In the words of author Sherril Jaffe, "Having a body is like having a big dog."[1] We have to walk our bodies and nurture our physical well-being with healthy eating, adequate sleep, enjoyable play, and regular exercise, all of which take time and discipline. Rabbi Simon Greenberg taught, "When the world does not look right, take a nap."[2] Our physicality affects our perceptions and thereby our thoughts and moods. This chapter will explore the miracle of our bodies and the interrelation of all that is physical with the emotional, intellectual, and spiritual planes on which we live our lives. Both honoring and honing our physicality are essential to wholeness.

http://youtu.be/
WYTHEnO3SUE

At a talk for my book *Does the Soul Survive?*[3] a member of the audience asked, "Do you believe in survival of the soul?" I replied, "Yes. Weighing evidence as a juror, I'm convinced that there is a quality of awareness that persists after death. And yet I'm not sure who I am without my body. When I think of Elie, I think of the person I see in the mirror and the voice that you are now hearing. So when I consider an afterlife, I'm unsure what an afterlife really means for Elie." Our identity is intrinsically linked to our bodies. All that we experience is filtered through our physical brains.

Some spiritual teachers across the spectrum of faiths have stated, "You don't have a soul. You *are* a soul. You *have* a body."[4] Such a viewpoint reduces the importance of our physicality by drawing a distinct divide between body and soul, or spirit. But they are profoundly interconnected. This perspective was expressed by the British poet and artist William Blake: "Man has no Body distinct from his Soul; for that called Body is a portion of Soul discerned by the five Senses, the chief inlets of Soul in this age."[5] Just as wine stains the inside of a clay jug and the vessel in turn imparts a particular flavor to the liquid, so soul and body interpenetrate. As soul is consciousness, our awareness is profoundly shaped by the use of our senses and the well-being of our bodies.

Each of Us Is Unique

When we speak of physical and spiritual wholeness, we also acknowledge that each of us is unique. As the early Rabbis marveled, "A king of flesh and blood stamps his image on a coin and all such coins look alike; but the King of Kings put the stamp on the first human and no person is like any other" (*Mishnah Sanhedrin* 4:5; *Sanhedrin* 37a). Consider how few features there are on a human face: skin and hair color, two eyes, two ears, a nose, and a mouth. And yet there never was another you. Rabbi Abraham Joshua Heschel, a twentieth-century sage, observed:

> Is not the human face a living mixture of mystery and meaning? Is it not a strange marvel that among so many hundreds of millions of faces, no two faces are alike? And that no face remains quite the same for more than one instant? The most exposed part of the body, the best known, it is the least describable, a synonym for an incarnation of uniqueness.[6]

Noticing the differences between faces, let alone how a single face changes from moment to moment, takes focus. Our physicality is distinctive, even between identical twins. Similarly, each of us also possesses a unique personality and inner life. As the Baal Shem Tov taught,

> Every person should know that since Creation no other person ever was like him or her. Had there been such another, there would be no need for him to be. Each is called on to manifest his unique qualities. And it is his failure to heed this call which delays the Messiah.[7]

Essential in our own unfolding toward wholeness is discovering that we are kaleidoscope-like: multifaceted, dynamic, and unique. And just as we invest in our appearance, so we have the power to consciously shape our inner composition.

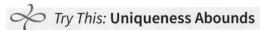 *Try This:* **Uniqueness Abounds**

Take two leaves off the same tree. Study the first leaf closely, paying attention to its shape, multiple colors, veins, texture, markings, and smell. Now examine the second leaf with equal patience. Compare the two leaves, becoming aware of their differences, both subtle and pronounced. Note how the veins of the leaf are similar to the veins on your hand. Appreciate your own uniqueness, aware that there is no other person on the planet who is exactly like you physically or in personality, history, and potential.

The Body as a Symbol of God

The human body is actually elevated in its significance in the Rabbinic mind to the highest conceivable level. Commenting on the biblical command that the body of a hanged criminal is not to remain on public display after dark (Deuteronomy 21:23), Rashi, the influential biblical commentator of medieval France, wrote, "Since a human being is created in the image of God, it can be likened to the twin brother of a king, who is a bandit and hanged for his crimes. People who see the body think that it is the king."[8] As recorded in the Creation story's account, humans were uniquely crafted *betzelem Elohim*, "in the image of God" (Genesis 1:27). Each person is a kind of banner, a representative of the Divine. Disrespecting another person's body or one's own is to shame God too.

To see our bodies as a symbol of God is to acknowledge our enormous significance and to see ourselves challenged to live up to that divine association. In moving toward wholeness we exercise the divine capacity of integration and creativity. At the same time, our physically fragile bodies remind us that we are not God. Our organs will ultimately cease to function, and during our lives we will experience aches and pains. And yet, through an examination of our physical workings, we sharpen our awareness that our bodies are also miraculous.

The Miracle of the Body

For the Rabbis, even bodily functions prompted wonder and gratitude. Abaye, a third-century sage living in Babylonia, uttered a prayer of thanks each time that he emerged from his morning visit to the latrine (*Berakhot* 60b). Today his words are included in traditional Jewish prayer books:

> Praised are You, Eternal our God, Ruler of the universe, who
> fashioned the human body with wisdom, creating openings,
> arteries, glands, and organs, marvelous in structure, intricate in
> design. Should but one of them, by being blocked or opened, fail
> to function, it would be impossible to exist and to stand before You.
> Praised are You, Eternal, Healer of all flesh, who sustains our bodies
> in wondrous ways.

Our physical well-being is not to be taken for granted. Sadly, I witness the suffering of friends who live with chronic, debilitating illness. There is no end to what can go wrong, no guarantee of a healthy body. And yet, most of the time, for most of us, our bodies serve us well and are fashioned to heal when ill. Although we will each meet physical challenges, our bodies, each of which remarkably began as a single cell, are a marvel of high-functioning integrated complexity.

Our brain is composed of a hundred billion neurons, of which there are thousands of types, enabling a trillion interconnections. The differences between people's brain connections lead to variations in thought and behavior, propensities and strengths. Recent research shows that the activation of genes is triggered by environment and culture. Particularly in the brain, genes may "jump" by making copies of themselves, migrating, and inserting themselves as a sequence elsewhere within a genome. The result is that even identical twins may differ in some of their DNA sequencing. We are each custom-made. Our bodies are pulsating in response to dynamic hardwiring and the ever-changing world around us.

Two Tales of Intentionality

Although our senses serve as our portal to the world and the source of so much pleasure in our busy daily lives, we are often oblivious to the changing colors of the sunset or the subtle flavors in our food. Vietnamese Buddhist teacher Thich Nhat Hanh has served as an instructor on the art of sensual wakefulness. I read several of his books on mindfulness before I went to hear him speak for the first time. I purchased a ticket from a scalper outside a sold-out lecture at the Santa Monica Convention Hall. Now there is irony: scalping for enlightenment. The great teacher's talk was often hard to follow because of his accent and soft-voiced delivery.

Years later, I do not recall insights from his dharma teaching. Yet he modeled an enduring lesson. After he had finished speaking, while an associate spoke about upcoming events, Thich Nhat Hanh reached down for a glass of water. Outside of the spotlight, he cradled the glass between his two palms, slowly raised it to his mouth, took a sip, paused, and then took another patient sip. His deeply focused attention to the act of drinking made a lasting impression on me.

Acting with great intention is also prized in Hasidism, whose sages used tales to illustrate core ideas, such as the following example:

> Once upon a time, a villager journeyed to the faraway study hall of the renowned eighteenth-century teacher the Maggid of Mezeritch. Upon his return, his neighbors gathered around him.
>
> "Tell us about the Rebbe," they chimed in. "What wisdom did you take away?"
>
> "I heard many teachings, but the greatest impact came from watching the Rebbe tie his shoelaces."
>
> Many of the listeners were baffled. Some even thought that their fellow villager was mocking them. Yet a few understood that in observing a sage perform simple acts with great intentionality, the observer may also refine devotion in the performance of sacred deeds.[9]

Try This: Sensual Wakefulness

Exercises that attune us to our physicality strengthen our appreciation for the gifts of body, enhance our concentration and sensuality, and further the integration of the physical with the emotional, intellectual, and intuitive. The following exercise cultivates physical mindfulness by elevating chewing with enhanced engagement of the senses.

> Hold a raisin and examine it closely. Observe the many colors, especially the differing shades of the same color. Be aware of all the wrinkles. See how the light reflects off the surface, casting small shadows. Consider how each raisin in its details is as unique as a fingerprint. Place the raisin between your fingers and squeeze gently. Feel the texture and squishiness. Notice how the skin around the fruit holds all the sticky moisture safely inside.

Put the raisin in your mouth. Observe where your tongue places the raisin in your mouth. Begin to chew with awareness of the motions of your jaw, noting the interaction of your tongue and teeth in maneuvering the raisin. Consider how your mouth seems to know just what to do with the raisin to extract its juices.

Chew slowly, savoring the various flavors and sensations on your palate. When the raisin feels fully chewed, use your tongue to explore for those little pieces that remain between your teeth or on your tongue. Pause to pay attention to the lingering tartness or sweetness in your mouth.

If you ate an entire meal with such patience and awareness, you would need a lot of time. You might lose some weight. And you would also find greater wonder and delight in an act that we perform several times each day. When we observe mindfully, we become aware of the textures, colors, and light; the tastes and smells; the sounds and silence around us. Such attentiveness takes practice, not unlike learning the skills of playing a sport or musical instrument. By deepening our awareness of the sensuality of our world, we enhance our appreciation for what we might otherwise take for granted. Appreciation leads to gratitude, and becomes a wellspring of contentment, compassion, and calm.

The Art of Meditation

We tend to multitask. In contrast, meditation is the art of doing only one task at a time, maintaining a singular focus. Meditation that enables greater calm and self-control is usually a three-step process leading to an altered state of consciousness:

1. Awareness of breath
2. Focus on a word or phrase
3. Passive disregard for fleeting thoughts and feelings

The physical benefits of meditation were first documented in the mid-1970s by Harvard cardiologist Herbert Benson. Dr. Benson and his research team demonstrated that regular meditators at his local Transcendental Meditation (TM) center had measurably decreased heart and breathing rates, blood pressure, and muscle tension and increased alpha waves in the brain as compared with a control group.[10] Dr. Benson recommended "secular meditation" sessions for ten to twenty minutes a day, twice a day, employing as a mantra a meaningful word such as "one." The resulting "relaxation response," he explained, was the opposite of the adrenaline-laden "fight-or-flight" reaction. Benson used his findings to emphasize the mind-body connection and to justify his prescription of meditation for stress reduction and health enhancement.

Women preparing for labor and delivery often study Lamaze breathing techniques, based on ancient Hindu yoga practices, to reduce their sensation of pain and to relax their bodies. Although the actual intensity of each contraction may not be altered by these breathing exercises, the experience of pain associated with each contraction is reduced.

The ultimate goal of spiritual meditation goes beyond physical benefits, seeking to let go of self-involvement to pave the way for an experience of oneness. Meditation practice takes a variety of forms in different faiths, including ancient Hindu mantras and yoga; Buddhist mindfulness techniques and imageries; Sufi practitioners' whirling dances; Catholics' rosary prayers (the recitation of the Our Father, Hail Mary, and Glory Be prayers over and over); Jewish chants of the psalms or a *niggun* (a repetitive, wordless melody). Although the focus may vary, breath is consistently a central component of each of these practices, even if not overtly acknowledged.

Awareness of Breath

Focus on breath is at once the simplest and most demanding of exercises. Thoughts and emotional yearnings continuously flow through us. Especially for beginning meditators, sitting still and staying focused is difficult. The mind is naturally active and avoids boredom by taking us down the road of a good story or producing itching sensations to distract us from the immediate task. During meditation, the thoughts that flow through us serve as vessels for emotional responses, physical needs, and spiritual longings that are both recurring and elusive. Helpful and practical thoughts may arise, such as priorities for the day or a solution to a problem, but it is wise not to interrupt a meditation to write the emerging ideas down, even when they seem profound. These are often a trick to distract us from the repetitive practice of mantra and focusing on the breath. Observe the flow of thoughts as if they were on a movie screen, becoming aware of them and letting them pass, while consistently returning to the focus on mantra and breath.

Meditation takes practice. When we first begin, we tend to sit for only as long as our predetermined goal, and even then it requires significant self-discipline and patience. But developing mental concentration is like building muscles: progress comes in stages, and there are many unanticipated benefits. Once you are in good physical shape from regular exercise, you have added capacity to explore and discover, hike hills and climb mountains, bicycle through landscapes, and play pickup basketball. Through regular meditation, you can listen more patiently, read with greater concentration, access intuitive thoughts more readily, and find greater calm despite ever-present distractions. Observing our breath provides a way to transition from the turmoil of daily life toward the peace that we seek. Meditation is a vehicle for wholeness making.

 Try This: **Walking Meditation**

When walking, we naturally breathe more expansively, enabling greater calm. The following walking meditation is an act of concentration, drawing our attention with each step to the interconnections between our various bones, muscles, and consciousness.

> Set a timer for twenty to thirty minutes. You can practice walking meditation either indoors or outdoors. The key is to do it in a place where you will not be too distracted by surrounding activity or noise. As you begin to walk, focus on the details of your body in motion: the movement of your legs and arms, the placement of your foot upon the ground with each step, and the rise and fall of your chest and abdomen with each breath.
>
> After gaining a steady rhythm, begin to take in your surroundings without labeling them, simply becoming aware of smells, sounds, sensations, and scenery. Then return to a focus on breath and the physical details of each step. Conclude the walk with a short prayer of gratitude for the capacity to move through space.

Shalom as Mantra Meditation

Meditation, the art of focused attention, enhances calm and prepares the body to deal with the ups and downs that come with each day. As an aid to sitting meditation, I often use the Hebrew word *shalom*, meaning "peace" or "wholeness." The meaning as well as the vibratory sound of chanting *shalom* elicits serenity and heightened awareness.

In Sanskrit, the ancient language of India that is still used for Hindu prayer, *mantra* denotes a word or phrase that is repeated over and over as part of breath meditation. The most commonly used mantra is *aum*, pronounced as three syllables: A ("ahh"), U ("ohh"), and M ("mmm"). *Aum* is treated as a sacred incantation that is chanted before and after the reading of the Vedas, the holy texts of Hinduism, or prior to reciting any prayer. Hindus believe that at the origin of Creation, the divine all-encompassing consciousness took the form of an initial vibration manifesting as the sound *aum*.

The vowel sounds articulated in *aum* are identical to those of the Hebrew word *shalom*. In both of these ancient words, the first vowel, the "ahh," comes from the back of the throat, the very sound that a doctor instructs us to make by opening our mouths widely. The second vowel sound, "ohh," is produced with our lips drawn into a circle, as the sound moves forward from the center of the throat. And the "mmm" sound is pronounced with our mouths gently closed, tickling our lips. In chanting *sha-lo-m*, we engage our entire vocal cavity, moving the breath forward and outward, producing a sequence of sounds that articulate wholeness.

There is an added significance to the choice of the word *shalom* as mantra when we consider the sound waves associated with the consonant sounds: the "sh" sound oscillates, while the "m" generates a nearly flat line. In chanting *shalom*, the wave frequencies of the sound shift from busy to calm.

Try This: *Shalom* **Meditation**

In this chant, become aware of how the sounds produce vibrations in your body, using *shalom* in the service of physical wholeness.

http://youtu.be/ abxz8_Yv9DM

Sit comfortably on a chair with your feet on the ground and your back straight, enabling you to breathe with ease. Breathe out all anxiety; breathe in calm. Breathe out all critical thoughts, and breathe in trust. Relax your body from your toes to your head. Focus on your breath. With each inhalation, feel the gift and goodness of life. On each outward breath, chant *sha-lo-m* with equal-length duration of each syllable. Do so six times.

Now chant *sha-lo-m* , emphasizing in sequence the following syllables on the exhale. Chant each iteration six times:

Long *sha* and short *lo* and *m*; then

Short *sha*, a longer *lo*, and a short *m*; then

Short *sha*, short *lo*, long *m*.

Now chant *sha-lo-m* six times giving each syllable the same duration during exhalation. You will notice that at this point your expression of the syllables lasts longer. You are breathing more fully and with greater ease than at the outset.

Continue to sit, quietly now, following the in-and-out of your breath. Choose a physical focal point—such as your nostrils or your chest, or that point in your lower diaphragm where your breathing switches from drawing inward to exhaling. While you are concentrating on your breath, other thoughts will arise in your mind. Just let them pass and refocus on your breath.

Continue to breathe, at once calm and alert. Be aware of breathing in and breathing out ... Know that just as the ocean's waves come in and go out, so your breath rises and falls. You are not only breathing, you are being breathed with a rhythm like the sea, breathing in and out ...

As you breathe in, welcome in the world. As you breathe out, know that you are distinctive. Just take another moment, following your breath, enjoying the gift of life, considering breath as the source of connection, at rest in your own calm and awareness.

Breathe in and out ... Slowly return to normal wakefulness. After opening your eyes, patiently continue to feel quieted, at once full of peace and fully awake.

Consider initiating a meditation practice by chanting *shalom* for ten minutes (with a timer) each morning soon after awakening or in the evening before bedtime. After repeating this daily practice for a week or more, gradually add to the time of each sit.

Remember: it is wise to set goals that are attainable. Upon reaching your goal, you will feel motivated to grow your practice. By building slowly, you can establish a daily meditation of at least twenty minutes.

The Jewish Tradition of Quieting the Mind

Inner calm is recognized in traditional Jewish teachings as a platform for prayer. In the Mishnah, an authoritative collection of Jewish legal writings edited in Israel around 225 CE, we are taught, "The early pious ones would quiet their minds for one hour before the prayer" (*Mishnah Berakhot* 5:1). "The prayer" refers to the standing *Amidah* prayer, which serves as the centerpiece of the traditional liturgy prayed by Jews morning, afternoon, and evening. In the sixteenth century, Rabbi Joseph Karo, the author of the most influential Jewish law code, the *Shulchan Arukh*, added that the early pious ones would not only quiet their minds for one hour before the prayer, but would then chant the prayer for a full hour.[11] Reciting the weekday *Amidah* for one hour equals a pace of seven seconds per word: an act of intense, sustained concentration.[12]

These descriptions from the Jewish tradition of quieting the mind and repeating familiar words as a vocal chant reveal a commonality between the faith traditions of the East and West. Questing for inner peace, people of diverse faiths have both learned from each other and independently discovered the power of breath techniques and concentration.

Sacred Text Study: Psalm 150

Breath is a key focal point for meditation because it is rhythmic, consistent, and necessary for life itself. The Babylonian Talmud (edited in what is now Baghdad around 500 CE) defines death as cessation of respiration.[13] Breath is life. Each breath that we take is also distinctive in duration, texture, and accompanying motion. For a master meditator, each breath is as unique as a snowflake.

Breath also connects us to the world around us. We are permeable and yet distinctively embodied. The air that we breathe emerges from plants and living beings, whether alive now or of a former time, going back to the dawn of Creation. When we exhale, we breathe ourselves into the world, and the world takes us in.

Each breath that we take in is transformed from oxygen into carbon dioxide, enabling a necessary exchange of gases with the plant life around us. Just as all of the waters on the earth pass from the oceans to the sky and return as rain, so all breaths on the earth pass from our bodies into the atmosphere and return to us as recycled air. Speech and song emerge as products of the flow of air through us. Focus on breath reminds us of the wonder of creation, the mystery of our own limited years, and our connection to the global community.

The author of the final line of the book of Psalms acknowledged the profound connection between breath and spirituality. The book of Psalms is part of the Hebrew scriptures, the compilation of Torah, Prophets, and Writings. The psalms are an integral part of Jewish and Christian liturgy, the source of such beloved verses as "The Lord is my shepherd, I shall not want" (Psalm 23:1). Each of the 150 psalms is written as a poem to God. Many are attributed to King David, who lived nearly three thousand years ago. The psalms express a broad range of emotions, including anger and rejoicing, fear and hope.

At the culmination of all the psalms is the following line: *Kol haneshamah*, "with every breath," *tehallel Yah*, "let us praise God"; *halleluyah*, "praised be God." Psalm 150 speaks of praising God with a variety of musical instruments and reaches a crescendo with breath alone as the instrument of praise. Two of the words of the line have a dual meaning: *neshamah*, meaning "breath" or "soul," and *Yah*, a biblical name of God that sounds like an airy exhalation.[14] In reciting Psalm 150:6, we underscore that each breath is a gift from God: "With every soul, let us praise God/*Yah*, praised be God/*Yah*—Source of breath."

The words of this verse, beginning *Kol haneshamah*, have been set to many melodies. Among them is a chant composed by the monks of Taizé, an interdenominational Christian monastery in Burgundy, France, and set to the original Hebrew by Rabbi Levi Kelman of Jerusalem. This chant has caught on in synagogues around the world. You can hear this chant by using the QR code accompanying this paragraph.

http://youtu.be/
N8k2QV_fv4w

 Try This: **Guided Meditation of Praise**

Offering praise requires that we shift our focus from emotional turmoil to a point beyond ourselves. Praise of God expresses gratitude and awe. The book of Psalms is composed of 150 poems that encompass the whole range of emotions, many marked by the word *halleluyah*, "let us praise *Yah*." Saying *halleluyah* is to exclaim "wow!" The final line of the final psalm in the book of

Psalms reads, "May each soul/breath praise God, *halleluyah*" (Psalm 150:6). After all the words of psalms is the recognition that each breath contains all that we could express. Each breath is a prompt of praise. Each breath offers the gift of life and interconnection. The following guided meditation evokes the mind-set of praise.

> While sitting in a chair or on the ground, close your eyes, sit up straight, and relax. Breathe out all tension; breathe in calm. Focus on your breath and join each in-and-out of your breathing with a syllable of the word *ha-le-lu-yah*. Repeat for five minutes.
>
>
>
> http://youtu.be/ cgJkv3AB0CQ
>
> Breathe out. Feel calm and awake as if the sun is caressing you. Feel praise bubbling up within you, emerging from your core and directed toward God. Experience at your center a hollow glass bead with a hole on either end. Through that center of your center a divine awareness flows and spreads out and surrounds you with a beautiful light. Allow yourself to feel held by that light. You feel whole and safe. A gentle smile spreads on your lips. Fill yourself with the goodness of life, curiosity, and the giving over of control. Embrace your power of choice and commitment, love and self-love. And from the deepest part of you, say *halleluyah* with your whole being. Repeat and when you get to the *Yah*, allow the breathy sound to reach far beyond you—linking you with a greater Presence, an enveloping whole of which you are an integral part. Feel love flowing through you as a waterfall, emerging from a nurturing divine source. Hold that experience of loving connection, and spontaneously express praise.
>
> After chanting *halleluyah* three times, you will slowly open your eyes. When you do, hold on to the sensations of light and love, aware that we are steady, skilled surfers on a dynamic sea. You are safe and the sea is good.
>
> *Ha-le-lu-yah, ha-le-lu-yah, ha-le-lu-yah.* Three, two, one. Now slowly open your eyes, feeling calm and centered.

Chanting *halleluyah* allows us to reach beyond ourselves toward a greater Presence, quieting our emotional struggles with a sense of something much vaster and more enduring than our troubles. Although our lives are fleeting, we are able to address the Eternal One. We are, in the words of Abraham and Job, but "dust and ashes" (Genesis 18:27; Job 42:6). The very act of praising God expresses the chutzpah, the audacity, of human prayer.

Blessings as a Spiritual Practice

Traditional blessings evoke and express gratitude.[15] Just before biting into an apple, we are invited to recite, *Barukh atah Adonai Eloheinu Melekh ha'olam borei peri ha'etz*, "Praised are You, Sovereign of the world, who creates fruit of the tree." Composed by the early Rabbis, the opening words of the traditional formula praise God's sovereignty, and the closing words identify the immediate prompt. The blessings tend to be quite specific. Such specificity cultivates heightened awareness of our world and multiplies the opportunities to express gratitude. The following are some of my favorite blessings:

> On seeing a beautiful person: "Praised are You, Sovereign of the world, who has such beauty in the world."

> On smelling a rose: "Praised are You, Sovereign of the world, who creates fragrant plants."

> On entering the presence of a person distinguished in learning: "Praised are You, Sovereign of the world, who has given of Your wisdom to flesh and blood."

> On observing a rainbow: "Praised are You, Sovereign of the world, who remembers the covenant, is faithful to it, and keeps promises." (This refers to God's oath to Noah to never destroy the world again by a flood in Genesis 9:14–17.)

> On hearing thunder: "Praised are You, Eternal our God, Ruler of the universe, whose power and might fill the whole world."

Rabbi Meir, a sage of the second century CE, encouraged a person to recite at least a hundred blessings a day (*Menachot* 43b). Yet the sheer act of saying a hundred blessings a day is not a guarantee of enhanced awareness and appreciation. Reciting formulaic blessings can easily take on the quality of repetitive, mindless behavior unless we infuse the traditional words with our own fresh feelings of genuine gratitude and even surprise.

⚘ *Try This:* **A Blessing Practice**

In the course of each day for a week, say five blessings. Do so in response to the food before you or events during the day, such as smelling a rose. You may do so in English, beginning with "Blessed are you, Ever Present One, who ..." and continuing with a few words describing the cause of your gratitude. At the end of the week, journal how the blessing practice shaped your awareness of what you might have otherwise taken for granted and how increasing your gratitude has impacted your attitude and deeds.

Sacred Text Study: The *Motzi*, the Blessing over Bread

Among my first teachers of meditation was Rabbi Jonathan Omer-Man. I still remember his visits to Congregation B'nai Israel nearly twenty-five years ago, when he guided five rabbis in my office in meditative chants. In his remarks to us, he drew our attention to the power of rituals as consciousness-raisers, such as the blessing over bread. That blessing, the *Motzi*, is a formula: *Barukh atah Adonai Eloheinu Melekh ha'olam, hamotzi lechem min ha'aretz*, "Praised are You, Eternal our God, Ruler of the universe, who brings forth bread from the earth." Bread in the Jewish tradition is the food staple, and the *Motzi* marks the start of a meal. (Note that the blessing expresses gratitude for bringing forth bread from the earth, and yet what grows from the earth is not bread but raw grain. Bread is a product of human partnership with God.)

Rabbi Omer-Man taught that in reciting a blessing before taking the first bite, we demonstrate human restraint. When saying the ten Hebrew words, we reach beyond ourselves, connecting to an extended community that has recited these words across the generations and around the world. And in expressing gratitude, we are prompted to pause to consider the many contributors to our meal.

Ben Zoma, a second-century rabbi, contrasted the toil involved in preparing bread from the dawn of biblical Creation with the custom of his own day:

> What labors Adam had to perform before he obtained bread to eat. He plowed, sowed, reaped, bound, threshed and winnowed and selected the ears. He grounded and sifted them. He kneaded and baked and then finally he ate. When I get up and find all these things, they are already done for me. (*Berakhot* 58a)

Ben Zoma could not have even begun to imagine packaged bread: sliced, infused with preservatives and vitamins, and wrapped in plastic.

The reciting of the *Motzi* invites us to consider the multiple contributors to the making of a loaf of bread or a bagel: the sun and fields, the seeds and rain; the farmer—plowing, planting, weeding, and fertilizing; the harvesters working by hand and on tractors; the mill workers who grind the grain into flour and place it into bags; and the transportation network that delivers the flour to the bakeries where bakers transform it into so many varieties of baked goods.

Today we commonly enjoy greater bounty on our tables than did the kings of the past. We may dine on fish from Alaska, cheese from France, honey from Australia, all combined with both locally and internationally grown vegetables and fruits. Aided by greenhouses, hydroponics, refrigerated trucks, and air transportation, modern agriculture allows us to indulge in daily feasts. We may elevate eating to spiritual dining by expressing gratitude, engaging our senses more fully, and expanding our perspective.

Rituals and Physicality

Rituals enable spiritual transformation by altering our perceptions and experience. Although all rituals engage our bodies, they also touch our hearts, minds, and spirits. Rituals have the ability not only to alter how we feel physically, but to heighten our awareness of the world around us and to prompt gratitude, wonder, and praise.

 Try This: **Blessings of Dawn**

The traditional morning prayer service, the first of three daily Jewish services, is designed to reframe our understanding of the day yet to unfold. The morning service begins with Blessings of Dawn. Called *Birkhot HaShachar* in Hebrew, the series of one-line blessings, which originated in the Talmud over fifteen hundred years ago (*Berakhot* 60b; *Menachot* 43b), awaken awareness of the miracle of our physicality. The following draws from the traditional series of morning blessings and incorporates them into a guided visualization. The blessings were initially prompted by a natural event, such as the crowing of the rooster at dawn or our first movements in getting out of bed.

http://youtu.be/
6zVjZINdYzA

Stand straight and breathe out anxiety. Breathe in calm. Feel the gift of your physicality.

Open your eyes to recite, "Praised are You, Ever Present One, Fashioner of the universe, who enables the rooster to distinguish between night and day." Close your eyes and hear in your mind's ear the sound of a rooster. Feel yourself becoming more alert, while remaining calm and focused.

With your eyes still closed, acknowledge the darkness and breathe out. Slowly open your eyes, but refrain from labeling objects. Simply take in sensations of colors and shapes. Pause to experience the wonder of sight. Now recite, "Praised are You who gives sight to the blind." Close your eyes again.

Breathe out. Stand with your feet set firmly on the floor, and slowly sway your upper body. Attend to how your muscles and joints enable mobility. Bend over and slowly rise up. Open your eyes and recite the following words: "Praised are You, Source of physicality, who enables the bent to stand upright." Hold the words as your own.

Close your eyes and fill yourself with a breath. Hold the breath for a moment, and as you breathe out, feel deep calm.

Breathe out. See yourself surrounded by a light that comes directly from above you, flows down your spine, through your legs, and into every cell of your body. And as that light passes and spreads through you, become aware of both the many components of your physicality and your physical unity. You will soon slowly open your eyes with a deep awareness of the gift of your body and a quality of calm. As you open your eyes, you will recite your own blessing of gratitude for your body. Now, open your eyes and begin: *Barukh atah Adonai*, Praised are You, Ever Present One ... (your own words).

Love and Lust: Overcoming Bodily Traps

Much of what drives us is unconscious. The sex act, for instance, contains mystery regarding attraction and arousal. The sources of "chemistry" are notoriously difficult to describe. (Paradoxically, they also reveal much about us.) Sexual cravings often lead to vivid fantasies so sensual that we may blur the lines between reality and wishful thinking. We are biologically wired to form attachments and in some cases do so irrationally. Freud said that "anatomy is destiny," which is largely true, but there is far more to the story.

I attended four sessions of sex education with each of my two sons when they were in fifth grade. The school nurse described body parts, warned about the dangers of venereal disease and unwanted pregnancy, and showed a film clip of the birth of a child. At the end of the last session, I could not restrain myself, and to my son's embarrassment and enduring amusement, I blurted out, "Monkeys don't need a class on how to reproduce! We're wired to do this. Understanding the physical dimensions of sex is important—but what this class lacks is a description of human sexuality at its most beautiful, even holy. You never addressed the emotional and spiritual dimensions of sexual relationship!"

The quality of an experience is judged by the aftertaste. When sex is only an instinctual, physical act, a release between nameless strangers and a chemical stimulation of the brain, it feels degrading. We yearn to express tenderness, trust, and love by connecting to a person we know—and like. On some primal level, sexual expression reveals our core self, which is why we euphemistically call it "physical intimacy." Only we humans wear clothing and cover our sexual organs, "our privates," for on a primal level sex is deeply personal. What excites us is often rooted in early memories or hardwiring, but we are also always changing. Discovering our own sensual needs and those of a partner is an ongoing process.

Sex at its best engages us as a whole person. The quality of long-term sexual relationships depends on the quality of communication, awareness, and imagination between the parties. Sex is a vital ingredient in marriage as a source of bonding and joy. Social psychologist Robyn Dawes showed that marital stability is predicted by a simple formula: a greater frequency of lovemaking than quarreling.[16] Quantity counts. There is also quality, which is a product of trust, play, and affection. In Judaism, enjoying sex is a positive expectation in the context of marital commitment, and refusal to engage in sexual intimacy is grounds for divorce.[17] The Rabbis emphasized that God seeks for us to enjoy permitted physical pleasures. As expressed in the Jerusalem Talmud, "Rabbi Chizkiyah said in the name of Rav, 'You will one day give an accounting for everything your eyes saw [that was permitted to you and] that you did not partake'" (Jerusalem Talmud, *Kiddushin* 4:12).

Sex, as all matters spiritual, is paradoxical: taking pleasure in giving pleasure; letting go of control yet remaining attentive; experiencing the momentary loss of self to experience oneness; seeking intimacy with a trusted partner while craving to expose a wild side. The challenge in a long-term relationship—"sex in captivity"[18]—is to know another intimately while honoring surprise and spontaneity. The Jewish mystics teach that sex realizes the divine image of unity in a physical act. Sex is complicated precisely because it touches on all four planes of our inner life.

Struggling with Pain

Our experiences are often held in our body. We speak of a gut-wrenching experience or a broken heart. Neurologists have shown with brain scans that physical pain and emotional pain impact the same parts of the brain.[19] In the words of Edward E. Smith, director of cognitive neuroscience at Columbia University, "When people say they feel pain from separation, do not trivialize or downplay it saying 'It's all in your mind.'"[20] We will all encounter physical and emotional aching and in some cases live with it as a companion.

In response to pain, we may detach from our body. We may even try to dull the sensation of pain by blanketing it with alcohol or medication. To live with greater harmony with our whole self includes observing our body—even its aches. Through the process of engaging pain, we may grow stronger. The hardest part of a bone is the calcification after the healing of a breakage. Likewise, although our pain may feel like a tormentor, it is also potentially a mentor, deepening wakefulness and wisdom. To overcome pain is to simultaneously acknowledge the location and source of discomfort and to identify ourselves as part of something much larger. When seeing ourselves enveloped and infused by divine light, our pain may be reduced and even dissolve.

 Try This: **Body-Mind Calm**

This body-relaxation exercise is an introduction to guided visualization. Going inward with imagination can allow for surprising and satisfying journeys. This exercise can be done lying down or sitting comfortably in a chair with your back straight and legs uncrossed. The goal is to breathe easily and to stay in balance, deeply relaxed and keenly attentive.

http://youtu.be/
qB7Zhum7Tvc

Close your eyes. Breathe out all anxiety. Breathe in calm. Breathe out all judgment, and breathe in trust. Breathe out all distraction, and breathe in steady focus.

Bring your attention to your feet. Curl your toes and release them, thereby intensifying your attention. Feel a soft but firm rubber ball rolling back and forth across the bottoms of your feet. Become aware of the massage sensations. Feel a release of the tension stored in your feet as it eases out through your toes.

Focus on your calves, then knees, then thighs. Inhale slowly and become aware of any sensations, any tension. Breathe in and out as you scan this area of your body. Exhale and allow your muscles to relax as tension slips away.

Focus on your stomach. Feel it rising as you inhale and sinking as you exhale. Become aware of this rhythm. Breathe easily and feel deep calm, while remaining attentive.

Become aware of your left hand and arm. In your mind, tighten your left hand and release. Tighten and release again, seeing tension easing away through your fingers. Repeat with your right hand and arm.

Now move your focus from your arms to your chest. With each breath, feel it rising and falling. Become aware of any tension in your chest and release it on each out breath.

Move your awareness to your neck and then to your jaw. Tighten your jaw and release. Mentally massage your jaw as if with your fingers, finding the tension soothed. Move your fingers to the temples of your face and massage your temples, releasing tension. Scan your face for any other tension and breathe it out.

See a beam of light descending from directly above you, traveling down the center of your head, through your spine, and spreading out through all parts of your body. See the light descending through your lower abdomen, down your thighs, and flowing into the earth. The light penetrates every cell of your body, healing and soothing. The light also surrounds you, like an aura, holding you, creating a deep sense of safety. Fully relax while remaining awake. Breathe in and out, feeling calm and whole.

Know that this place of peacefulness is accessible to you. You can always pause and return to this sensation of deep calm and wholeness. Take another moment to just savor the ease that you feel.

You will now slowly begin your return to the place where you began. Count from five to one backwards and slowly open your eyes. Take your time to readjust. Pause and feel deep calm as you look around the room and reorient yourself to wakefulness.

It is not uncommon for novices to fall asleep when listening to a voice guide them toward releasing tension. With practice, you will be able to stay more consistently focused, maintaining a balance between relaxation and mindfulness.

Our bodies and the earth beneath our feet steady us and enable us to leap forward. And yet the physical, including aesthetics, health, and natural grandeur, is only part of a larger whole. As we saw earlier, the physical and emotional inform each other. When we are out of breath, we are emotionally constricted too. Paying attention to our physical needs grounds us, reducing stress, increasing our energy, and enabling greater resilience.

HEART

Fueling Engagement

Emotions fuel our engagement with the world. Our range of emotions is as varied and colorful as a painter's palette. At the same time, emotions seem to have a life of their own, floating in and out of consciousness. Employing the resources of meditation, prayer, and sacred text, we can steady ourselves amid the swirl of life's emotions.

http://youtu.be/
sVX4gyJvV3U

When we keenly observe the feelings of the heart, we become more aware of their transience, significance, and underlying sources.

Have you ever noticed defensive thoughts as you enter a new space, perhaps a conference room or a café? As you scan the room, you might find yourself thinking, "This meeting is going to be a waste of time." Such negative orientation is rooted in the self-defensive concern to guard against disappointment or even rejection. But our protective emotions are often exaggerated, if not outright irrational. Most of the time we are not consciously aware of the fleeting critical thoughts that shape our outlook. Once we have a realistic assessment of our surroundings, the tide of feelings and the chatter of critical thoughts will dissipate and even disappear.

With greater self-awareness, we become more attuned to our thoughts and how they are often vessels for elusive emotions. Emotions may be prompted by triggers in the present, especially impulses of the body's yearning for food, sleep, sex, or release from tension, which can emerge as moodiness or oversensitivity. Perhaps because we are jetlagged and cranky we expect a meeting to go poorly, or perhaps something about a certain situation reminds us of a previous rejection. Once they arise, negative emotions can fuel rumination on other disappointments, regrets, and resentments. If we address these thoughts consciously, we may counter the underlying emotion.

Sometimes these exaggerated thoughts are directed against ourselves. Fueled by feeling frustrated in not finding a job, betrayed in romance, or ashamed for having acted selfishly, we may begin to mentally pound on ourselves. A dangerous loop may ensue: feeling flawed leads to further berating ourself with distorted thoughts, which evokes more hurt and negativity.

In the extreme, this can lead to such severe pain that we might compulsively want to turn the pain off. In my book *Healing from Despair: Choosing Wholeness in a Broken World*, I deal with the dynamics of suicidal thinking. Here, I want to focus more on the everyday rise and fall of emotions, which includes shades of darkness.

In dealing with depression, research has demonstrated the efficacy of "cognitive behavioral therapy," a process that begins by assessing whether our thoughts are objectively fair. When a voice arises in our mind chastising us, saying something like, "You always act selfishly," examining the thought may enable a healthy reassessment. During a mindful pause, we might challenge the voice: "That's untrue. I often act caringly." When the berating thought arises again, rebut. Identifying our emotions and attendant thoughts, then accepting them or challenging them, may release us from many of our emotional struggles and anxiety.

⚯ *Try This:* Quieting the Inner Drama with Touch Points

When you feel upset, an inner drama may unfold and capture your attention. You may play out differing scenarios of a past hurt or obsess over a threat by producing fantastic exchanges. Over and over again a thought returns. The obsessive voice in your head becomes like static that distracts you from attending to the present moment. As you exist on the physical, emotional, and intellectual planes simultaneously, you can quiet your thoughts and calm your emotions by shifting attention to your body, including a focus on touch points.

Whether you are standing, sitting, or lying down, become aware of the touch points of your body. Concentrate on where your body contacts a surface; note how your hands are placed and where they are touching your body. Feel the pressure of these contact points and become aware of the positioning and balancing of your body.

Placing your attention on these touch points creates an immediacy of awareness, offering an alternative to obsessive thinking. As you attend to your touch points, become aware of the power to choose where you place your attention. Breathe out and refocus on the present moment.

Cognitive behavioral therapy is akin to stepping up onto a balcony to examine inner turmoil, gaining some emotional distance and a broader perspective. Meditative practices such as attending to touch points allow us to shift our attention away from the tugs of inner drama. Expressing an intention to let go of certain patterns of thought may also help in doing this. And listening patiently to someone else in emotional pain offers awareness of our strengths and contributes to our appreciation that life has its ups and downs. Speaking with God, perhaps by offering a blessing on behalf of another person, also gives perspective and draws on our deepest feelings.

The Gifts of Blessing Another

Exchanging blessings can be a powerful exercise in expressing long-held emotions in times of crisis. I recall visiting my colleague Rabbi Allen Krause when he was dying of cancer at his home. Every fifteen minutes he pressed a button on a pump to relieve his pain with medication. Fortunately his mind was clear. My friend had served as a caring pastor until the age of seventy. His preaching and scholarship had emphasized social justice. Like the prophets, he accepted even rejection by some of his constituents. Sitting before him, I wanted to express my gratitude for his mentorship and to pray for his gentle passing. But it felt presumptuous to initiate a blessing upon an elder of such wisdom and goodness. Instead I asked him to bless me. He closed his eyes and spoke slowly and haltingly. At times the pauses were so long that I was unsure if he had fallen asleep. I listened patiently as words emerged. I experienced his expression of care and affection as a precious gift. I then took his hand in mine and, in the context of addressing God, shared his importance to me and my most deeply held wishes for him and his family.

Ten days later my colleague passed. I led a memorial service on one of the nights of mourning in his home. Before we began, I privately asked his wife, Sherri, if she had any requests, and she asked me to guide the group in a visualization meditation. I readily agreed. Toward the end of the traditional prayers, I described how Allen and I had exchanged blessings. I invited anyone who wished to participate in a guided visualization of blessing to do so. I then led them in the following exercise, "Receiving and Giving a Blessing."

At the close of the guided imagery offered on behalf of Allen, I opened my eyes and scanned the quiet room. As others opened their eyes, many wiped away tears. Participating in such a guided visualization of blessing had allowed those present to access and experience profound emotions that they may not even have had the words to fully articulate.

 Try This: **Receiving and Giving a Blessing**

Sit comfortably with your back straight, feet flat on the ground. Close your eyes and breathe out tension. Breathe in calm.

See before you a person whose blessing you seek. Become sensually aware of his or her presence.

http://youtu.be/
Wv2MyD5EkYc

Notice the color and texture of your loved one's hair, the color of the eyes, the shape of the face. Take your loved one's hand in yours.

Now listen. Your loved one has words of blessing to give to you. Listen to the blessing spoken to God on your behalf. Allow yourself to be surprised by the words that arise spontaneously.

Now, still holding hands, bless your loved one.

Pause and feel the goodness of your loved one's presence. Share an embrace. Let go and allow him or her as a lit figure to slowly fade away. Linger for a moment, feeling the goodness of having had this relationship and recalling the words that you exchanged.

Hold on to the words of the exchange. Remember your loved one's blessing and recall what you spoke as well. Feel the goodness of the heartfelt words. These words will endure for you as a gift.

Breathe out and open your eyes.

Prayer in Times of Chaos

In times of emotional turmoil, prayer can serve as an aid to self-expression, awareness, and connection. In the midst of illness, our prayers may emerge spontaneously. A poet hospitalized for the first time in his adult life at the age of sixty-eight told me that words of prayer emerged spontaneously, as if thrust out from him. Feeling disoriented and vulnerable, his words expressed yearning for connection, healing, and grounding. Yet prayer does not magically determine an outcome. In the words of Rabbi Abraham Joshua Heschel, "Prayer may not save us, but prayer helps make us worth saving."[1]

In thinking about God and prayer, we wisely ask questions: If God is caring, why is there evil? Does God answer prayers? These questions challenge and clarify our faith and serve as a check on wishful thinking and unexamined promises of intervention. And yet when it comes to the act of prayer, we suspend the work of theology. Analysis is paralysis if it prevents us from identifying and expressing heartfelt emotions. Prayer is speaking *as if* God were before us. In Hebrew, prayer is called *avodat halev*, service of the heart. Analyzing God is akin to psychotherapy, an arm's-length examination of relationship, helpful but different from living the experience. Prayer is the leap into a relationship.

Letters to and from God

The Western Wall in Jerusalem is the last vestige of the Holy Temple, destroyed by the Romans in the year 70 CE. For generations, Jewish pilgrims gathered there to express their yearnings for the rebuilding of the Temple. The association of tears of longing with the stones explains the popular name the "Wailing Wall." Many who gather there also write personal notes to God.

Before I left on my first trip to Jerusalem over forty years ago, my mother gave me a handwritten letter and instructed me to place it at the holy site. To my surprise, the wall was filled with papers. I then understood that the writing of a letter to God was a distinctive Jewish folk practice. I tore a corner from a sheet of paper and wrote spontaneously. I do not remember my words, but I recall feeling moved by the candor and catharsis of opening myself up to God.

Today there are so many bits of paper in the crevices between the massive stones of the wall that only a tightly wadded scrap has a chance of finding a slot at "God's mailbox." Among the visitors in recent years who have placed personal notes at the Western Wall are Pope Francis, President Obama, and Madonna.

 Try This: **Corresponding with God**

> Please consider writing a letter to God. Do so for five minutes with a set timer. Do not anticipate what you will write. Begin with "Dear God," and let the words flow spontaneously.
>
> Look back over your letter. Notice what surprises you, and consider:
>
> What have you learned about yourself?
>
> How does it feel to talk to God?
>
> When I begin a "letter to God" by expressing anxiety, uncertainty, fear, or anger, I usually find that at some point my words turn to gratitude, as if gaining a broader perspective. You will find that once you have begun identifying sources of gratitude, additions will emerge.
>
> Now write back as if God were answering, again setting a timer for five minutes. Begin "Dear (your name)," and allow the words to flow. If you finish and there is still time, just sit and wait. You might find that more words will soon emerge. Once the time is complete, reflect:
>
> What was the nature of God's response?
>
> How is God's response different than the way you normally perceive yourself (or a problem in your life)?
>
> What did you learn?

As a rabbi, I have used writing letters to God as an introduction to prayer and as a tool in counseling. In everyday life, we filter our words, whether in speaking with family, friends, or colleagues. Even in addressing a therapist, who gets paid for hearing the confessions of our dark side, we monitor our words, because we want the therapist to like us. But when we address God, we do so openly because God knows us. When writing a note to God, we articulate our deepest feelings, which may surprise and comfort us. Prayer is a distinctive form of honest conversation.

Writing back to ourselves as if God were responding offers a whole other vantage point for seeing ourselves. Such a note is an act of cosmic empathy. When a person finds this too big a stretch, even an act of heretical hubris, I suggest writing to God to explain why role reversal does not feel proper. Most people do write back from God's vantage point, aware that this is an act of empathy and not substitution. Rarely do these spontaneous letters offer Ouija-board-like yes-or-no answers. "God's answers" are process oriented, drawing on our deepest values and offering a broader perspective than our daily frame of reference. The "letters from God" also tend to be more concise than our letters to God—and more loving.

 Try This: **Harvesting Gratitude**

The following exercise harvests awareness of the goodness in our lives.

> For one week, make a list of seven items each day for which you are grateful, not repeating any item as you expand the list. On the final day, make it eight items, so as to have a total of fifty. When it is completed, examine your inventory of gratitude and reflect on the goodness in your life. How does it make you feel? What actions does it prompt?

Modeh Ani: Wakeful Words of Gratitude

Expressing gratitude on awakening can shape the emotional unfolding of the day to come. Alfred Adler, a contemporary of Freud and pioneer psychologist, said that if you want to know a person quickly, ask for her earliest memory, because what a person holds as the first memory distills her identity.[2] In music and literature, what appears on the first pages or in the early stanzas often foreshadows what will follow.

Modeh Ani is the first prayer of the day, uttered when we open our eyes. This single sentence conveys the essence of prayer. Composed by Moses ibn Makhir of sixteenth-century Safed, Israel, a center for luminaries of Jewish mysticism,[3] *Modeh Ani* is commonly found toward the beginning of most Jewish prayer books. The words are as follows:

> *Modeh ani lefanekha*—Grateful am I before You,
> *Melekh chai vekayam*—Sovereign, dynamic, and
>   steadfast,

shehechezarta bi nishmati—that You have returned
   my soul/breath within me,
bechemlah—with graciousness;
rabbah emunatekha—great is Your faithfulness.

With a close reading, each word prompts reflection—for each word is multifaceted, self-contained, and part of a larger setting.

Modeh, "grateful," bids us to say thank you when we first open our eyes each morning. Consider the effect of beginning each day by expressing gratitude. This opening word invites us to ask ourselves what things evoke our gratitude—health, shelter, safety, family, or an anticipated event. Pausing on this one line exposes what we might otherwise take for granted. *Modeh ani*, "Grateful am I": The second Hebrew word, *ani*, begins with the letter *aleph* (א). In Hebrew, the letter *ayin* (ע) at the outset of a word corresponds with the external, and the *aleph*, whose numerical equivalent is one, refers to the inside. In modern Hebrew both of these letters are silent, only taking on the sound of the vowel attached. For instance, the Hebrew word pronounced *or* can mean "skin" (with an *ayin*) or "light" (with an *aleph*). When the word *ani* begins with an *ayin*, it means "impoverished," while *ani* with an *aleph* means "I." To be an "I" is to possess the gift of inner light, being enriched by self-awareness and the capacity to give presence to others while retaining our true self.

Modeh ani lefanekha, "Grateful am I before You." We ultimately live before God as the Other. For life to matter, you have to feel that what you do matters to somebody. On the religious plane, our lives are of infinite value because what we do matters to God, a caring, ever-present Consciousness. To live before a loving God is to believe in accountability, responsibility, and the essential goodness of the world. And so *modeh ani lefanekha* is a mind-set, a chosen way of seeing ourselves in relationship with God.

"Grateful am I" for my life lived "before You," a caring Divine Presence, *Melekh*. *Melekh* translates as "sovereign" and as "the one who guides." Grateful am I before You who guides me, who calls to me with a still, small voice of awareness that beckons and directs me to actualize my potential.

We characterize this *Melekh* with two words, *chai vekayam*. *Chai* means "alive," conveying dynamic change. *Vekayam* means "established" or "fixed." Our lives are fleeting before a greater, eternal Presence. But that

Divine Presence is paradoxical: always changing and fixed at the same time, just as our world is characterized by constant change and familiarity.

And what is it that we are grateful for? *Nishmati*, "my soul/breath within me." A conscious breath prompts recognition that life is a gift, always changing, always fragile. Each breath may elicit the awareness that our existence is a product of God's grace. With each breath there is reason for gratitude.

Bechemlah, "with graciousness": Grace means giving without expecting anything in return. God's acts of compassion in the Bible are referred to as *chemlah*. For example, in Genesis 19:16, we are told that Lot, Abraham's nephew, lingered before leaving Sodom, but *bechemlat Adonai alav*, "the grace of God was upon him," saving him despite the destruction of his town. When we acknowledge God's presence as *bechemlah*, we are prompted to see ourselves as unconditionally loved and safe.

The final words of the *Modeh Ani* prayer are *rabbah emunatekha*, "great is Your faithfulness." The key to any relationship is trust. The most commonly repeated exhortation in the Bible is *Al tera*, "Do not be afraid."[4] People have always lived with fear and uncertainty. In saying "great is Your faithfulness," we express trust that God will help us through times of pain and darkness. To believe in God's trustworthiness is to affirm a foundation of goodness that underlies and links all facets of Creation. To have such a belief is also to see ourselves as potentially and essentially unified, a microcosm for the larger world. Acknowledging goodness beneath the surface of Creation contributes to experiencing sacred wholeness.

The phrase *rabbah emunatekha* can also mean "great is your trust [in us]." With such a reading, the *Modeh Ani* conveys God's faith in us—a boost to our own sense of worth and the recognition of our potential to use our resources to help ourselves and others. The test of prayer is whether it increases our compassion and willingness to act on God's behalf in the world. This one-line affirmation points us toward action.

The *Modeh Ani* lacks God's explicit name. Unwashed and still in bed, we refrain from formal prayer, and yet our initial words carry great weight. This one line declares that we live in a loving relationship with God. We pause to propel ourselves forward with gratitude and faith, enabling greater inner wholeness and motivating us to increase wholeness in the world.

Try This: **A Daily Recitation of the** *Modeh Ani*

To utilize the *Modeh Ani,* copy the words and place them on your nightstand. (To hear the words chanted, access the video that accompanies this exercise. Note that for a female the opening word is *modah.*) Tell yourself that when you open your eyes in the morning you will recite these words, pausing to consider elements of gratitude in your life.

http://youtu.be/
u-JF2V0xXjw

At the outset, determine to recite the line each morning for one week. You might miss one or two days. Be gentle and understand that habits take time to form.

Memorize the words and continue for a second week. Then consider making the recitation a daily practice.

Reciting the *Modeh Ani* each day prompts you to pause before burrowing into busyness. The *Modeh Ani* will remind you of life's goodness and offer a more balanced perspective for the day ahead. Seeing yourself in relationship with a loving God will reinforce your own lovable qualities and your capacity to love. Beginning your day with gratitude will ripple forward into a mind-set of increased wholeness.

Sacred Text Study: God's Complexity

Although gratitude and sunny thoughts feel good, dark emotions are also part of life's weave. Consider the aftermath of the Golden Calf episode in the Torah. Moses has climbed Mount Sinai and is spending forty days and forty nights before God. Meanwhile at the foot of Mount Sinai, the Israelite people have panicked and reverted to the familiar, idolatrous ways of Egypt. They have demanded that Aaron, Moses's brother, build a Golden Calf for them to worship, and he has complied. The Almighty, as if peering down from the top of the mountain at their idolatry, erupts and vents to Moses, "I see that this is a stiff-necked people. Now leave Me alone when I unleash my wrath against them to destroy them. I will then make of you a great nation" (Exodus 32:9–10).

Moses implores God to consider how poorly it would reflect on God's reputation among the nations if God wiped out the Israelites. He reminds

God of the promises made to the Patriarchs to bring their descendants into the Promised Land, "and the Eternal renounced the calamity that God had planned to bring upon the people" (Exodus 32:14).

In this dramatic episode, the greatest surprise is not that God displays such intense anger, but that Moses has the capacity to persuade God to reconsider. The Rabbinic commentators often devote their writings to filling in the gaps in the Torah text, and one Talmudic sage, Rabbi Abahu, describes Moses's response with imaginative vividness. Before offering his explanation, the sage warns, "If the explanation was not written in scripture, it would be impossible to say it," acknowledging the audacity and perhaps danger of what he is about to present. He continues, "By God saying 'leave Me alone,' we understand that Moses grabbed the Almighty like a person seizes a friend by the jacket lapels, and said, 'Master of the universe, I will not let You go until You forgive and pardon them'" (*Berakhot* 32a). And God did.

God is surely the most emotional personality in the Bible. The intensity of the despair and joy, rage and sorrow experienced by God draws us into the text and provides insight into our own complex emotional lives.

Dr. Peter Pitzele, a psycho-dramatist, showed me that we can find ourselves in the artfully composed biblical stories when we imaginatively enter into them. While I was a rabbinical student at The Jewish Theological Seminary in New York City, Dr. Pitzele once stood before our class and explained, "Although I am Jewish, I never had a bar mitzvah, and I feel intimidated teaching a group of soon-to-be rabbis. Yet as a psycho-dramatist, I do have a skill to share with you. Here is what I propose. I will stretch myself by acting the role of a rabbi, and I'd like one of you to volunteer to speak as a biblical character who seeks counseling."

A male classmate took the seat opposite Peter. "My name is Sarah," he began. "My husband Abraham recently tried to kill our son. He disgusts me. Either he's crazy or his God is. I can no longer look at Abraham. I want to leave him. What is your guidance?"

I had read this story many times and was aware that in the chapter immediately after "the binding of Isaac," Sarah dies (Genesis 23:1–2). I had read commentaries by rabbis from ancient times (called *midrashim*) in which they imagined Satan revealing to Sarah that Abraham had attempted to sacrifice Isaac and Sarah dying in that moment of a broken heart.[5] Yet these accounts had only reached me on the intellectual level. Now, listening to a gripping, painful exchange, I was riveted.

That bibliodrama presentation forever changed how I read sacred text. In experiencing the Bible through identification with the emotional turmoil of the characters, I continue to uncover aspects of myself, including selfishness, fear, generosity, and faith. As God in the text repeats familiar patterns, even unhealthy ones, so do I in my own life. The power of the Bible is that the stories present challenges laden with frustrations and yearnings, jealousies and gratitude that endure across time and around the world.

Negative emotions are part of the Bible's tapestry of dark threads amid brighter colors, teaching us to acknowledge anger, sorrow, and loss as part of life's mix. And yet we are also encouraged to ritually transform painful emotions into positive feelings. For instance, it is the Jewish custom for a groom to break a glass at the end of a wedding ceremony to signify that even in our moments of greatest joy, we should remain aware of the incompleteness of our world and our responsibility to work toward change. At worship services we pause for the mourner's *Kaddish* prayer to honor those who have passed and to recognize sorrow as part of life. On Passover we recline with pillows to celebrate freedom, but we also remember the pain of our ancestors' slavery by eating eye-watering bitter herbs and tasting tear-like salt water. Happiness is rarely experienced as a pure emotion. Uncertainty and disappointment, fragility and loss are our constant companions. Yet we have the power to elevate emotions found in darkness in order to live with less fear and more hope.

Try This: **A Quick Bibliodrama**

The spontaneous filling in of gaps in the biblical story through bibliodrama offers insight into the text and into our own lives.

There are various ways to explore this exercise, either with a partner, as a journal entry, or as a guided imagery (below).

If you have a partner, take turns with one person being the biblical character and the other a counselor. As the biblical character, allow yourself to be surprised as you describe your dilemma in detail. Be aware of the emotions attendant to your description.

Then, as the counselor, after listening nonjudgmentally, ask questions to gain clarity. Summarize what you have heard, allowing the biblical character to add or clarify. And then, as the counselor, offer guidance.

Now, out of character, share what surprised each of you about the exchange and what you learned both about the story and yourselves. Switch roles.

If you lack a partner, you might also try the previous role-play as journal entries, taking on each of the roles in turn.

Here is the experience of Bibliodrama as guided imagery:

> Close your eyes and breathe out. Feel deeply relaxed and focused.
>
> See yourself as a biblical character in need of counseling. Who are you? Describe your appearance. What is the problem or situation for which you seek clarity? What are your emotions?

http://youtu.be/
RBvbUeaLUvg

> Breathe in the tension and hold it for a moment.
>
> Breathe out in a relaxed fashion, and as you do, become aware of a spontaneous resolution.
>
> What do you now understand as a clue to the resolution of the problem? What would you do practically to build on this recognition?
>
> Breathe out, retaining a clear memory of the experience. Breathe out and open your eyes.
>
> Pause to reflect:

> What insight into the biblical story did you gain?

> Why do you think you chose the biblical character that you did?

> What insight did you gain that might help you with a current problem?

Dealing Realistically with Fear

Emotional potholes are scattered along the road of life. We will each encounter danger and disappointment. We are each vulnerable to random violence, financial hardship, deteriorating health, loss of loved ones, and betrayal. It is natural to experience hurt and anger, hate and sadness, aversion, and even despair. Beyond natural disasters, there is the reality of human evil, acts of senselessly cruel behavior. Sometimes our emotional wounds are profound, even disabling.

Popularly attributed to Mark Twain is the quip "I am an old man and have known a great many troubles, but most of them never happened."[6] There is the tendency to anticipate and exaggerate physical and emotional dangers by thinking in terms of possibilities rather than probabilities. When looking through the lens of fear, we distort reality, so focused on dangers that we overlook goodness, including love. The Buddha taught that when we let go of attachments—whether to loved ones, property, or aspirations—we are released from suffering. My hesitation about the Buddha's guidance as applied to daily life is that attachments, especially relationships, are also the source of much that is worthwhile and joyful in life.

Grandiosity, insularity, superstition, selfishness, and greed are warped emotional manifestations of our need to protect ourselves from dangers, real and imagined. In the words of Eleanor Roosevelt, "You gain strength, courage and confidence by every experience in which you really stop to look fear in the face. You must do the thing which you think you cannot do."[7] With our minds we may distinguish between realistic and exaggerated fears. Although it is dangerous to run out into rushing traffic, it is also unhealthy to live like a hermit, insulated from all dangers.

We are wise to view our problems within the frame of a larger context. Rabbi Pesach Krauss, who served as a chaplain for patients at Memorial Sloan-Kettering Cancer Center in New York City, would show patients a white page with a black dot and ask, "What do you see?" Most of the time they would say, "A black dot." He would then comment, "Yes, there is a black dot. But mostly, there's a white page. Although you're confronting uncertainty and pain, now is also the time to appreciate all the white, all the goodness that defines your greater life."[8]

Inner peace depends on a realistic outlook, which means acknowledging both darkness and light. Rabbi Nachman of Breslov, the Ukrainian sage of the mid-nineteenth century, taught: *Kol ha'olam kulo gesher tzar me'od, veha'ikar lo lefacheid klal*, "All the world is a narrow bridge, but the main thing is not to fear at all." Rabbi Nachman lived during a time in Eastern Europe when Jews struggled with poverty and persecution. In his own life, he also suffered from depression. His own fears and dark moods do not discredit his guidance; rather they fueled his quest for understanding.

Although achieving a life of perpetual joy is an unrealistic goal, choosing to act as if we are happy can positively influence how we feel. And yet it is foolish to ignore pain, whether physical or emotional. Our challenge is to examine our darker emotions—hurt, anger, resentment, fear—and to identify and strengthen the impulses that lead us toward goodness and trust.

In times of stress, whether provoked by troubled relationships, financial hardships, or grave illness, chanting a sacred phrase can bring a pause and emotional peace. After repeating your chosen phrase many times, allow yourself to sit in the expansiveness of the silence. The line above by Rabbi Nachman has been set to a popular melody. When a moment of distress seems to be descending on our emotions, consider chanting or singing the words of Rabbi Nachman: *Kol ha'olam kulo gesher tzar me'od, veha'ikar lo lefacheid klal*, "All the world is a narrow bridge, but the main thing is not to fear at all." (To hear these words chanted, access the video accompanying this paragraph.)

http://youtu.be/ WadOjouocwA

Daily Jewish Prayer as a Spiritual Journey

Jewish prayer cultivates a loving relationship with God, offering belonging and purpose. The thrice-daily service is structured as a journey through the four dimensions of our inner life, culminating in expressions of our yearning for peace for the entire world. The prescribed morning service begins with the physical. The opening words, called *Birkhot HaShachar*, "blessings of dawn," are about gratitude, a list of fifteen blessings thanking God for making us in God's image, making us free, giving sight to the blind, clothing the naked, providing for all our needs, and restoring vigor to the weary. This collage of blessings emphasizes our bodily gifts.

The second phase of the service engages us emotionally. Called *Pesukei Dezimra*, meaning "verses of song," the words are largely taken from the psalms. Consider the opening words of Psalm 100, which have been incorporated into the morning prayer service: "Acclaim the Eternal, all people on earth. Worship the Eternal in gladness; come before God with joyous song." Since music amplifies emotion, these psalms are often sung. We praise God, expressing the wonder and goodness of life.

The third phase is mind oriented. This set of prayers begins with a communal call to prayer, as if the words until this point were only a warm-up.

This section characterizes the nature of Israel's relationship with God as Creator, Teacher, and Redeemer. Each of these descriptions is prompted by an image: the rising of the sun; the gift of Torah; the redemption from Egypt. At the center of these three images of relationship is the reading of three paragraphs from the Torah, which begin, "Hear O Israel, the Eternal our God, the Eternal is one" (Deuteronomy 6:4).[9] This touchstone of Jewish faith is called the *Shema*, named for its opening Hebrew word, which translates as "hear" or "listen." The teaching calls on the people to "love the Eternal your God with all your heart, your spirit, and your physical means ... to teach these words diligently to your children ... and to write them on the doorposts of your house" (Deuteronomy 6:5–9).

After describing in the *Shema* that God gives and expects love, we are now prepared to literally stand up, step forward, and converse with the Divine. The fourth section of morning prayer prompts conversation with God, which entails imagination and intuition. The central prayer of this unit is the *Amidah*, the "standing" prayer, which we will examine more closely in the chapters on spirit and inner peace. For now, let's examine the *Shema* as a prompt to engage the heart, specifically with a focus on love.

Love and the *Shema* Prayer

Wholeness hinges on love, both feeling beloved and the corresponding desire to give graciously to others. The centrality of love is evident in the *Shema* prayer and its surrounding three blessings. Introducing the first blessing, we identify God as Creator with the chant "God renews Creation each day with goodness." In the second blessing, we focus on God as Teacher, who gave us the love letter of Torah. The liturgy reads, "Deep is Your love for us, Eternal our God, boundless Your tender compassion." In the biblical text of the *Shema* that follows the second blessing, we are commanded to love God, suggesting that God too yearns for relationship. This focus on love is at the center of both Hebrew and Christian scriptures. When Jesus was asked what is the most important command, he responded with two verses from Torah: "Love the Eternal your God" (Deuteronomy 6:4) and "Love your neighbor as yourself" (Leviticus 19:18; see Matthew 22:37; Luke 10:27). Love as an emotion is complex and paradoxical, a potential source of worry and guilt, and the foundation of wholeness and purpose. Celebrating God as Redeemer, we return to the moment of the

Israelites' safe passage to freedom, and we echo their song upon reaching the shores of the Sea of Reeds: "Who is like You, Eternal, among all that is worshipped? Who is like You, majestic in holiness, awesome in splendor, working wonders?" (Exodus 15:11).

Nurturing relationships with those who are closest to and most dependent on us is at the heart of emotional and spiritual work. Martin Buber, the twentieth-century German-Israeli theologian, taught that the Divine is manifest where there is an I-Thou relationship marked by being fully present for another person. When we give of ourselves expecting nothing in return, we are acting with profound love. The same insight is conveyed in the numerical equivalents for "love" and "God." In the *gematria* system, each letter of the Hebrew alphabet is assigned a numeric value, comparable to a = 1, b = 2 ... k = 11 ... The numerical value of *ahavah* (love) is thirteen and *YHVH*, the intimate name of God that is not pronounced, is double that: twenty-six. This numeric approach conveys that when two people genuinely love each other, God is manifest.

Beyond the I-Thou, Martin Buber acknowledged the legitimate value of I-it relationships. Relating to an "it" is relating to another as if an object, which we experience in the practical dimension of many of our interactions. For instance, in a restaurant, we will pay for someone else to cook, serve, clear, and clean our dishes. If we are considerate, we will leave a tip to express gratitude and treat those who serve us respectfully. Even our close friends are valued for what they do for us. And yet when we listen and speak—or even engage in silence—with the immediacy of connection, unfettered of expectations, we experience I-Thou, creating a space between us and the other person in which the Divine is present.

Our desire to love is a function of both nature and nurture, both hard-wired and impacted by life experience. Rene Spitz, an Austrian-American psychoanalyst who studied institutionalized children after World War II, found that children's early interactions shaped their human development. Children deprived of affection as infants literally lost their desire to live and in many cases withered away. The love that was bestowed on each of us as children, even when flawed, serves as a reservoir we may draw from to share with others. We add to that reservoir when we act lovingly and when we acknowledge the goodness that continues to flow our way. When prayer focuses us on our blessings, it inspires loving acts: smiling at a child; picking up trash in a public space; writing a check for a good cause; devoting time to someone in need; listening attentively in our daily encounters. Opening our hearts with courage and compassion is vital to increasing our wholeness.

The Wisdom of the Healing Hand

As a rabbi performing life-cycle events ranging from baby namings to funerals, I regularly encounter others' emotional wounds. Life-cycle moments are family reunions that often bring suppressed feelings to the surface: memories of hurt and distrust, as well as yearnings for greater closeness and ease. By expressing gratitude and love and offering forgiveness, we enable healing and increase our emotional well-being.

With an approaching death, I witness how often relationships are incomplete, even in close, loving relationships. There is a quality of honesty that comes with this last phase of life, especially for the person who is dying. At the bedside of a dying person, life is quite real. Such moments are holy due to the transparency of emotions and the preciousness of limited time. Honest words in the final days and hours can allow for fuller acceptance of life's incompleteness, forgiveness, and the healing of relationships, enabling closure and enhanced ease in the last phase of life.

The five statements below provide a "healing hand."[10] They offer focus and concrete actions for meaningful, honest words, whether in bidding farewell or in living in closer relationship with loved ones now.

1. *Thank you.* Express gratitude personally, whether for something quite simple or more profound.
2. *Forgive me.* Ask your loved one to forgive you for your shortcomings or for a particular act that caused pain—the more specific, the more helpful. Sincerity is essential. The larger goal of reconciliation trumps who is right.
3. *I forgive you.* Let the other person know that you forgive him or her for the specific ways that he or she has hurt or disappointed you. To forgive is not to condone hurtful behavior, but to gain release from it. The work of forgiveness is to accept the other person and to embrace compassionately the whole person, including and despite shortcomings.
4. *I love you.* With forgiveness comes an opening of the heart and a larger capacity for compassion and love. Expressing love is a great

gift. Nothing feels better than being told that we are loved. We should never assume that it is known. Putting our love into words makes an enormous impact on both the person to whom we say the words and ourselves.

5. *When you are ready, you can go.* In a deathbed situation, it helps to give the dying person permission to leave. Doing so conveys, "Do not worry; I can manage; I am willing to let go of holding on to you so that you can be released from pain." In other relationships, it is important that we let go and give our loved ones permission to choose their own path.

Even after our family members have passed, we can aid our own healing by writing a letter to the departed using the five statements of the healing hand. Furthermore, we need not wait until the end is near to do the courageous work of healing and expressing our love. The sage Rabbi Eliezer taught, "Turn one day prior to your death." His students asked, "Master, how can anyone know what day is one day prior to his or her death?" He replied, "Therefore, turn today, because tomorrow you may die" (*Shabbat* 153a). Using these five steps in fullness of health allows us to live now with greater ease, joy, and vitality.

Forgiveness is essential in all relationships. We will fall short of doing as much as we could for those we love. We may also harbor anger for selfish and even abusive behavior that was inflicted on us. Many of us hold on to our justifiable rage. And yet holding on to painful memories inflicts ongoing harm on ourselves. To forgive is not to say that the wrongdoing was excusable; rather, it is to acknowledge that there is now a need to move forward. In the words of Christian theologian Paul Tillich, "Forgiveness presupposes remembering, and it creates a forgetting, not in the natural way we forget yesterday's weather, but in the way of the great 'in spite of' that says: I forget although I remember."[11] We have succeeded in forgiveness when on hearing the other person's name we respond with a smile, rather than a grimace. When we let go of a hurt, we have given ourselves a gift of greater emotional freedom.

Giving our loved ones permission to choose is also important in how we relate to those closest to us. As a parent, I am aware of my tendency to want to tell my children what choices to make. After all, I have far greater life experience than they do and more fully appreciate the consequences of their decisions. My children are young adults who no longer depend on me to protect them. I let my children know that when they ask, I am available for guidance, but also that I trust they will act with the values that we share. And when I express my gratitude and love for them and their mother, I hear my words sincerely reciprocated—and that sure feels good.

We are also wise to actively extend the healing hand toward ourselves: feeling gratitude for the goodness in our lives; forgiving ourselves for unworthy behavior; readjusting unrealistic expectations; feeling lovable; letting go into new beginnings. Feeling loved, we more easily love others. We have faith that we will manage capably, caringly, and responsibly and so are prepared to step into the unknown.

No Absolute Peace

Life is dynamic and invariably incomplete. Rabbi Adin Steinsaltz, the contemporary translator and commentator of the Talmud, cautioned:

> The very concept of the Divine as infinite implies an activity that is endless, of which one must never grow weary.... The Jewish approach to life considers the man who has stopped going [on]— he who has a feeling of completion, of peace, of a great light from above that has brought him to rest—to be someone who has lost his way.[12]

Inner peace is never fully achievable, only tasted for fleeting moments. These tastes are more readily accessed and sustained through spiritual practices. Emotional balance is likewise dynamic. And yet to live closer to the fulcrum of the natural seesaw of life's emotions is to savor life more fully, because it means to live more fully in the present. Engaging the present also means having a strong connection to the past and to the future. When we live with greater emotional wholeness, we express love with greater ease and more consistently feel lovable, effective, and at home in the world.

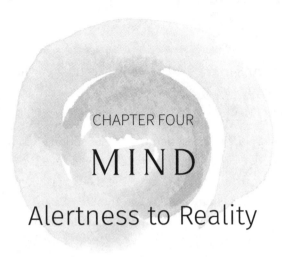

CHAPTER FOUR

MIND

Alertness to Reality

Information is never fully objective but is colored by disposition, personal history, reflection, and what we expect to find. As a story told by the Baal Shem Tov illustrates, our experiences are always an interpretation of what is before us:

http://youtu.be/
ejfN2K7pGuQ

> Once, a talented musician came to town. He stood on a street corner and began to play. Many who stopped to listen could not tear themselves away, and soon a large crowd stood enthralled by the glorious music whose equal they had never heard. Before long they were moving to its rhythm, and the entire street was transformed into a dancing mass of humanity. A deaf man walking by wondered: Has the world gone mad?[1]

What we notice and how we understand it defines our reality. Our own limitations, including preconceptions, will skew and narrow our perceptions. We cannot control much that happens to us, but we can pay close attention, choose our interpretations carefully, and thus shape the impact of events on us.

The mind cautions us of dangers and identifies those people whom we can trust and even love and offers a worldview that determines many of our attitudes. The mind can enhance a life of wholeness, rather than get in the way, when we openly notice the world around us and carefully choose our ideas.

I had a wonderful teacher, Rabbi Simon Greenberg, who taught for fifty years at The Jewish Theological Seminary. After turning ninety years old, he spoke to a group of rabbis in celebration of his birthday:

> People ask, "How is it that you have lived so long?" My longevity was decided in *Yeshivah shel Ma'lah*, the Heavenly Court. My quantity of years is not due to anything that I have done. Yet I can say why my life has provided a great quality of satisfaction. In my early twenties, I made a choice that has made all the difference. I chose to see myself as living before a loving God and to see the world as a creation of that God. That decision has allowed me to experience each day as a gift.

This chapter begins with a substantial account of my own religious journey of shifting beliefs, a journey marked by doubts. I begin this chapter on mind with an exploration of whether there is a caring Presence that transcends our limited years and how to understand why many people fall far short of the ideal in their espoused religions. I delve into faith because ideas matter, especially the big ideas that shape our worldview. As a rabbi I have invested deeply in learning about my tradition and in teaching others. And yet even with that commitment there is room to wrestle and wonder. My hope in sharing this personal account is to prompt your own reflection on what you believe about God, for that profoundly influences how you see the world.

Spiritual Crisis in the East

A decade ago I had the privilege to spend forty weeks traveling to seventeen countries with my wife and three children. Most of the countries we visited were located in Asia, where we could keep costs down, explore new terrain, and begin to learn about Eastern religions. Our sons were in high school, and we arranged for them to take their classes online. I also designed a course on comparative religion for them, using Huston Smith's classic *The World's Religions* as our text.[2] In his introduction Professor Smith states that just as a textbook on the history of art would present only the great artworks, so his book would describe each faith tradition at its best. As I read about Hinduism, Daoism, Buddhism, and the Jains, I was inspired by the distinctive wisdom of each of these ancient faiths.

In Bali we attended a Hindu ceremony in honor of ancestors. I was drawn to the song, dance, and silence, and the use of flowers and rice as part of the symbolic celebration. On an intellectual level, I was curious about the use of colorful ritual, meditation, and yoga as expressions of this spiritual path. I asked our tour guide if he could arrange for us to meet his Hindu priest. He looked a bit concerned by the request. He revealed that in the course of thirty years he had never had a private conversation with his spiritual leader, for fear that if the priest was offended by his words he would be cursed.

The elderly priest did agree to meet, and we sat with him a few days later at an outdoor temple shrine. Our guide served as the translator. We spoke for forty minutes about the priest's daily work. When he handed me his handheld bell, which the guide had earlier described as infused with the power of the spirits and reserved only for the priest, my guide's eyes opened wide. I rang the jewel-encrusted bell as a fellow professional.

Just months before our encounter the massive ocean waves of a tsunami had devastated the region. I asked the priest, "How do you explain the tsunami?"

"It is clear," he replied without hesitation. "It was intended as a punishment for the Muslims."

"But many Hindus were killed too, correct?" I responded.

The guide failed to translate my challenge, perhaps to protect me from offending his power-laden priest, and instead explained, "Yes, but mostly Muslims." Ouch. I was pained by the wide gap between the theory of a universal, loving Hindu God and the narrow belief of this Hindu leader and his follower.

In Thailand I sat outdoors conversing with a twentysomething Buddhist monk. I had previously spent time with Buddhist practitioners who had greatly aided me in developing my meditation practice. I had also heard Buddhist sages, including the Dalai Lama and Thich Nhat Hanh, whose teachings on human nature I found insightful. The young man described how he had grown up in a poor village and that he chose to join a monastery after seeing a film about monks engaging in martial arts. He remained because of the education and his Buddhist faith. When I asked him about future goals, he replied that he yearned to visit an ashram in India to experience the land where the Buddha had walked and taught. After I offered him a small contribution toward realizing his dream, the young monk asked if he could bless me. When he finished, I asked him to translate. The words of his blessing were similar to the words that I would have shared on behalf of a congregant or friend. "But to whom do you say your blessing?" I asked. "I thought that Buddhists did not believe in a Supreme Being, a God who blesses."

"There are powers all around us," he replied. "For instance, in each of these trees," he said, pointing to our surroundings, "are spirits who impact our lives." I was surprised by the gap between the purity of abstract Buddhist principles and this youth's magical worldview informed by animism.

Near Udaipur, India, my family and I visited a Jain temple. In preparation for our travels, I had read *Holy Cow*, a book that Professor Smith had personally recommended.[3] The author, an Australian journalist, described her search for spiritual wisdom in India and concluded that the Jains, whose faith had developed as an offshoot of Hinduism, lived with extraordinary devotion to lofty principles. The Jain monks, for instance, are so pure in orientation that when they walk the countryside, they do so naked while whisking a broom before each step so as to protect all living creatures. In the Jain holy shrine near Udaipur, beautifully carved marble columns containing figures with eyes of inlaid black stones filled the expanse around the central altar. We eventually made our way over to the spiritual leader of the temple. In his late forties, he looked like the actor Sean Connery's James Bond, but with a jet-black beard and a lively twinkle in his eyes. He described sleeping for only a few hours each night, using the stillness of the darkness for meditation and writing inspired insights. So great was his spiritual devotion, he said, that in his entire life he had never watched television nor read a single newspaper.

"The only other Jain believers that I have met in India," I said, "were jewelers. How can Jains also be businesspeople?"

"When we want to do business, we are quite successful," he replied. Then he added, "Not as successful as the Jews, but far more generous. The Jews spend their money on war."

His anti-Jewish statement surprised us. My fifteen-year-old son immediately challenged, "But you said you don't follow the news. On what basis do you make such a claim?"

"There are many visitors to our temple," the priest replied. "I watch the Jews and they do not come before the altar and make contributions."

"I am a priest for Jews," I told him. He looked surprised but maintained his calm demeanor.

"And as a matter of faith, we do not make contributions before the altars of other faiths. But we are a generous people," my wife added a bit indignantly.

The priest continued to smile and twinkle but soon excused himself, ending the conversation.

Once again I felt the air knocked out of me. Here was a revered religious leader who had formed a worldview that allowed for ignorance and bigotry. My hope of finding followers of the Jain faith who lived up to the ideals of their teachings was crushed.

An Even Greater Trauma in Israel

Among those of my own faith, I would soon encounter the greatest disappointment in my search for spiritual wisdom, humility, and integrity. After our time in Asia we traveled to Israel, where we rented an apartment for ten weeks. On our first Friday afternoon, on the eve of Shabbat, an old friend called my wife with a request: "Our thirteen-year-old daughter is suffering from terrible headaches. May we bring her over to see you tomorrow night?"

After examining the young woman, Linda, a neurologist specializing in epilepsy, said, "There aren't clear physical signs of a cause for the headaches. It might just be a product of the onset of menstruation. And yet I do detect a slight wobble in her gait. So be sure to take her to a hospital tomorrow and get a CT scan of her brain."

The imaging revealed that the young woman had a brain tumor. On Wednesday the family met with a neurosurgeon, who scheduled the operation for the following Sunday morning. Meanwhile, a son-in-law said to the father, "I know a former chief rabbi who is a great mystic. Here is his phone number. Call him for a blessing."

When the father telephoned, the chief rabbi offered to meet: "Come to my home in Jerusalem on Saturday night. In the meantime, visit with a local rabbi, who will guide you," and he gave the father the contact information. The local rabbi directed the father to gather earth from two graves of famous rabbis, then place the earth in a bandanna and wrap it around his daughter's head. The rabbi also gave him a vial of olive oil to pour onto the spiritual bandage. As his wife sat in the hospital with their daughter, the father crisscrossed the country to obtain the sacred soil.

On Saturday night the father went to the chief rabbi's home, feeling privileged to have a personal audience. The elderly sage gave him a book in which each verse of Psalms was organized by its first letter and directed my friend to journey to the Western Wall in Jerusalem to recite the verses that began with the letters that spelled out his daughter's three-letter name, and then to proceed for prayers to the grave of a saintly rabbi. As the father rose to depart, the chief rabbi added, "I sense that your efforts have already made a difference and that your daughter will be fine. Do not proceed with the surgery."

After leaving, the father immediately called the surgeon, who was also an observant Jew, and told him what the chief rabbi had said. In the previous two days, the young woman had begun to lose her peripheral vision due to the tumor pressing on her optic nerve. The surgeon was firmly opposed to any delay. The father was now caught between the holy man and the physician. Several phone calls later, the chief rabbi agreed that if a CT scan showed that her tumor still existed, they could proceed with the surgery. The tumor had grown. The surgery commenced.

My wife and I visited the girl in the hospital a few days later. All were relieved that the surgery was over and that the young woman was recovering.

Her father said to me, "Elie, would you read a letter that I have written to the chief rabbi?" In the letter, the father thanked the rabbi for his care and concern. I was struck by how magical thinking had prompted the father to continue to curry favor from a rabbi who possessed "spiritual powers." Once again I observed fear as an underpinning of faith and a religious leader who was unwilling to acknowledge his limitations, which in this case had posed a dangerous threat.

I felt angry and injured. How could religious leaders behave with such hubris? As a rabbi for close to twenty years, I knew intellectually that even religious leaders falter. I knew that fear motivates faith for many. And yet I felt deeply shaken. In the midst of exploring the new, I had raised my emotional expectations that these traditional religious leaders would embody wisdom and integrity. Deeply wounded, I questioned both my own faith and my work as a religious leader.

Reorientation

For many months, I found it difficult to pray as I grieved the loss of my trust in so many clergy and the awareness that religion often emerges from fear and magical thinking. Once back in California, I sought out admired teachers to guide me in processing my spiritual trauma, including Rabbi Jonathan Omer-Man, who was a member of the first Jewish delegation to meet with the Dalai Lama in India, in 1990.[4]

Rabbi Omer-Man, never one to mince words, said to me, "You sound like someone who has had a bad experience with the rabbi at his bar mitzvah and is using that as a justification to dismiss Judaism in its entirety. When we traveled to meet the Dalai Lama in India, there was a group of secular Tibetans who asked for a meeting. At the end of a polite and uneventful conversation we asked, 'Why did you want to speak with us?'

"'We understand,' one of the leaders responded, 'that Jews control the press in Beijing. We hoped that you would convey our plight to the Jewish media.'

"Now because these secular Tibetans were wildly misinformed, do you think I should judge all secular people negatively?"

Rabbi Omer-Man's directness and wisdom allowed me to step back and acknowledge that the spiritual leaders who had disappointed me did not define the whole enterprise of religion. Although some religious leaders are small-minded and self-serving, this is true for people in all walks of life. We do not judge medicine or law by the failings of some physicians or judges. Intellectually I knew this to be true, but when my expectations for goodness and wisdom among religious leaders were dashed, I responded emotionally. It took Jonathan's critique, and some time, for me to cease nursing my wounds and examine my experiences in a more mindful way.

Yes, religion may emerge from fear, but it is also prompted by the best in us: the yearning for transcendent connection, meaning, and service. Rituals in particular may cultivate enduring values, nurture a sense of belonging, and evoke genuine goodness. When a Jewish woman lights candles on Friday night, for instance, it marks the start of the Sabbath, offering a pause from the week during which she surveys her blessings, yearnings, and belonging across generations. When a person recites a blessing before eating, it is a mindful pause that elevates feeding to sacred dining. The symbols of a wedding offer vessels for sacred transformation that cannot be put into words. Religion may refine that which makes us most human.

My conversation with Rabbi Omer-Man did make an impact, because I respected his integrity. And yet in describing the conversation as a turning point, I recognize that I had already given much thought to my relationship with God and religion. Intellectual exercise had made a way for my emotional reorientation.

Even so, I was left with a vexing question, the key challenge to religious faith: What is God's role in suffering?

God's Place in Tragedy

Among the most distressing of the many funerals that I have attended was that of a nine-year-old relative, Jordan, who died from undiagnosed diabetes. The December burial in Boston took place in frozen ground, but it was the challenge to faith that left me shuddering. At the funeral a beloved rabbi eulogized that Jordan had been a pure soul whom God had chosen to retrieve. Those words, intended to bring comfort, disturbed me as a distortion of tragedy. I knew Jordan and loved him, but he was only human. His death was due to the lack of a medical diagnosis. Artificially sweetening the bitterness felt wrong.

A few weeks before the funeral, I had a public conversation before my California congregation with Rabbi Harold S. Kushner, whose book *When Bad Things Happen to Good People* addressed his own shaken faith in response to the suffering of his son, Aaron, who died at the age of fourteen from progeria, an incurable genetic disease that causes rapid aging and death.[5] Kushner, then a pulpit rabbi, analyzes the book of Job in his best seller. In that biblical account, the saintly Job suffers unimaginable loss and ongoing physical pain, which challenge his faith in the justice of God. Toward the end of the book, God responds to Job's cries, "Who is it that gives counsel without knowledge?... Where were you when I laid the foundations of the earth?" (Job 38:2, 4). Rabbi Kushner interprets God's rebuttal as essentially saying, "Yes, I created the world, but have chosen not to intervene. It is a good world and I am loving, but I am limited in power." This understanding departs from most traditional Jewish commentators, who interpret God's words as declaring, "My power, knowledge, and intentions are beyond your human grasp." Kushner would explain his motivation forthrightly, "As my son was dying, I needed a God to whom I could pray and who was not responsible for his suffering."[6]

After Jordan passed, I had the opportunity to visit with Holocaust survivor and Nobel Peace Prize laureate Elie Wiesel in New York City. I asked his opinion of Kushner's theology. "I don't agree," he replied. "I cannot say that God's power is limited. God is a mystery. God, for me, is a question mark."

Later I called Reb Zalman Schachter-Shalomi, a master teacher of Jewish mysticism and the founder of the Jewish Renewal movement. "How do you understand God's role in tragedy?" I asked him.

"I approach it on the four levels of traditional mystical teaching," Reb Zalman replied, "the physical (*assiyah*), the emotional (*yetzirah*), the intellectual (*beriah*), and the intuitive (*atzilut*). First, I want to know what has happened. I inquire as to the physical causes of the death. Next, I just seek to hold those who mourn, embracing them in their pain. On the intellectual level, I can only go as far as Kushner. As the Talmud teaches, *Olam kiminhago noheg*, 'The world operates according to its order' [*Avodah Zarah* 54a]. God created a good world, but not a world that is perfect. Bad stuff happens. And finally, on the intuitive level, I glimpse that life in its unfolding is whole and purposeful. Although that realization is elusive, it is also foundational and informs my humility and acceptance."

Reb Zalman's teaching has offered me a religious response to loss that reinforces the very thesis of this book: We live on four planes simultaneously. I accept human limitation. I identify with God as described by Isaiah, "My thoughts are not your thoughts; My ways are not your ways" (Isaiah 55:8). I do not expect as a human being to understand the mind of God. At the same time, my aversion to easy answers on God by "holy clerics" persists. I do not worship an abusive God or justify the Holocaust as part of God's plan. I am a child of Holocaust survivors: my mother spent the war years in Auschwitz and my father in a Hungarian forced labor camp; both had family members who were murdered. And yet I learned from how my parents chose to lead their lives to believe in a God who calls on us to "choose life" (Deuteronomy 30:19) despite unknowns and traumatic loss. To live with such a faith is to still believe that the world is good and that God cares, offering the gifts of feeling beloved and hopeful. And yet I have also learned to reject easy explanations of God's role in suffering. Acknowledging evil is necessary in a world of unnecessary suffering.

Blasphemy

When I was in my twenties, I visited the Kotel, the Western Wall, as I mentioned in chapter 3. Just behind me, a group of young men dressed in white shirts and black pants were celebrating their pilgrimage with a song and a circle dance. I grabbed hands and joined their celebration. Abruptly their religious teacher proclaimed, "Please stop. I have an important story to share." He proceeded:

> Once upon a time there was a young artist. He climbed a steep mountain with a friend to paint the beautiful landscape. He set up an easel and grew more and more focused on his art. After painting for a while, he started to walk backward with his thumb extended to judge the perspective displayed on his canvas. Behind him was a cliff. His friend shouted, "Stop!" but the artist was oblivious. Desperate, his friend picked up a rock and heaved it. As the stone burst through the canvas, the painter leaped forward. In doing so, the artist's life was saved in the nick of time.
>
> So it was before the Second World War. The Jews were assimilating quickly. God needed to grab their attention to prevent a total loss. The Holocaust was God's drastic effort to save the Jewish people.

This story knocked the air out of me. It was revolting to justify the murder of a million and a half children and a total of six million Jews. Later I would read Elie Wiesel's *The Trial of God*, the playwright's angry protest against those who would characterize God's role in the Holocaust. Wiesel has emphasized that it is blasphemy to explain God's intentions in the Holocaust.

There are no answers to God's place in tragedy or willful human cruelty that satisfy me. Faith requires critical thinking if we are to avoid falling into the trap of believing a colorful story as truthful wisdom. It is natural to seek clarity, but if the price for simple answers is intellectual dishonesty, then the price is too high. Faith and skepticism can coexist and actively engage each other. Robust faith can honor doubt.

 Try This: **Identifying Holy Moments**

When I ask people, "Do you believe in God?" there is often a hesitation. After all, what are the definitions of "believe" and "God"? Who can be sure as to the nature of a God without a body when all that we experience is mediated by our physicality? And yet I find that our descriptions of sacred experiences evoke profound and surprising responses.

> Write down three moments when you have felt close to God.
>
> After writing, consider how these episodes in your own life manifest certain facets of God, such as caregiver, comforter, shield, or fearsome power. How have these holy moments shaped your worldview?
>
> Now turn your description into a short prayer of praise.

In culling my own holy moments, I believe that God is a caring Consciousness that pervades creation. From time to time, both in moments of surprise and as a product of preparation, I experience God as a flow of love and unity within the world and, at other times, as a still, small voice that informs conscience, calling on me to live out core values. Living with a belief in God enhances my orientation of being beloved and at home in the world. Such a faith contributes enormously to my inner peace. Such a faith feels real, both emotionally and intuitively, and meshes with my life experience. My mind honors that faith, knowing that it cannot be intellectually proved or disproved. By transcending instinct and assessing our experiences with an analytic mind, we cultivate our spirituality.

The Distinctive Human Mind

Erich Fromm, an Austrian Jewish psychologist of the nineteenth and twentieth centuries, defined primal human angst as stemming from a paradox of mind: "We are distinctly intertwined with nature and aware of our separateness."[7] When experiencing ourselves as an extension of nature, we feel a quality of unity. In the words of Joseph Campbell, "The goal of life is to make your heartbeat match the beat of the universe, to match your nature with Nature."[8] And yet upon reflection, we are set apart too. As a Zen poet wrote in the *Zinrin Kushu*:

> The wild geese do not intend to cast
> their reflection;
> The water has no mind to receive
> their image.

In contrast, a biologist examining the makeup of a cell or an astronomer peering at the sky is engaged in an intentional act, a pursuit grounded in curiosity and choice. We have the facility to transcend instinct. We may discover our deepest selves by utilizing our ability to see the big picture and to uncover the essence of things. We have the capacity to defy immediate self-interest, such as choosing to fast in order to express contrition, self-discipline, or belonging. Our sense of right and wrong is shaped by culture, is honed by self-reflection, and emerges from conscience. Although we are inclined to give in to hardwired cravings of appetite, we may choose to set long-term goals and to abide by moral action. We are each an "I," a self-reflective knowing, before an "Eye," a grand consciousness that underlies all knowing.

Dr. Elizabeth Spelke, a Harvard professor who has dedicated her career to the study of the unfolding intelligence of children, says that human language is the secret ingredient that gives us the capacity for using numbers, spatial relations, and social constructs to connect forces, cultivate ideas, and catapult us toward new horizons. "What's special about language is its productive combinational power," she says. "We can use it to combine anything with anything."[9]

Humans are uniquely unable to communicate with each other due to differing languages (currently estimated at nearly seven thousand) and yet simultaneously may use language to convey ideas across generations and the globe. Each species has its own attributes, its own unique expression of spirit. To fully express our humanity, we need to cultivate our kinship with the larger world by using language to create and commune. We use our minds to speak and to listen. The *Shema* (meaning "listen") is a central prayer in the daily flow of the traditional service. Listening is the essential activity that allows for language, learning, and love.

Listening as Meditation

Listening is more than a physical act. To listen well requires intention. Listening at its best is a form of meditation, a taking in of another's words with steady focus. When counseling, I will listen with no expectations, being as fully present as possible as a receiving vessel. I will then reframe concisely what I have heard while amplifying intuitively the emotional dimension. My goal is both to convey that I have listened and to evoke what might have been unsaid. I will ask the person before me to respond to how I have reframed his or her words. Through responding, the speaker gains catharsis, clarity, and the gratification of being heard. I will then shift and react to what I have heard as myself, honestly conveying what challenges or discomforts are present and how I might respond if I were in a similar situation.

⚮ *Try This:* **A Listening Exercise**

This exercise demonstrates the satisfaction of feeling heard and the annoyance of feeling ignored.

> Find a listening partner and set a timer for two minutes. You will each take a turn as the speaker and the listener. When listening to the other person, do so initially as a model listener: make eye contact, lean forward intently, refrain from interrupting.
>
> Once the alarm sounds, reset the timer for one minute. The good listener will now become a poor listener by looking away, whether fidgeting with socks or staring off into space.
>
> At the end of the two-part exercise, have the speaker share how it felt to be listened to closely and how it felt when the listener ceased to pay attention.
>
> Switch roles and do the exercise again.[10]

In sharing reactions to this simple exercise, I have found that when a person feels listened to, words flow easily, but when the listener stops making eye contact, the speaker is stymied and stumbles due to distraction and annoyance. Reflexively the speaker wonders, "Why is she not listening to me? Am I so boring?" This is true even when people know that the listener has been instructed to look away. Ideas falter as the person unconsciously wonders, "How do I get her attention back?" This exercise reveals the power of reflexive, hardwired emotions to quickly overcome the objective mind. Satisfaction, empowerment, and greater self-control come with hearing others and feeling heard.

The *Shema* Prayer's Focus on Listening

In the previous chapter, I looked at the *Shema's* focus on love. As an engagement of mind, the *Shema* and its blessings also draw our attention to three key paragraphs of the Torah that convey the nature of relationship with God and emphasize the centrality of listening. By once again examining the *Shema* prayer, we gain insight into what we are expected to hear in order to forge a relationship with God. The first two units of traditional daily prayer (*Birkhot HaShachar*, the blessings of dawn, and *Pesukei Dezimra*, verses of song) have evoked gratitude for our physicality and they have prompted emotional praise. With the *Shema* and surrounding blessings, we engage our minds by recalling the nature of the Supreme Being. We do so to prepare for conversation with God, the apex of our daily prayer journey.

We begin by acknowledging God as Creator, Teacher, and Freedom-Maker. At the center of this three-fold description of God are several paragraphs from the Torah that describe God's expectations of us, including the need to listen, to affirm God's oneness, and to love God (Deuteronomy 6:4–9, 11:13–21; Numbers 15:37–41). The opening paragraph of the three passages begins with the word *shema*, which means "listen" and gives the entire paragraph its name.

To elicit concentration, Jewish practice is marked by placing a hand over one's eyes while saying the opening line of the *Shema*. This prayer is chanted traditionally during morning and evening services and before falling asleep each night. So important are the opening six words as a touchstone of Jewish faith that they are the last words a person traditionally recites before dying. Those words, taken from Deuteronomy 6:4, are *Shema Yisrael Adonai Eloheinu, Adonai echad*, often translated, "Hear O Israel, the Eternal our God, the Eternal is One."

Moses originally spoke these words as part of his farewell before turning power over to his successor, Joshua, who would lead the people into the Promised Land while Moses stayed behind on the far side of the Jordan River. After recapping his people's history, including the revelation of the Ten Commandments at Mount Sinai, the 120-year-old Moses formulates the essence of their faith. As he looks out over the Israelite flock, Moses begins with *Shema!*, "Listen!" as if to draw their full presence to what he will proclaim. When we chant the *Shema* we are part of a chain of listeners. We listen as if Moses were before us. When we draw the echo of those sounds inward, we may make the words our own.[11] A traditional reading of Torah texts approaches each word as purposeful and multilayered in meaning. Even the sound of each letter is viewed as a distinctive packet of energy.

Rabbi Aryeh Kaplan, an important twentieth-century writer on Jewish meditation, pointed out that when chanting the word *shema*, the sounds move from "sh," which produces the most wave motions on an oscilloscope, to "mm," which as a wave is almost a flat line.[12] (This is true of the word *shalom* as well, as I pointed out in chapter 2.) The *ayin*, the final Hebrew letter of the word *shema*, has no sound, and the name of the letter means "nothingness," another name for God, who in essence eludes all description. When chanting the three syllables *sh-mm-'*, we move from motion to calm to silence, and in that silence we may pause to feel the coming together of life's vitality. The following is a meditation on the sounds of the Hebrew word *shema*, sounds that evoke a subtle journey toward achieving quiet from within.

 Try This: **Shema Meditation**

Sit straight, feet flat. Breathe out tension; breathe in calm.

http://youtu.be/
OYcuytazeG8

Chant softly the following three syllables while exhaling: first, the sound of "sh"; "mm" on the next exhale; and on the third exhale, just experience silence. When other thoughts arise, label them with one word and let them gently pass as you return to the chant. (Continue doing this sequence for five minutes.)

Now in your mind's ear continue to hear the sound of "sh" as you breathe out. Attach the sound of the "sh" as if encountering the motion of a wave (one minute).

Now hear the "sh" as a blowing wind, feeling the motion (one minute).

Shift to focusing on the sound of "mm" and experience the "mm" as the sound of calm (two minutes).

Allow yourself to stay with your breath, breathing in and out with calm focus. Know that this is the silence of the Hebrew letter *ayin* (ﬠ). See yourself as a grounded vessel. Listen to what flows through you. Open to receiving intuitive insights (four minutes).

Count from three to one, returning to wakefulness, aware of any insights that you might have gained, while remaining open, calm, and alert.

Limitations of the Rational Mind

An unknown author taught, "The longest journey a person must take is the eighteen inches from the head to the heart." Our minds, which offer divine-like power, are often disconnected from what we feel and do. We know we should exercise but we fail to make the time. Emotions prompt us to buy a luxury item, and we then justify our purchase. We tell ourselves creative stories to explain our self-serving behavior. Past injuries, often hidden in the recesses of memory, put us on guard and prevent us from seeing clearly or reacting wisely. We attune our senses to the familiar, often ignoring fresh experiences and insights.

In his book *Thinking, Fast and Slow*, Nobel Prize–winning economist Daniel Kahneman uses social psychology research to demonstrate the gap between rational analysis and how we actually make decisions. Outcomes are often determined by mental shortcuts, skewed by how questions are posed, or influenced by a well-told coherent story, even if it is false. For example, 84 percent of physicians hypothetically chose to do surgery when presented with a one-month patient survival rate of 90 percent; while only 50 percent favored doing the surgery when presented with outcomes of 10 percent mortality in the first month. The two statistics point to the same medical outcome, but the way the information was presented led to the doctors making dramatically different choices.[13] Kahneman also argues that we tend toward cognitive ease (thinking fast) over the demands of intellectual analysis (thinking slowly) and that we tend to avoid decisions.[14]

Our ability to understand how the world works is also limited by unending layers of knowledge. In the words of Ecclesiastes, "However much a person toils in seeking, he will not find it out; even though a wise person claims to know, she cannot find it out" (Ecclesiastes 8:17). The world around us invites inspection, and the output of data increases exponentially. Yet the unknown only grows.

According to traditional commentators, the Hebrew word for "world," *olam*, shares the root for "that which is hidden."[15] Whether delving into an atom or searching the stars, the more we discover, the more we become aware of mystery. In 1930 the scientist Abraham Flexner wrote, "No scientist, fifty years ago, could have realized that he was as ignorant as all first-rate scientists now know themselves to be."[16] If that was true then, it is much more true for our own day. For instance, in examining the physical evidence of the big bang and evolution, imponderables emerge: What existed before the big bang? Where did the physical material come from? How did the rules of evolution emerge? How did physical material morph into consciousness? If the big bang is a singularity, a unique event, what other singularities might define our reality? Our ability to ask these questions is itself a mystery. In the words of Rabbi Abraham Joshua Heschel, "The most incomprehensible fact is the fact that we comprehend at all."[17]

The Mind's Role in Nurturing Inner Peace

Much of this chapter on mind has focused on big and lofty questions. For inner peace, we need to also examine how we see ourselves and the world around us. Most of us live with an undertow of vulnerability, marked by anxiety and overreaction. We seesaw from feeling strong to weak. Part of our vulnerability is universal and deep-seated. Even children raised by stable parents in safe neighborhoods worry about monsters under the bed, a response to the natural, primal anxiety of a child's small size and vulnerability. Maurice Sendak, the author of the beloved children's book *Where the Wild Things Are*, was criticized for scaring children. He wisely recognized, confirmed by the popularity of his books, that frightening images are already present for children. His books describe how it is possible to befriend the monsters. When we look a monster in the eye with quiet confidence, it becomes transformed into a gentle friend or just slides away. Similarly, by using our minds to examine our fears, we can determine if we are overreacting. When we look fear in the eye, we can usually tame it.

How we experience immediate challenges is colored by previous vulnerabilities. Alfred Adler, the great psychologist, emphasized that our identities and energies are often directed to overcompensating for the perceived shortcomings in our youth. For instance, an accomplished physician in my community shared that his immigrant parents depended on him as a ten-year-old to serve as their translator. He recalled feeling overwhelmed when speaking on behalf of his parents to lawyers concerning the sale of real estate. Even as an adult he continued to feel intense anxiety when engaged in legal proceedings, which he does on a regular basis.

I advised him to enter into a quiet mind-set and to address the young boy that he carries within. I asked him to hold the boy and reassure him that he is not fully responsible for his parents' successes or failures and that he was remarkably strong to have even served as his parents' translator. With the young boy's hand in his, I asked him to revisit the original situations and to perceive that the outcomes were not as dependent on him as he previously experienced and that he was a talented and beloved youth. When I met with the physician a week later, he shared that he had followed up on my guidance and had been able to reassure the child within. A few weeks later, he said that he had continued to feel greater confidence and less anxiety in addressing legal matters. I invited the adult physician to also thank the child within for enabling him to have become a successful physician as an adult.

Exaggerated anxiety may still exist for this doctor, but now he knows that he can use his mind and imagination to recalibrate and soften reflexive responses. Such cognitive-behavioral therapy trains us to defuse the power of upsetting thoughts by challenging their accuracy and validity. In seeking inner peace, we bring the analytic capacity of our minds to examine reality both subjectively and with a detached perspective.

Context is essential in judging behavior. For instance, when a car speeds by, we may feel angered by the behavior of a "dangerous driver" or sympathetic if it is clear that the person is rushing to the hospital. We can train ourselves to seek out a broader context and a more detailed assessment of a situation. Many of our overreactions are due to labeling events as part of a larger pattern rather than seeing a specific action in its own particular context. For instance, one spouse may throw away a used tea bag that the other has kept out as the last of a favorite flavor to be used one more time. He experiences this moment as, "She is *always* throwing everything away, including what I need." Her inner commentary is, "He *never* throws anything away, which is why he is so disorganized." A minor event explodes into a major confrontation. This is only one example of the danger of using words like "always" and "never" and of overgeneralizing and labeling.

The mind's ability to reassess thoughtfully is powerful. And yet some emotions may linger even when the mind has gained clarity. When we intellectually untie an emotional knot, the metaphorical string remains a bit crooked and even frayed. It is only natural to live with some emotional strain and overreaction.

∞ *Try This:* **Discerning Patterns and Directing Your Future**

Use the following as journal material:

Looking back:

> Examine when you have most recently felt upset.
>
> What was the incident?
>
> What bothered you about it so much?
>
> How did you react?
>
> Is there a discernible pattern to the upset?
>
> How might you reinterpret such incidents to allow yourself to feel more balanced in future responses?

To enhance inner peace, it is essential to look to the future. We are as profoundly shaped by where we see ourselves going as by where we have been. Research shows that the anticipation of a vacation or a reunion with loved ones shapes our well-being even more profoundly than the events themselves.

Our minds steady us through observation, interpretation, and goal setting. Choosing goals and acting on them shapes our self-identity and perception of life's goodness. It is wise to choose a one-year goal. It might be a big family trip or learning a new skill, but it is necessary that the goal be attainable. It is also healthy to have a longer-range goal, a three- or five-year goal, such as earning a degree, building a business, or saving a set amount of funds. Now use the following as journal material:

Looking inward:

> What are several of your strengths?
>
> What are your sources of joy?
>
> What are several of your prime worries?
>
> How can you better manage your worries?

Looking forward:

> What is a significant goal for the next year, whether in obtaining a long-sought possession, making progress in work, or improving a personal relationship?

What are the steps needed to make that goal a reality?

Break down those steps and identify a timeline to meet them.

Looking forward five years, see yourself as having attained a longer-term goal. Describe the goal that you have achieved.

How do you feel?

What was the most important ingredient in having reached your goal?

Valuing and Transcending Mind

Ideas have advanced the quality of our lives. Ideas build on each other and by determined study create the foundation for innovation. Democracy, for instance, has led to greater individual dignity. Technological improvements in medicine, transportation, agriculture, and communication have enhanced the quality and quantity of our days. The computer on which I am typing is but one example of how intellect has fashioned tools that make our lives better.

Although the analytic mind is essential, its knowledge is incomplete. There is more to reality than fits into a formula. As Freud sagely taught, "When making a decision of minor importance, I have always found it advantageous to consider all the pros and cons. In vital matters, however, such as the choice of a mate or a profession, the decision should come from the unconscious, from somewhere within ourselves."[18] Likewise, in forging a relationship with God, while we need to use reason as a check on irrational, harmful beliefs—such as the claim that people injured in an earthquake or a train accident were being punished by God—love and faith in others and in the Divine are ultimately nonrational, intuitive expressions that emerge from our core.

Mindfully Alive

To honor the mind, here is a closing prayer and meditation. To hear the words recited, go to the video accompanying this paragraph.

http://youtu.be/
yFy1_2RNfSc

> *Ribono shel ha'olam*—Master of the revealed
>   and the hidden,

May I delight in the unfolding kaleidoscope of
   Your creation.
May I use all my senses to breathe in, feel, and
   taste the glory of One.
May I value the precious mystery of those yet
   unknown and may I honor them as family.
May I hear Your voice expressed in the speech and
   unspoken words of others.
May I see the world and intuit Your Presence with
   greater clarity, honesty, and love.
And may You provide me with wisdom as a sturdy
   staff for the journey ahead, so that I will exude
   compassion on Your behalf.

Try This: Intensive Meditation with a Focus on Mind

For one week, start your day with twenty to thirty minutes of meditation
with a focus on mind. Pay attention to the rise and fall of thoughts, labeling them as they arise, and each time returning to your breath. After each
day's meditation, journal the types of thoughts that arose, the emotions
contained in the thoughts, and any recurring patterns.

CHAPTER FIVE

SPIRIT

Intuitive Wisdom

Spirit is by definition elusive and intangible. In English the word "spirit" is derived from the Latin *spiritus*, which means "breath." This is also true in Hebrew, where the words *ruach* and *neshamah* both mean "breath" and "soul/spirit." Just as breath is our essential link to life, so spirit is identified with our life force and essence.

http://youtu.be/
x82IU5O7He8

Scripture teaches, "The lamp of the Eternal is the *neshamah* of a human" (Proverbs 20:27), and "It is the spirit [*ruach*] in a human being, the breath [*neshamah*] of the Almighty, that allows for human understanding" (Job 32:8).

We access the wisdom of spirit intuitively, often using imagination as a bridge. Such wisdom often contains surprising insight, which may feel immediate and unmediated. In this chapter, I offer guided meditations to help you access the intuitive wisdom of the soul and to glimpse the divine flow and flowering at your center. I also explore how Torah is a product of collective intuition and how prayer links body, heart, mind, and spirit to the Divine.

Finding Answers Within

We access our intuitive spirit-wisdom when we turn inward with attention. Guided imagery is a vehicle for accessing the intuitive. I once counseled a couple six weeks before their wedding, when the groom began to feel uncertain about marriage. To prepare for our meeting, I called Marielle Fuller, my master teacher of guided meditation, and she offered the following advice: "Have them dig in the sand for three items to give to each other. And if either presents handcuffs, the wedding is off."

With the couple before me, I instructed them as follows: "In a moment you will close your eyes and relax, and I will guide you inward. You will see yourself on a beach, where you will find a shovel in the sand. You will each dig and uncover a wrapped object, which you will present to the other. You will dig three times. As you unwrap each object, allow yourself to be surprised by what you find. Consider the significance of each object. Present it and pay attention to how your gift is received."

The young man began, "I have an object, which I now unwrap. It is a jar of herbs that will help Emily in her work as a healer."

"Okay," I say, "dig again and see what you find."

"Another small object. As I unwrap it, I see that it is a clock. This will help Emily manage her time better."

Oy, I think with concern. *These gifts are way too practical.*

"You have one last object to find," I emphasize. "This time dig even deeper. Take your time and allow yourself to be surprised."

"I have found a very large object," he says with a note of concern.

"You will have no problem picking it up or unwrapping it," I assure him. "What have you found?"

After a long pause he replies, "It's me."

"Present yourself and see Emily's response."

"She welcomes me with open arms and holds me close. It feels good."

As I drew the guided imagery to a close, both had tears in their eyes. They stood and hugged. The invitations went out a few days later, and in six weeks we shared in a beautiful wedding at sunset overlooking the Pacific. Years afterward that same couple greeted me and with delight showed me pictures of their children.

Sometimes analysis is paralysis. The rational mind is stymied. We cannot align our feelings with our thoughts. When tallying pros and cons, we are unsure what weight to give the variables. We are unsure how to proceed. To tap into the wisdom flowing at our core, we need to relax and trust that we will access insight. Guided imagery, also called wakeful dreaming, quiets our minds so that intuitive spirit-wisdom can surface. Sometimes the spirit-wisdom surfaces like an "aha," conveyed with striking resolution. Usually we gain only incremental awareness by bringing the dreamlike material to the surface of our consciousness. Imagery needs interpretation, rarely offering a yes-or-no answer.

And yet not all thoughts that feel spontaneous are necessarily expressions of the deepest self, let alone a gift from a larger consciousness. Feelings are not facts. Sometimes our hunches are simply rapid expressions of deeply held prejudices, compulsive yearnings, or base emotions. Just because it *feels* true does not mean that it *is* true. You may feel that *this time*, after losing most of your money, you will win at the craps table. But I would not bet on it. Our hunches and deeply held feelings warrant examination to ascertain if they correspond to reality, and yet we may indeed gain enduring wisdom intuitively.

 Try This: **Intuitive Answers**

> Pause and become aware of a question that you would like answered. Write the question down and put the writing aside. Set an alarm for fifteen to thirty minutes. Now shift your focus to following the in-and-out of your breath. When thoughts arise, even possible answers, just allow them to pass, and return to breath. Once the alarm sounds, sit for another minute or two. Now in a state of calm, remember your question and become aware of any intuitive insight on how to proceed.

What Is Intuition?

The word "intuition" is derived from the Latin *intueri*, which means "to look inside." What is it that we are looking at? What is the nature of such immediate perception? Some say that such information is simply a product of the mind's ability to quickly discern cues and patterns grounded in memory and experience. Others state that intuition is another kind of mental capacity entirely, and mystics go even further by claiming it accesses a Grand Consciousness.

Gary Klein, a psychologist and a rationalist, characterizes intuition as "recognition primed decision" (RPD).[1] He illustrates with an account of a fire captain who had led his men into a home with a fire in the kitchen. Suddenly, the captain yelled, "Get out now!" Moments later, the floor collapsed, the supports burned through by flames from the basement. The firemen had escaped in the nick of time. The captain could not initially explain his sudden recognition of danger. Upon reflection, he noted two unusual cues: the pervasive quiet and the intense heat on his ears. For Klein, intuition is not magic, but the everyday experience of memory and recognition. Enough experience with fires leads to the perception of subtle cues. This is also true for a chess master who can see several moves ahead on the board due to accumulated experience and the rapid ability of the mind to make calculations, as cognitive psychologist and economist Herbert A. Simon explains.[2]

Daniel Kahneman, author of *Thinking, Fast and Slow*, approaches intuition as a developed skill of rapidly identifying patterns based on cues. He states that a physician who makes a complex diagnosis from a brief interview with a patient is simply employing the same recognition faculties as a child who, after learning to distinguish a dog from other animals, will say "doggie."[3] Kahneman concludes that the confidence we have in our intuitions or hunches is not a reliable guide to their validity. Intuition depends on stable regularities in the environment, and in the absence of valid cues, "intuitive 'hits' are due either to luck or to lies."[4] Even "moral intuitions," Kahneman writes, are often empty, a product of how a problem is presented (framing), rather than the substance of a situation. For example, participants in a study were asked to respond to the following choices:

> Imagine that the Unites States is preparing for the outbreak of an unusual Asian disease, which is expected to kill 600 people. Two alternative programs to combat the disease have been proposed. Assume that the exact scientific estimates of the consequences of the programs are as follows:
>
> If program A is adopted, 200 people will be saved.
>
> If program B is adopted, there is a one-third probability that 600 people will be saved and a two-thirds probability that no people will be saved.

A substantial majority of the participants chose program A, preferring the certain option over the gamble. They were then asked to choose from two other options for the same scenario:

> If program A' is adopted, 400 people will die.

If program B' is adopted, there is a one-third probability that nobody will die and a two-thirds probability that 600 people will die.

In this second scenario, respondents largely preferred the second option. Close analysis reveals that there is really no difference between A and A' and B and B'. The researchers attributed the difference to whether the choices were presented as lives lost or saved, coupled with a reflexive tendency to prefer a sure thing (risk aversion) when the outcome is good and a willingness to gamble (risk seeking) when both outcomes are negative. Participants were then shown their inconsistency: in the first choice they were willing to save 200 lives for sure, and in the second they preferred to gamble rather than accept 400 deaths. The response was usually embarrassed silence.[5]

Making the choices described above takes effort and discernment. We tend to look for shortcuts, responding to verbal and emotional cues, and prefer answering a simpler question than the one that is really being asked. The slow, methodical mind carefully examines the words and consciously processes the information. The fast, decisive mind may lose to misconstructions or fallacies what is gained in efficiency. Optimally, the slower approach serves as a check on the rapid decision-making mind. For Kahneman, what we call intuition is the fast mind at work with remarkable skill and ease—and the danger of false assuredness.

There is an alternative approach to defining intuition that elevates it above the normal processes of thought. For Albert Einstein, once a scientist has gathered information, intuition enables surprise and coherence that transcends analytic thought. To quote Einstein, "[empirical] knowledge is necessary too. An intuitive child could not accomplish anything without some knowledge. There will come a point in everyone's life, however, where only intuition can make the leap ahead, without ever knowing precisely how. One can never know why, but must accept intuition as fact."[6] Einstein emphasized, "Intuition is the father of new knowledge, while empiricism is nothing but the accumulation of old knowledge. Intuition, not intellect, is the 'open sesame' of yourself."[7]

As to the source of intuitive knowledge, there is a continuum of approaches, from the naturalistic to the more mystical. Neuroscientists contend that intuitive processes use the brain pathways identified with emotion, music, and art, rather than those pathways associated with factual and mathematical analysis. Intuition is thus a particular kind of creative brain activity.[8] For mystics across faith traditions and for many artists and poets, intuitive insights are experienced as a gift from beyond the self or drawn from the center of one's true self. Carl Jung explained that intuitions are drawn from the unconscious, containing products of one's own life experience along with archetypal, collective wisdom that is drawn from the transcendent divine mind.[9] Psychics or mediums claim the ability to function like receivers that are attuned to information drawn from beyond themselves, not unlike a radio translating unseen radio waves into music. As an example of receptivity, I am fascinated by accounts of twins. For instance, an Episcopal minister, formerly a banker, told me of awakening with severe pain in her wrist. A couple of hours later the minister called her twin and learned that she had broken her wrist earlier that morning.

Psychologist Elizabeth Lloyd Mayer, in her book *Extraordinary Knowing*, examined the scientific literature on extrasensory perception (ESP) and other forms of paranormal knowing.[10] Although there was a lively debate on methodology, she determined that many mainline scientists resisted credible findings about telepathy and extrasensory perception. Mayer grew to believe that psychics do acquire information intuitively, without the aid of rational analysis or use of their senses. She began to consider how this mechanism might work from her perspective of modern psychology and its recognition of conscious and unconscious knowledge. In experiments on "subliminal priming," a subject's exposure to a flashing word can significantly improve that person's ability to fill in missing letters when presented with that incomplete word a week later.[11] Even more fascinating is the evidence that when people are subliminally exposed to the phrase "Mommy and I are one," there is remarkable adaptive improvement, whether increased success in quitting smoking or gaining higher scores on high school math examinations.[12] Mayer also pointed to "entrainment," the synchronizing of two people's physiology, whether the timing of menstruation or excitement. Our brains contain mirror neurons, which translate subliminal observations into emotionally contagious responses.[13] In an even more dramatic example, she pointed to studies in which subjects are separated by a wall, with one sending images and impacting the mood of a recipient toward greater calm or anger.[14] Even when a subject has no conscious awareness of an experience, information may exist in the mind that has great influence on consciousness.

Mayer posited a human ability to receive information in ways that we cannot explain materially, a capacity of knowing that transcends the normal working of the mind. This kind of awareness supports the mystics' claim of communion with an abiding Consciousness, whether gaining deeper understanding or connecting with a greater unity. Although I am cautious, even skeptical, when hearing claims of telepathy, let alone an ability to predict the future, I do believe that people can acquire information in ways that transcend the normal analytic workings of the mind.

Another model for a continuum of knowing and the power of intuition is learned from examining the nature of dreams. Most dreams are superficial. They serve to release emotions produced by events of the day. And yet there are dreams that may transcend an immediate prompt. For Jungians, dream imagery reveals deeply held universal symbols, or archetypes, which are connected to enduring universal ideas. We identify more profound dreams by their recurrence and vivid intensity. Jungian psychotherapists seek to discern the symbolic meaning and emotional content of all dream material. Close to two thousand years ago, the sages of the Talmud observed, "A dream that is not interpreted is like a letter unread" (Rabbi Chisda, *Berakhot* 55b).

Gradations of Intuitive Wisdom

Intuitions, like dreams, exist on a continuum of profundity. In certain cases, intuitions are experienced as a gift from beyond our own psyche. In the words of Philo, the first-century-CE Alexandrian scholar:

> On other occasions, I have approached my work empty and suddenly become full, the ideas falling in a shower from above and being sown invisibly, so that under the influence of the divine possession I have been filled with wild frenzy and been unconscious of anything—place, persons present, myself, words spoken, lines written.[15]

The most profound intuitive insights depend on accumulated learning and keen wakeful observation. Accessing intuition takes practice and preparation. Consider Einstein's hypothesis that energy and matter are interchangeable. This theory explained that a small amount of radioactive matter could explode into a massive outburst of energy. Einstein, who had a strong foundation in physics and was a careful observer of natural phenomenon, explained his creative process: "There is no logical way to the discovery of these elemental laws. There is only the way of intuition, which is helped by a feeling for the order lying behind the appearance."[16]

As in the story of the young groom, adding up pros and cons may not lead to a clear decision. For a scientist, finding a pattern that lends itself to a formula may go beyond gathering data. Suddenly, after we let go of analysis, we encounter a flash of illumination. Intuition is experienced across a spectrum ranging from shallow hunches to more profound levels of wonder and creativity. People may intuitively commune with the Divine, accessing love, conscience, and wisdom that encompass and transcend time and place.

Intuition, in my experience, exists on a continuum: from the insights of the creative brain to a core awareness of our deepest self to drawing wisdom from a grander Consciousness that transcends the human mind. In deep moments of meditation, I have visualized a hollow bead of knowing at my center (as in the meditation on Psalm 150 in chapter 2). The bead is a visual metaphor for an observing part of my inner self, an "eye" that is set apart from the thoughts and feelings of "I," which percolate into consciousness as if projected onto a movie screen. The inner eye is more fully "me" in stability and wisdom than the ever-shifting kaleidoscope of sensations of ego-self. In a state of quiet mind, I visualize the bead at my core with a hole at its center as if hollowed out. Instead of string, light flows through that bead, producing an awareness of unity with all that exists. My inner eye depends on a light from beyond myself with which to see, know, and experience a more abiding reality. That divine light has a texture of illumination, tastes like love, and permeates creation. Is this indelible experience of light, love, and knowing just wishful thinking? I cannot prove it either way, but I can say that it feels fully true, motivates me to live at my most loving best, and is not contradicted by analytic mind.

Complementary Qualities of Awareness

Our imagination is the bridge to spirit, a vehicle of intuition that allows us to create and to see this world more clearly. Finding a balance between the states of analytic mind, characterized by a cautious, adultlike approach, and open mind, with the spontaneity of a child, is necessary for wisdom, inner harmony, and effectiveness. The Maggid of Dubno, who lived in Lithuania in the eighteenth century, beautifully illustrated this quest for inner balance with a parable, which I recraft here.[17]

Once upon a time a father told his daughter a bedtime story of a magnificent palace. "And when you reach this palace," he said in a hushed voice, "and stand in its entryway, you are bathed in the golden light of God's embrace." Repeatedly, the little girl insisted that her father retell the enchanting story of the long journey to the destination of delight.

One morning the child said to her mother, "You know the palace that Father described? I want to go there. Can we go for a long walk and try to find it?" Her mother agreed and they set off toward the mountains. When they reached a river with rushing water, the mother picked up her daughter and carried her safely across. When they climbed up a steep hill and the young girl's legs began to ache, she pleaded, "Mother, can you carry me?" And her mother picked her up and carried her until she could continue on foot and then they advanced hand-in-hand.

"Mother," the young girl said, eagerly pointing toward the distance, "there's the palace!" Together they rushed forward. When the mother grabbed the handle of the massive door and pushed, it would not budge. The door was locked. Both stood motionless, exhausted from the long journey and from disappointment.

"Look," the young girl exclaimed, "there is a window. Pick me up one more time and put me on your shoulders. I can enter the palace through the window, climb down, and open the door from the inside." Sure enough the young girl reached the windowsill and with determination pulled herself up, eased downward, and opened up the palace door from the inside. Her mother entered. Together they stood in the entryway with golden rays streaming down on them. They experienced the bliss of being caressed by a loving, indescribable light.

The Maggid of Dubno concluded that there are certain places that we as adults cannot enter alone. Only with childlike trust and imagination can we access the inner realm of awe and faith. And yet the adult, analytic mind is a necessary check against false beliefs and danger. When the adult and child are united within us, we may experience the divine light that is always around us and that flows through us. The story honors not childish thought but the capacity to draw forth childlike wonder from the deepest part of ourselves, from our intuitive center.

Try This: Conjured Sensuality

"Imagination" and "magic" share the same linguistic root. Neuroscientists cannot explain the science or magic of how we imaginatively taste an ice-cream cone in our minds or how we soothe our nerves with the sound of the surf even when on the seventh floor of a hospital. Researchers have shown that the same parts of the brain are activated whether subjects are looking at a tree or thinking about the image of a tree. The imaginative process is paradoxical: marked by both intuitive surprise and accumulated experience; requiring both letting go and having a direction. Imagination enables us to create art and music, fosters self-expression, and amplifies our sensual awareness.

To experience your imagination's capacity of vivid sensuality, please consider the following exercise:

http://youtu.be/
OCienFCxziM

Sit comfortably. Breathe out. Feel an ice-cream cone in your hand. Bring the cone to your mouth and take a lick. Enjoy the ice cream's texture, the cold sensations, and the flavor. Take another lick and pause to feel the pleasure of it. Now place the ice-cream cone in a stand located on your right side within easy reach.

To your left is a beautiful flower. You will have no problems with allergies when you smell it. Pick the fresh flower up and take in a deep whiff. Hold the flower's fragrance for a long moment and breathe out slowly. Inspect the flower, noting the colors of the petals and the overall shape. Gently feel the texture of the flower. Take in one more deep breath of the flower's scent, hold the fragrance, and exhale.

Now put the flower down. See in front of you a bowling ball. Pick it up and feel its heft. Feel the muscles on your arms pulling downward as you lift it in your arms. Feel the smoothness of the ball. Put the bowling ball down.

Pick up the ice-cream cone again for one final lick. Enjoy. Put it back down.

After a count from three to one, you will slowly open your eyes, profoundly aware of the sensual sensations of these three objects.

The power of the mind to tell a good story or to create a full-bodied experience is quite profound. On the most lofty level, Rabbi Abraham Isaac Kook, the first Ashkenazic chief rabbi of Israel, taught:

> The fierce power of imagination is a gift from God. Joined with the grandeur of the mind, the potency of inference, ethical depth, and the natural sense of the divine, imagination becomes an instrument for the holy Spirit.[18]

The intuitive mind can enable us to tap inner wisdom that is often symbolic in form and is remarkably helpful in resetting priorities with renewed hope. The following wakeful dream will enable you to draw on intuitive resources by journeying inward.

 ## Try This: **Intuitive Gifts**

Sit comfortably and breathe out. Relax all your muscles and stay alert.

Breathe out. See yourself walking up a mountain path. Your energy is good, and your legs and breathing are relaxed and strong. You come to a clearing, where you see a table. On the table are three

http://youtu.be/
5cfRv6onZEA

wrapped objects. Each contains an item that is useful to you. Behind the table stands a sage. You may ask the sage any questions, including the significance of each object.

Breathe out. Unwrap the first item and allow yourself to be surprised. What is it? Use your senses to examine the object. What is the value of this object for you? What insight does it offer? Ask the sage. Listen. Understand. Place it back on the table.

Breathe out. Unwrap the second object. Examine it. Ask the sage for the value of this object in your life and any insight that it offers. Place it on the table.

Breathe out. Unwrap the third object. Place it in your hands. It now reduces to fit inside your palm. Toss it upward so that it reaches so great a height that you lose sight of it. Transformed, another object falls back down. Pick it up. What is this new object? The sage explains the value of this object to you. Place this third object on the table. You may ask the sage an additional question. Listen. Understand.

Breathe out. Look at all three objects. Pause to hold in mind the lessons that each represents. Now look and see if there is a relationship between the three objects. What is the lesson that you needed to learn? The insights will come to you as an intuitive gift. Hold the lessons in mind when you begin to return to this space.

Breathe out. Walk back down the mountain. Your energy and breathing are strong and comfortable. You will return to the seat from which you began. Pause to remember the three objects that were presented to you. Recall the significance of each and their relationship to each other.

Breathe out. Feel the seat beneath you. Slowly open your eyes.

Journal what you experienced, including drawing a diagram of each object and its significance. Add the overarching insight that you took away.

Sacred Text Study: God's Call at the Burning Bush

Even our most riveting insights may lack enough clarity to prompt immediate action and may take time to sink in.

Consider Moses at the burning bush. God speaks to him for the first time and essentially says, "I've got a job for you." Now if God spoke to you, what would you say? If you knew that the Supreme Being was giving you an order, you would probably salute as if in the army and exclaim, "At your service!" Yet in reading God's call to Moses in Exodus 3:1–4:17, we find that Moses begs off not just once, but *five times*. It is hard to believe that this man who would come to exemplify leadership and loyalty would begin his career with such strong doubts.

After God describes the suffering of the Israelites in Egypt, the need for action, and God's decision to send Moses to Pharaoh to enable redemption,

Moses responds, "Who am I that I should go to Pharaoh. And how can I possibly get the Israelites out of Egypt?" God reassures him, but Moses protests, "But I do not even know what name to call you when they ask." God first offers an elevated response, saying, "I will be what I will be," and then responds more concretely, "You must say to the Israelites, 'YHVH, the God of your ancestors, the God of Abraham, Isaac, and Jacob ... will bring you to a land of milk and honey.'"

You might think that Moses would at last be satisfied, but he continues to protest, "But they won't believe me." God, still patient, offers impressive signs. God instructs Moses to cast the staff he is holding to the ground; the staff becomes a serpent and then returns to its form as a staff when he grabs it by the tail. God then tells Moses to place his hand inside his robe, and the hand becomes leprous, as if dead white tissue, and then becomes normal again. Moses now pleads, "I beg you, O God, I am not a man of words—not yesterday, not the day before ... I find it difficult to speak and find the right language." God grows firmer, as if irritated: "Who gave human beings a mouth? Who makes a person dumb or deaf? Who gives a person sight or makes him blind? Is it not I—God? Now go! I will be your mouth and teach you what to say." Moses is out of excuses, but he persists, "I beg you O Eternal, please send someone more appropriate!" In response, "the Eternal was angry with Moses," and yet God offers the concession that Aaron, Moses's brother, will do the talking in Egypt. And Moses accepts the call to action, a call accessed as a divine yearning for a profound mission.

Every divine call is filtered by our own history and personality, vulnerabilities and aspirations. God's beckoning voice needs interpretation. Revelation is uncertain and challenges us with an invitation into the unknown. And yet Moses ultimately answers the divine call. His service will not only liberate the Israelites, but provide hope for the oppressed around the world ever after.

We are not told why God sought Moses for such a demanding task. The Bible recounts that Moses grew up in the palace. Perhaps such privilege distinctly offered him the capacity and status to confront the Pharaoh. When Moses the shepherd spots the burning bush, he marvels. Rabbi Lawrence Kushner adds that you have to really pay close attention to a burning log or bush to notice that it is not "being consumed."[19] Moses's greatness was that he was fully present, noticed the miraculous, took the call seriously, and chose to act. Moses, attuned and attentive, left the burning bush with a determined mission.

Discerning whether a divine voice is authentic or just wishful thinking takes practice. Genuine prophetic calling goes against immediate self-interest and prompts doubt, yet simultaneously feels profound, real, and urgent. Moses began a new phase of his life as God's servant and as leader of a diverse people. The journey ahead would be fraught with difficulties, including rebellions against Moses's authority. And yet Moses would persevere and bring the people to the edge of the Promised Land. Moses, the reluctant prophet, would over time forge an intimate relationship with God. God would uniquely characterize their exchanges, "I speak with him mouth to mouth" (Numbers 12:8). As a great leader, Moses would prepare the Israelites to proceed on their own, guided by memory, clarity of divine expectations, and core values.

The tale of Moses at the burning bush reflects our own encounters with conscience, consciousness, and the mystery of Divine Presence. Bible stories are dreamlike in that they are multilayered and highly symbolic. The narratives are not history or science, but value maps that guide us toward meaningful living. The biblical personalities may have existed in history, but they also abide in each of us as role models and archetypes. Intuitive listening on a deep level may lead to transformative action that takes us beyond our comfort zone and makes an impact that transcends our limited years.

 Try This: **Hearing Your Calling**

Close your eyes, relax, and breathe out. See yourself in the desert before a burning bush that is not consumed. Stop and stare at the sight before you.

http://youtu.be/
i6-L1790C44

Breathe out and feel wonder. Remove your shoes, because you stand on holy ground. Feel the ground under your feet.

Breathe out. Listen for your name being called out. How does it sound? What is the significance of your name?

Breathe out. The echo of the divine voice, the *bat kol*, is addressing you. What does it say?

Breathe out. What is your mission, the task for which you are chosen?
Breathe out. See yourself taking the next step in pursuing the calling.
Breathe out. See yourself having fulfilled your task.

Breathe out. What obstacles got in your way in fulfilling the task, and how might you better address them in the future?

Breathe out and open your eyes, remaining aware of your call and the initial step for you to take now.

Identifying the authenticity of a call depends on discerning if it emerges from your core. It often helps to discuss your experience with another person to ascertain if what you believe is your calling correlates with your true values and whether it is helpful and doable. A call need not be grandiose. Rather it can be quite simple and easily accomplished. To believe that a task is a response to a higher call gives it greater purpose and meaning. A test of a call is whether it simultaneously feels natural and emerges from a perspective that transcends your narrow frame of reference.

The *Amidah* Prayer as Conversation with God

The *Amidah* prayer is the spiritual destination of the daily prayer service. Having engaged body, heart, and mind, we use imagination to stand before God and to share our gratitude and petitions. We speak on behalf of others and then for ourselves, and ultimately we let go of words and intuitively feel touched and reassured with hope and called to act by encountering God's caring presence.

When reciting the words of the *Amidah*, we represent the Jewish people and speak for the whole of humanity, an audacious task. We ask God to bring redemption for the Jewish people and peace to the world, culminating with such words as "Grant peace to the world, with happiness and blessing, grace, love, and mercy ..."

We are given a script in the form of the nineteen blessings included in the daily recitation. The first three blessings serve as an introduction, which are accompanied by movement so that we can visualize leaving our immediate surroundings by entering into the sublime presence of God. We take three steps forward as if entering before God's throne. We bow as we introduce ourselves as descendants of the Patriarchs and, in contemporary texts, the Matriarchs as well. We conclude our opening statement with another bow. We then acknowledge God's power both to help the living and to determine the fate of the dead: "Blessed are You, *Adonai*, who revives the dead." The *Amidah*'s middle thirteen blessings are a petition articulating an outline for God to fulfill the prophetic promise of universal peace.[20] After each blessing, the person praying is invited to share personal petitions. The final three blessings are a thank-you and a humble farewell, marked by ritual bows. On the Sabbath and holy days the middle thirteen blessings are removed, and a paragraph suited for the day and the service becomes our statement before God, with the frame of opening and closing blessings remaining the same. Most mornings when I chant the daily prayers, nothing profound happens. I barely consider the content of my recitation. And yet daily prayer shapes my religious identity.

Researchers have found that young people who dine with their families on a regular basis are better adjusted.[21] Apparently the very act of regularly sitting together conveys belonging and care, offering a foundation of stability and motivation. By virtue of sitting across from each other, we invariably share, if only in bits and pieces, what is going on in our lives. My own daily prayers provide a context of belonging and a habit of sharing that allow me to reach out to God when I feel the need.

To pray is to express ourselves honestly and openly before a Higher Being, enabling catharsis and self-discovery. And when I listen for an answer, I find a perspective beyond my own predictable musings. At my best in prayer, I seek only to experience God's presence. Imagination, such as seeing myself standing before God, is the booster rocket that allows me to rise upward. And then suddenly there is a letting go of self-awareness.

Among the masters of Jewish prayer is the eighteenth-century sage Dov Ber of Mezeritch, who described the sublime dimension of prayer as moving through the four worlds of being (the physical, emotional, intellectual, and spiritual) as follows:

> As God turns to look at the ascending word, life flows through all the worlds, and prayer receives its answer. All this happens in an instant, and all this happens continually; time has no meaning in the sight of God. The divine spring is ever flowing; make yourself into a channel to receive the waters from above.[22]

✤ *Try This:* **Experiencing Daily Prayer**

For one week, set aside fifteen to twenty minutes in the morning for communal prayers after meditation. The touchstones of prayer are the *Shema* and the *Amidah*, which you will find in a traditional Jewish prayer book. Alternatively, use prayers from your own religious tradition. Chant them out loud, whether in English or Hebrew.

As with meditation, there is value in finding others with whom to pray in order to increase motivation and for the enhanced energy of group activity. Journal about your experiences at the end of the week:

What words surprised you by grabbing your attention during your prayer, and what do those words signify for you?

How does it feel for you to pray?

Was there a moment in which you felt intuitively drawn beyond yourself toward a greater Presence? If so, describe.

Experiences of Prayer with Words and Silence

Prayer's goals are connection and expression. Prayer is first and foremost a conversation with God that enables self-discovery through self-disclosure. Traditional liturgy offers words to express gratitude, evoke praise, and echo a call to action.

There is a complementary quality to meditation and prayer. For over twenty years, I have sat for a designated period of time most mornings, observing my breath and clearing my mind before commencing my traditional daily prayers. During meditation I become more aware of the "radio stations" that play in my mind, so that I can steadily turn down the volume and even experience the silence between stations. Stilled within, I am at once more calm and attentive as I begin to pray the prescribed words.

When Elie Wiesel was asked if there is a tradition of silence in Judaism, he quipped, "Yes, but we don't like to talk about it." To deepen my Jewish meditation and prayer experiences, I have spent time in both Buddhist and Christian retreat settings. Doing so has underscored the complementary nature of meditation and prayer. On a ten-day silent Buddhist retreat, activity alternated between sitting meditation (focusing on the rise and fall of breath) and walking meditation (close observation of the body in motion). Awareness of the other people around me engaged in similar practices increased my concentration. During another meditation retreat, when reciting my morning prayers from memory, my mind slowed down and words popped out, drawing me to reconsider their significance. In an altered state, I have paid detailed attention to the act of eating or become transfixed watching ants crawling (not necessarily at the same place or time). Deeply calmed, I have experienced a flow of love passing through me, evoking indescribable feelings of unity, as if shedding my own particularity.

Recently I spent five days at Taizé, a monastery in Burgundy, France, which was created after World War II as a center for Christian reconciliation. Over fifty monks live at the monastery, coming from Protestant, Orthodox, and Catholic backgrounds from around the world. They share a commitment to simplicity, celibacy, and service. The monastery is famous for melodic chants offered up in many languages. More than one hundred thousand youth pilgrims come here to pray each year. While sitting on the floor in worship for three services a day, I was drawn to the power of the words and melody. I sensed that these prayers enabled connection between worshippers and pointed us toward a loving God.

When publicly praying each morning at the monastery, I wore my tallit (the traditional prayer shawl), and tefillin (phylacteries, the leather boxes and straps of daily prayer). One day at the close of services, a stranger about my age approached, placed his hand on my shoulder, and whispered in a German accent, "Thank you for being here. Your presence opens my heart." I placed my hand over my heart to express gratitude. The mood in the prayer space was not conducive to conversation, so our brief exchange ended. After services concluded the next morning, I looked around and saw that the man of the previous day was seated alongside a woman. His eyes were closed, and he sat cross-legged with bare feet. Slowly he raised his arms above his head, and tears began to stream down his face. I wondered at the underlying emotion. Was it guilt, joy, or something else? His companion reached over and gently placed her palm on his foot. They both remained in silence, holding their positions. As I watched, I was deeply moved. The act of connection and presence between the two worshippers struck me as emblematic of the prayer service's quest to experience the embrace of a loving God.

Meditation and prayer overlap and are each distinctive and complementary. Silence is an essential part of prayer, although prayer also entails words. Prayer actively directs our words outward for connection with a caring Presence. And yet at the center of the forty-five-minute Taizé worship service is close to ten minutes of silence. In the midst of a Buddhist retreat there is also a commonality of shared practice. During meditation I have felt deeply stilled within and detached from the world around me. With monotheistic liturgy I have felt intertwined with community, self-reflective, and even uplifted toward God.

The Mystical Shape of the Divine Name

At the start of Moses's mission to redeem the Israelites from slavery in Egypt, God announces, "I am *YHVH*. I appeared to Abraham, Isaac, and Jacob as *El Shaddai*, but I did not make Myself known to them by My name *YHVH*" (Exodus 6:2–3). The name *YHVH* would soon take on special significance, used when referring to God's intervention in history. Although God had used the name *YHVH* previously in scripture, the sages widely understand this biblical statement to mean that God's desire for human liberation would only become fully manifest from this point forward.

The Hebrew of *YHVH* is a conflation of tenses—was, is, and will be—conveying that God is ever present. Jewish mystics would identify the four letters of the Hebrew word with the four planes of self—the physical, emotional, intellectual, and intuitive. The *yud* (י), the first letter, is the smallest of the twenty-two letters in the Hebrew alphabet. It appears on the page as a seed dangling in midair, representing the intuitive mind. The second letter is *hey* (ה), which in form is like an open hand receiving ideas from above. It is the role of intellect to examine ideas for their correspondence with reality and to develop them with language. The third letter is a *vav* (ו), a straight line shaped like a spine, descriptive of posture and suggesting energetic, emotional flow. The final letter is another *hey* (ה), the physical level of grounding and doing, and a receptacle for all above it.

Try This: **YHVH Meditation**

These reflections on *YHVH* form a foundation for the following guided meditation as a vehicle for experiencing wholeness.

http://youtu.be/
KsJfYi6BEPM

> Sit comfortably, back straight. Close your eyes. Breathe out.

Bring to mind the letter *yud* (י). Straighten out your head, as the *yud* represents your head. Breathe in calm and alertness. Breathe out the cloud of fatigue. Breathe in awareness of the expanse around you; breathe out constriction.

Breathe out and bring to mind the letter *hey* (ה). Identify your shoulders and arms with *hey*, and become aware of the posture of your upper body and the receptivity of your arms and hands. Breathe in with *hey* awareness, which allows you to reach and examine the world beyond your body. Receive the *yud* with your *hey*, turning the seeds of ideas over for understanding and truth.

Breathe out. See your spine as *vav* (ו). Become aware of your posture. Breathe out all anxiety, and breathe in calm. Feel your back relaxing and your spine becoming more erect. Feel the increased ease of your breathing. Feel the stability of your emotions, an alignment of the positive and negative.

Breathe out. See your legs as *hey* (ה), grounding you. Breathe out any unfinished business, and breathe in fixed steadiness. See your lower body supporting your spine, your back and arms, and your head. Draw from the earth the energy of the soil, an energy that fills you with quiet presence.

Breathe out. Now mindfully follow your breathing. When thoughts come to mind, allow them to pass easily and return to your breath (five minutes).

Scan your posture—your head, upper body, spine, torso and legs. Feel aligned.

Return to following your breathing (five minutes).

Feel your own inner unity as an expression of the wholeness of creation. Experience your own inner steadiness. Breathe in and out three times. See your body as a receptive vessel for the presence of the Divine.

Breathe in and out, feeling love flowing through you, a love that tastes like a sweet nectar and is composed of light. Hold the light and allow it to penetrate each of your cells. Breathe in and out, feeling steady and imbued with love and balance.

Breathe out. The light of love surrounds you, and your head tilts slightly upward. An additional light comes down from above; it flows through you and connects with the energy coming from the earth. You are bathed in light and ease. You feel held and safe.

Breathe out. Watch your mind within as a movie screen. Pay attention to an image that appears that offers you wisdom. Stay with the image and see if another appears. Now pause to intuitively know the meaning of each image. Listen to the quiet voice that is accessible within you. Listen for any guidance or call to action. Pay attention to any fears attendant to the call. Return to the voice and listen.

Breathe out. In a moment you will return to this space. When you do, you will remain calm and alert and aware of the feeling of intense love that has flowed through you and that has encircled you. The love will give you heightened awareness of the goodness of life. Retain awareness of the images that appeared on your inner screen and the message conveyed. And most importantly, hold on to the inner call and consider how you might proceed to fulfill it. Breathe in. Pause. Breathe out.

Three: See your body as composed of the four letters *Y* (י) *H* (ה) *V* (ו) *H* (י).

Two: Return to awareness of your physical body.

One: Savor the enduring presence of *YHVH* uniting yourself and the whole of creation.

Open your eyes and slowly readjust.

Translating Epiphany into Words

When we are stilled from within, we may intuit a guiding voice or inner eye calling on us to act as our best self.[23] Despite the constant presence of human conflict and suffering, we may intuit an underlying unity and goodness. Faith is faithfulness to those riveting, holy moments when we have felt close to God. In going inward, we may become spiritually aware that we are part of a vast cosmos. We are stardust with the unique capacity to marvel over celestial order and expanse. In the words of Dr. Daniel Matt, *Zohar* translator and dedicated student of cosmology:

> We are infinitesimal, yet part of something vast. Being aware of this, we strive to comprehend the entirety. On this quest, spirituality and science are two tools of understanding. Their approaches to the question of our origin are distinct and should not be confused; each is valid in its domain. Occasionally, though, their insights resonate. By sensing these resonances, our understanding deepens, nourished by mind and heart.[24]

Our years are fleeting and our impact is trivial in comparison with the vastness of the universe and the expanse of time. And yet we are of enormous significance for the people in our lives and for our experiences moment to moment. With the scientific mind we observe the world and design technology to explore, comprehend, and improve. We also have the capacity from the inside out to experience connection to the entirety of creation. We may marvel at the expanse of the night sky and our ability to connect with another human being through discrete words. With an intuitive faith in God, we relate to a divine unfolding of presence amid mystery. Prayer gives voice to our deepest yearnings for connection and draws us with awe toward wholeness and belonging.

Mystics have stretched their own consciousness in yearning for divine union and unity. In sixteenth-century Safed, Israel, during the time of Rabbi Isaac Luria, mystics would dress in white and go out into the fields on Fridays in the late afternoon. They would sing hymns of welcome for the Sabbath bride, seeing the impending sunset as the beginning of not only a new day, but of the possibility of a longed-for messianic harmony. Among the questing souls of that place and time was Rabbi Elazar ben Moshe Azikri, who composed the following poem, with the first letter of each stanza combining to form God's name, *YHVH*. This Hebrew poem, *Yedid Nefesh*, is often recited in our own day at the start of the Sabbath prayers on Friday night. Read the following words out loud as an expression of your own longing to experience God's presence, or use the QR code to access a video of this prayer, and simply listen.

http://youtu.be/
DVi6Mc0sOoA

Friend of soul, Source of tenderness, shape my
  inner nature to Your will.
Like a deer I will run to You. Before Your
  splendor, I will humbly bow.
Your love is sweeter than the drippings of the
  honeycomb, than any taste.
Glorious, beautiful radiance of the world, my soul
  is lovesick for You.
Please God, heal her now by showing Your tender
  light so that my soul can recover strength and
  gain wholeness, enabling enduring service of You.
Ancient of days, let mercy be aroused; please
  bestow pity on Your beloved child.
Long have I yearned to witness the harmony of
  Your strength.
Such my heart has desired—hurry; do not hide
  Yourself.
Reveal Yourself, please, and spread over me, my
  Beloved, the canopy of Your peace,
Let the earth shine with Your glory, we will revel
  and rejoice in You.
Rush, my Love, be quick. Now is the time. Let
  Your grace favor us as in former days.

❧ *Try This:* **Intensive Meditation with a Focus on Spirit**

For one week, start your day with twenty to thirty minutes of meditation with a focus on spirit. Pay attention to the rise and fall of breath; when thoughts arise, note them and return to your breath. Appreciate the sweet stillness between breaths. About halfway through your sit, expand your awareness so that you are in a state of "big mind," as if you are breathed. After each day's meditation, journal your experience.

CHAPTER SIX

HAND

The Power to Touch

http://youtu.be/
eWhIG7ouGio

Our deeds reflect the priorities that we set for our limited time and energies. Our interior world is the vessel from which we draw the wisdom and will for the work of our hands. All four dimensions of that inner life are engaged when we reach beyond ourselves: our body, as the vehicle for action; our heart, as a source of connection and motivation; our mind, as a check on irrational behavior through thoughtful discernment; and our intuition, allowing us to prioritize, empathize, and surprise ourselves with insights. Bringing these all together, our actions increase our wholeness when we artfully act kindly and justly.

Sacred Text Study: To Be a Blessing

Ancient myths contain accounts of the gods bestowing power and wealth on chosen heroes. In the biblical account, too, God promises Abraham abundance, including children. God distinctly adds a promise and a mighty challenge when saying to Abraham in Genesis 12:2,

> I will make of you a great nation,
> And I will bless you;
> I will make your name great,
> And you shall be a blessing.

What does it mean to become a blessing? In short it means to serve with goodness on behalf of God.

Rabbi Abraham Joshua Heschel taught that the essence of faith in God is to know that God cares.[1] In the Torah we find that God, the sole

Creator, acts as a Parent. God cares about the well-being of creation and most centrally about humanity's righteousness. Nothing gives a parent greater joy than seeing his or her children act lovingly toward each other. And there is no more ready upset than witnessing our children hurt each other. To be a blessing is to see the world through God's eyes and to dutifully care for God's creation, especially treating other people as fellow children of God.

The enticements of acquiring abundant material goods often lead to the temptation to take advantage of others. The prophet Amos, writing over twenty-six hundred years ago, decried, "For silver, they sell the upright; they sell the poor to buy a pair of shoes" (Amos 2:6). In our own day, we are at risk of skewing priorities too. In the competition to accumulate and to achieve enhanced security and status, we may lose our moral bearings. How we treat those who are weakest in society—the biblical equivalent of the dependent widow, orphan, and stranger—defines the quality of our culture and our own character. Serving as a blessing entails placing our own wants into the larger context of actual needs and the welfare of others.

In Hebrew, the root for the word "blessing," *berakhah*, is the same as the roots for "knee" and "a pool of water." To live as a blessing is to live with humility, as when we kneel, and to recognize the miracle of our creation from amid water, a symbol of life. To live with humility is to know that we are fleeting and fragile as human beings and yet that in God's eyes each of us is precious. To live with humility is to identify with the pain of others and to exercise our ability to alleviate suffering, whether in addressing the needs of the poor, the abandoned, or the oppressed. We serve as a blessing when we reach beyond ourselves with small acts of care and justice. These acts create a ripple effect contributing to community-wide hope in the possibility of change. Our intentions represent but a starting point. We are a blessing through action, including our words.

When Abraham addresses God about the planned destruction of the evil residents of Sodom and Gomorrah, he audaciously challenges, "*Chalilah lekha!* Far be it from you! To do such a thing, to bring death upon the innocent as well as the guilty, so that innocent and guilty fare alike. Far be it from you! Shall not the Judge of all the earth deal justly?" (Genesis 18:25). Abraham begins his negotiation with genuine humility, stating,

"Here I venture to speak to my Lord, I who am but dust and ashes" (Genesis 18:27). And yet the patriarch quickly wields the tremendous power that is potentially in each of us, speaking on behalf of those who lack a voice. In his bid to save all the residents of the towns on account of a small number of righteous ones, he negotiates with God until they agree that even for ten righteous souls, the entire population of these evil communities would be saved. When Abraham speaks out for compassion and righteousness, he enables both God and himself to be their best.

And yet the Bible presents a startling counterpart to the story of Abraham's willfulness on behalf of Sodom and Gomorrah. Only a few chapters later, the text reads:

> Some time afterward, God put Abraham to the test and said to him, "Abraham," and he answered, "Here I am [*hineini*]." And [God] said, "Take your son, your favored one, Isaac, whom you love, and go to the land of Moriah, and offer him there as a burnt offering on one of the heights that I will point out to you." So early the next morning, Abraham saddled his donkey and took with him two of his servants and his son Isaac. (Genesis 22:1–3a)

This awful story is the most challenging in the entire Bible: the divine call for the patriarch to slay his son. It ends all right, with God sending an angel to stop Abraham as he wields a blade above his familial bound offering. A ram is substituted. Even so, the "test" was traumatic. In the text, Abraham and Isaac never speak again, nor do God and Abraham.

We are left to ponder: Could God be so cruel? Did Abraham fail or pass the test? Was the test ultimately for Abraham to learn the depth of his own faithfulness to God? This story is multilayered and complex. Some contemporary rabbis would choose to edit the entire story out of the sacred text, leaving only the image of Abraham's challenge to God. In contrast, the ancient sages so honored this episode that they made it the Torah reading on Rosh Hashanah, the celebration of the New Year, using it to illustrate the merit of Abraham's supreme love of God, which bestowed favor on his descendants.

The Bible presents stories of extreme dilemmas to prompt reflection. The *Akeidah*, the "binding of Isaac," challenges us to consider when it is appropriate to engage in audacious protest and when the better response is quiet acceptance and even radical submission. To make moral distinctions between good and better and bad and worse, the service of the hand relies on all four aspects of our inner life. To act as a blessing, we tap our conscience and simultaneously reach beyond ourselves, envisioning the broadest perspective while drawing values from our core. When seeking to act from God's point of view we increase the odds of enduringly useful action, while humbly knowing that we are not God and are simply trying our best.

Open Hands and Their Rewards

When my aunt Shari, my mother's sister, passed away in Israel at the age of ninety-five, over a thousand people came to provide comfort for her family during shivah, the seven days of mourning. For twenty years, Shari had volunteered several days a week in nursing homes, feeding her feeble peers, listening to them, and singing and dancing before them. She had the good fortune to live independently and gave graciously of her time and energy. When she died, her three children experienced the vacuum of their mother's love and life-affirming spirit. They were aided greatly by the combination of set rituals to mourn for her and the flow of visitors, many of whom shared a story of how my aunt had touched their lives. When we live in community and draw on the wisdom of the generations before us, we gain a path to honoring and retaining a memory of a loved one who serves as an enduring blessing.

Recent studies have shown that deeds of helping others correlate with living longer. The title of one such research article is "Providing Social Support May Be More Beneficial Than Receiving It."[2] A study of twenty-eight hundred Americans over the age of twenty-four found that the outcomes associated with volunteering, when assessed one year later, correlated with increases in happiness, life satisfaction, and self-esteem and decreases in depression.[3] Neuroscientists using imaging technology have found that acting kindly activates the reward and meaning centers of our brains, prompting physical signals of pleasure and purpose.[4] Giving literally feels good.

Wharton Business School professor Adam Grant explores the benefits of being a "giver" in his book *Give and Take*.[5] He defines givers as those who prefer to give more than they take, which he contrasts with "takers," who like to get more than they give, and "matchers," who seek reciprocity.[6] Givers are usually the minority in the workplace, which Grant attributes in part to the assumption that givers lack the determination to get ahead in a competitive environment. He sought to prove to his students that skillful givers were actually among the most successful in the workplace and in life. He marshaled much research, including a study of Belgian medical students. In their first year of training, givers earned lower grades than most, apparently due to time devoted to helping others and behaving less competitively. By the second year that changed, and givers were slightly outperforming their peers. By the sixth and seventh years, the givers were among those at the top of the class. As the emphasis shifted from course work to collaboration with colleagues and concern for patients, the givers excelled.[7] Cultivating caring relationships proves indispensable not only in medicine, but in all areas of work and life.

In an address to the World Economic Forum, Bill Gates said, "There are two great forces of human nature: self-interest and caring for others," and the greatest success is achieved when a person is driven by a "hybrid engine" of the two.[8] Generous people are unsuccessful when they allow others to take advantage of them, whether as a product of too much trust, too much empathy, or too much timidity. Giving entails risk and therefore is best done thoughtfully. According to one study, givers are twice as likely to be victimized as takers.[9] In another finding, "employees who reported strong concern for benefiting others and creating a positive image for themselves were rated by supervisors as being the most helpful and taking the most initiative."[10] Those who exercised giving in a balanced way made more sustainable contributions in the workplace than selfless givers, takers, or matchers. Giving at its best combines an open heart, a discerning mind, and intuitive judgment. Appropriate giving is an art form that uplifts the receiver and the giver and is the right thing to do.

Sacred Text Study: Moses in Midian

The impulse to give defines Moses in the Torah. As a young prince adopted by the Pharaoh, he ventures out of the palace and into the fields of slavery, where "he witnessed an Egyptian beating a Hebrew, one of his kinsmen." Moses strikes down the Egyptian and hides him in the sand (Exodus 2:11–12). On the very next day, he intervenes in a fight between two Israelites.

The aggressor snarls, "Who made you chief and judge over us? Do you mean to kill me as you murdered the Egyptian?" (Exodus 2:13–14). Moses flees Egypt as a wanted man. His attempts to effect justice had led to rejection and failure. His adoptive father, who had raised him in protective splendor, now seeks his life. After even the Israelites had rejected his attempt of just intervention, we may imagine Moses wanting to shout, "Enough! I don't need to be a hero. I am ready to enjoy quiet and to worry only about myself!"

Despite this, Moses will later return to Egypt to effect changes for others. His future conduct is quite different from the account in Homer's *Iliad* of a group of exhausted sailors. Upon reaching an island, the sailors eat a lotus plant that eases away worries and their sense of obligation. Lord Alfred Tennyson characterized the "Lotus Eaters" in a poem first published in 1833:

> Most weary seemed the sea, weary the oar,
> Weary the wandering fields of barren foam.
> Then someone said: "We will return no more;"
> And all at once they sang,
> "Our island home is far beyond the waves;
> We will no longer roam....
> Let what is broken so remain.
> The gods are hard to reconcile;
> Tis hard to settle order once again."[11]

These lovers of the lotus faced the physical exhaustion of their voyage, the emotional trauma of separation from home, and the spiritual demands of pleasing the gods. In response, they chose a lifestyle of self-involved, drug-induced bliss.

In contrast, when Moses comes to rest at the well of Midian, he does not do so for long. When he sees shepherds bullying young women, he acts. As the story in Exodus describes, "They came to draw water, and as they began to fill the troughs to water their father's flocks, other shepherds arrived and tried to drive them off. Moses rose and saved them [*vayoshian*] and he watered their flock" (Exodus 2:16–17). We would understand if Moses in his dejected state had ignored the needs of the sheik's seven daughters. And yet he intervened. The Hebrew word that is used to express Moses's action—*vayoshian*, he "saved them"—appears here for the first time in the Bible, foreshadowing Moses's calling. This particular word, *l'hoshea* (to save), will appear repeatedly in the description of God and Moses's efforts to save the Israelite slaves in Egypt.

And here we come to a strange confluence of the stories of Moses and the lotus eaters. Rabbi Moshe Halfon lived in the nineteenth century on the Mediterranean island of Djerba, located off the shores of Tunisia. In legends dating back to Greek mythology, Djerba was identified as the Island of the Lotus Eaters.

Djerba had an unusual history in that most of its Jewish residents linked their origins to the ancient priests who fled Jerusalem after the destruction of the First Temple by the invading Babylonians in 586 BCE. The Jews of Djerba held that their El Ghriba synagogue was the oldest place of Jewish worship in continuous use. On this physically idyllic island, Muslims, Berbers, and Jews lived peacefully for many centuries. For Rabbi Moshe Halfon, the story of Moses demonstrates moral development. Despite a life of ease in Pharaoh's palace followed by exile suffered due to intervention, Moses responds immediately when justice beckons. Rabbi Halfon, the sage of Djerba, concludes,

> From the actions of Moses we should learn that even when a person lives in serenity and security, even when he lives in peace and comfort in his own home, even when wealth and honor surround him, even then he should not think: "I have peace in my own home. What do I need to care about my brothers, my sisters, or anyone else who is suffering?"[12]

From Moses we learn that we are bidden to do what is right despite fatigue, previous frustration, or even abuse. Despite the temptation to check out, we are morally bidden to get involved. Our actions may make only a small difference relative to the expansive needs of a broken world, yet it is our duty to act. In the words of Rabbi Tarfon, who lived in the immediate aftermath of the destruction of the Second Temple in Jerusalem in the year 70 CE, "The day is short, the task is great, the workers reluctant, the reward bountiful, and the Master insistent. It is not upon you to complete the task, nor are you free to refrain from engaging with it" (*Pirkei Avot* 2:20–21).

The Attitudes of Giving

How we give matters too. Maimonides, the twelfth-century sage of Jewish law, ranked eight types of giving, ranging from giving less than is needed and with an attitude of disdain to giving generously with compassion where both parties know each other, and, on the next to highest level, giving in such a way that the giver and the recipient are anonymous due to a caring intermediary. The highest level of giving, he emphasized, is investing in recipients so that they can become self-sufficient, whether with the gift of tools or an education.[13] Maimonides's guidance is for self-assessment of moral development rather than as criteria for judging the generosity of others. And for a person in need, what essentially matters is action.

On a spiritually high level, giving is done unconditionally. Rabbi Abraham Isaac Kook built on the statement of the Talmudic sages that the Roman's destruction of the Temple in Jerusalem in the year 70 CE resulted from baseless hatred between Jews (*Yoma* 9b). This great mystical teacher wrote, "If we were destroyed and the world with us due to baseless hatred, then we shall rebuild ourselves and the world with us with baseless love."[14] As described in the teaching of Adam Grant, a "giver" is motivated by the satisfaction of giving itself. If we lived in a world in which givers were the norm, greater joy and harmony would surround us. The following exercise offers a taste of the satisfaction of one-sided giving.

 Try This: **Baseless Generosity**

> For one week, consider doing one small act of kindness each day for a stranger or a friend. Among the possibilities: pay a toll and say, "This is for the car behind me"; bring some vegetables from your garden or a favorite cup of coffee for someone in your office; buy a bagel and give it to a hungry person you encounter on the streets. You might initially find coming up with ideas for such surprise gift giving a challenge. And yet you will likely find many opportunities once you begin. Pay attention to how your gift is received and how it makes you feel. Consider continuing to perform such random acts of kindness on a regular basis.

Responsible Giving

The Torah declares, "Do not harden your heart nor shut your hand against your needy sibling" (Deuteronomy 15:7).[15] The Rabbis of the Talmud directed that a person should give 10 percent of net income to charity.[16] Understanding that giving bestows dignity and accomplishes good on behalf of God, the Rabbis decreed that even a person who received charity had a responsibility to give to others (*Gittin* 7b). Maimonides, the great codifier of Jewish law, translated the biblical command into everyday terms: "Whoever sees a poor person asking [for assistance] and ignores the person and does not give *tzedakah* [charity] violates a biblical command."[17] And yet the same Rabbis who emphasized that generosity was a duty sought to deter reckless giving by placing a cap on how much a person should give away, namely no more than one-fifth of their total assets in any one year.[18] They emphasized balanced giving lest the donor become impoverished too.

With giving comes the risk of deception when the recipient is a faker, a maligner, or a manipulator. How assured should we be before giving? The eighteenth-century rabbi Moshe Leib of Sasov, Ukraine, modeled a pietistic response. When the sage gave all the money in his pocket to a man who had a poor reputation for honesty, his disciples were disturbed. The sage explained, "Should I be more picky than God, who gave it to me?"[19] Offering the benefit of the doubt to a beggar, Rabbi Abin, in third-century Israel, stated, "When this poor person stands at your door, the Holy One, Source of Blessing, stands at his right hand, as it is written, 'God stands at the right hand of the needy' [Psalm 109:31]."[20]

Other rabbis of the Talmud, who debated Jewish law from the first century BCE through the fifth century CE, advised caution in responding to requests, acknowledging that resources are limited and that bad behavior does not warrant reward. When givers are taken advantage of, the result is cynicism and even callousness, which is at odds with the impulse and obligation to open one's heart and hand to those with legitimate claims. Rabbi Sheilah of Naveh warned against the needy who were cheaters.[21] Rabbi Abba did not want to embarrass the poor so he would wrap coins in a long kerchief and drag it behind him as he walked by the houses of the poor, but the Talmud states, "Out of the corner of his eye he looked for cheaters" (*Ketubot* 67b). The Talmud contains a debate on when to make a presumption of honesty, concluding that in an urgent situation of human suffering, specifically a request for food, givers should assume that the need is real. But in the case of a person who asks for a change of clothing, the giver may err on the side of caution and investigate the need.[22] With regard to communal charities, the Talmud and the later Jewish codes declared that known, trustworthy, competent people should supervise such funds, which usually entailed a lag time from gift to disbursement.[23]

The Hebrew word *tzedakah*, often translated as "charity," more literally means "righteousness." Giving is a duty on behalf of God, an act of righteousness. God the Parent is concerned about the welfare of all of God's children and the entirety of creation. *Tzedakah* alleviates pain in the world, sustains the planet's welfare, and extends hope. To give wisely demands more than emotion. In the words of the Psalms, "Happy is the person who understands [the needs of] the lowly" (Psalm 41:2). Commenting on this verse, Rabbi Yonah taught in fourth-century Israel that a person needed to examine a situation thoroughly to determine how to best make a contribution.[24]

 ### Try This: A *Tzedakah* Box Practice

Opening our hands as a sacred act opens our hearts, minds, and spirits too. And yet just as the ability to play a musical instrument is a natural gift that improves with practice, so too the giving of charity benefits from study and experience. It is Jewish custom to keep a *tzedakah* box at home. Traditionally it is forbidden to even touch money, a tool of commerce, during the Sabbath. Women customarily place money in a *tzedakah* box immediately before the lighting of Shabbat candles. Doing so just before entering the sacred day of rest signifies that at the final moment when people are still permitted to touch money, we do so on behalf of others. Likewise, it is customary to place money into a *tzedakah* box in the course of communal weekday morning prayers as an act of opening our hearts and conveying that we are God's hands in the doing of good.

Designate a *tzedakah* box in your home. Each day place a single coin or more into the box, so as to cultivate the habit of giving.[25] Offer additional funds as part of either daily prayer or Shabbat preparation. Whether in honor of a milestone or after filling the *tzedakah* box, decide to whom or to what cause you wish to give, and make a distribution, reinforcing that small, steady acts add up toward a significant contribution.

Giving as Empathic Justice

Abraham and Sarah are portrayed in the Bible as eagerly greeting passing strangers with the humble invitation of rest and water and then providing a lavish meal (Genesis 18:1–8). The Rabbis teach that it was Abraham and Sarah's generous hospitality that earned them a close relationship with God and their appointment as the spiritual ancestors of generations to come. The whole of creation is of personal concern for God and is the necessary concern of religion.

The Bible is radical in its social legislation. God as universal Parent wants to see all people living with basic needs met and the hope of new beginnings. Every seventh year debts were to be canceled and indentured servants released, and on that Sabbatical year anyone could enter into a field and take the produce (Leviticus 25:1–7; Deuteronomy 15:1–3, 12–15). The needy had rights in any year to any fruit or sheaths of grain that were overlooked or fell to the ground in the process of harvest (Deuteronomy 24:19–22). The corners of the field were to remain for the poor and the stranger to take (Leviticus 23:22). A tenth of the harvest every third year was to be given as tithes to aid those without fields of their own (Deuteronomy 14:27–29). And in the fiftieth year, the Jubilee, land was to revert to its original tribal owners (Leviticus 25:8–17). God is the actual owner of all and insists on food for all God's children and the cyclical renewal of hope and opportunity.

In biblical times, when economies were based on working the land, whether by farmers or shepherds, the widow, the stranger, and the orphan were particularly vulnerable. God, as Parent of all peoples, offers the poor the right to gather their own produce. The premise of the biblical legislation is that "the earth is the Eternal's" (Psalm 24:1). Ownership is better understood as stewardship.

In our own day, how we relate to the person who waits on us in a restaurant, delivers our mail, or washes our car is a test of our character. Creating social safety nets is not communal charity but a duty. People are not objects we may treat as invisible. The Bible's teaching is that each person is a child of God who deserves respect and care.

Biblical morality hinges on empathy. The collective memory of slavery is repeatedly evoked: "Remember you were slaves in Egypt" and therefore allow the slave to rest on the Sabbath day (Deuteronomy 5:15); take care of the widow and the orphan by providing for their physical needs at harvest time (Deuteronomy 24:18–22); make sure that the same law applies to the resident and the visitor (Numbers 15:15);[26] release the chains of bondage of Israelite slaves in the Sabbatical year (Deuteronomy 15:12–15). Remember the loneliness of feeling like a stranger: "When a stranger resides with you in your land, you shall not wrong him. The stranger who resides with you shall be to you as one of your citizens; you shall love him as yourself, for you were slaves in the land of Egypt. I am the Eternal your God" (Leviticus 19:33–34). The collective story of slavery establishes national identity, prompting the religious mandate to tend to the needs of the oppressed and weak. How that mandate gets actualized depends on context and the weighing of priorities in allocating limited resources. The Bible's attitude of care prompts conversation across the generations and guidance from sages.

The *Shulchan Arukh* describes *tzedakah* as a duty in concentric circles.[27] We are first and foremost responsible for meeting the needs of our family. Although *tzedakah* begins at home, it does not end there. We are obligated to give charity to those in our local worship community, then to our town, and finally to a communal fund that tends to the needy regardless of origin. A person is to put some money into each of these categories, actively expanding the categories of "me" toward "we." The more broadly we define the boundaries of self, the more profound our purpose and the greater our identification with God as caring Creator. And yet there is a need for balance: self-identity amid group identity; protecting self while sharing with others.

Living in a consumerist culture that often encourages selfishness adds challenge to parting with our possessions and our time. This was a lesson driven home to me by Rabbi Jonathan Omer-Man when he worked for the Los Angeles Jewish Federation, engaging in outreach to cult members. I had heard him described as an insightful spiritual teacher, so I scheduled an appointment with him. We met at a local McDonald's, which he later explained is the most neutral meeting place in America. As we sat in a booth, I asked him his thoughts on growing spiritually. "Most of the values of spiritual discipline, such as humility, chastity, or modesty, are not an active part of the vocabulary of secular culture. We live in a materialistic age," he said, turning and pointing to the large billboards outside. "In that light, start with acts of generosity. Learn to give some of your funds and time to others and you will grow spiritually too." In giving, each of us is to know that, but for the goodness of circumstance, we could be the ones in need and that to give is to share what is passing through us from a greater Source.

 Try This: **Prioritizing Charitable Giving**

To discern the needs of recipients and to prioritize the amounts you give, set aside time to review your charitable giving at least once a year. Consider what causes most matter to you, and, as if rebalancing your stock portfolio, designate funds generously and purposefully. Decide when you will disburse those funds during the year ahead. If you have children, consider conducting a family meeting to discuss where to prioritize family giving. And then write the checks.

Acts of Loving-Kindness

Acts of loving-kindness, or in Hebrew *gemilut chasadim*, "are even greater than the giving of material objects," the Rabbis teach (*Sukkah* 49b). *Gemilut chasadim* encompasses welcoming guests, visiting the sick, feeding the hungry, clothing the needy, and burying the dead.[28] Loving-kindness is bestowed on all people, rather than just the poor; on both the living and the dead, including attending a funeral or tending a grave; and is effectuated either with money or the gift of time (*Mishnah Pe'ah* 4:19). By giving of ourselves we manifest power and purpose, offering dignity and hope, thereby increasing our own sense of self-worth and joy.

The following is an illustration of how giving attention to another in need can literally save the lives of both the giver and receiver. Dr. Daniel Gottlieb, a psychologist in Philadelphia, was driving on the turnpike when a wheel came off the truck in front of him, crashed through the windshield of his car, and broke his neck. When he awoke in the hospital a few hours later, he was a quadriplegic. As he sat in his chair in the intensive care unit of Jefferson University Hospital a couple of weeks after his accident, he really did not know if he would be able to live or if he even wanted to live as a helpless human being.

With his broken neck, he was encased with a plaster cast from his head to his waist, with just his face exposed. He looked like a mummy. From a "halo," stainless-steel rods came straight down and were fixed to a fiberglass vest to keep his head from turning.

He was in such great pain that he wished to die—until he heard the voice of a woman sitting near his bed, asking if he was a psychologist. She then spoke of her own personal suffering, of her own suicidal thoughts. And from his bed, unable to move his head or any other part of his body, Dr. Gottlieb was able to counsel the woman, give her a referral, and help her navigate her way to a path of healing. At the same time, he discovered his own will to live, to help others, to make a difference in the world despite his physical disability.

This story illustrates that if we are to live meaningful lives, we need to feel that we have the ability to help others—and we can have that even as a quadriplegic. Most of us will not have such a severe limitation nor make such a significant impact and yet the lesson holds true. Each person longs for contact, compassion, and comprehension. We all suffer in the face of impotence and loneliness. When we pay attention to another person, when we genuinely listen, it makes an enormous difference for giver and receiver.

 Try This: **A *Gemilut Chasadim* Practice**

Consider a person or an organization whose work you identify with and offer your time—whether tutoring children, helping direct traffic at a place of worship, writing grants, putting stamps on envelopes, counseling, or regularly hosting visitors for a meal at your home. The more consistently you give, the more it will provide satisfaction, allow you to feel effective, and prompt you to give more.

(A caution on the quality of experience in volunteering: supervision may be poor; the needs may be overwhelming; the team may be working at cross-purposes. And yet by adjusting your expectations and becoming aware of your positive impact, you can still find much satisfaction.)

Setting Limits

In the words of a Yiddish folk saying, "Do not be too sweet or the world will eat you up." Those who have high others-interest and low self-interest are unhealthy.[29] For a giver to avoid becoming a pushover, it is helpful to identify with the thoughts of a potential recipient, rather than the emotions. In doing so, we are more prone to objectively examine the needs and the reasoning of the person before us.

In negotiating a contract or seeking payment, it is wise to see ourselves as asking for funds on behalf of a larger group, whether our employer or our family. Research shows that people make more accurate and creative decisions when they are choosing on behalf of others[30] and they negotiate with greater persistence.[31] Balanced, thoughtful people must maintain the control to decide when, where, how, and to whom to give of ourselves.

In our caregiving, the most important factor in maintaining determination and avoiding burnout is seeing a positive impact on another person. Literally putting a face on our efforts matters. In a study of radiologists in Israel, attaching a patient's photo to a CT exam increased diagnostic accuracy by 46 percent, and close to 80 percent of key diagnostic findings came only when the radiologists saw the patient's photo.[32] In another study, student callers on behalf of a university scholarship fund were losing motivation. (One of the dispositional givers had a note above his desk: "Doing a good job here is like wetting your pants in a dark suit; you get a warm feeling, but no one else notices.") When those callers met scholarship recipients and heard how the scholarships had made a difference in their lives, the energizing effect was dramatic: revenue went up fourfold.[33]

Avoiding burnout has less to do with the amount of effort than the amount of feedback that the effort genuinely matters to someone else and is appreciated. Avoiding burnout is also a product of realistic expectations and empowering others. In the Bible, Jethro, Moses's father-in-law, observes Moses judging the people from morning to night and asks Moses to explain. The elder leader then counsels, "The thing that you are doing is not right. You will surely wear yourself out, and these people as well. For the task is too heavy for you; you cannot do it alone" (Exodus 18:17–18). Jethro advises Moses to create a hierarchy of leadership, leaving it to Moses to "take to God" only the tough cases.

When I took my first sabbatical in my tenth year as a solo rabbi in a blossoming synagogue, I spent the year with my family in Jerusalem. During that year, I recognized my exhaustion and made a commitment to greater balance: more time with my family; more time writing, reading, and exercising; more efforts to enable my congregants to care for each other, both in terms of visiting those in need and in teaching each other. I have learned that I cannot solve every problem, that there is always unfinished business, and that I need some rest after a major life-cycle event. I cannot claim that I have fully succeeded. Fatigue is a regular companion, but I have improved in my ability to fashion realistic expectations and to create a healthier balance. I expend energy as a skilled caregiver because I find that my constituents are grateful and because my service feels meaningful.

Power is the ability to effect change. When we know that our efforts matter, we are energized. To feel your power, consider giving chunks of time rather than "sprinkling," that is, contributing in small increments. Just like cleaning the house, picking up only a few items at a time rather than clearing an entire area may fail to reinforce that real change is being made.

Recharging may also result from changing your charitable focus. Nearly a century ago psychologists asked subjects to engage in repetitive tasks such as writing a word over and over again. One participant persisted until "his hand felt numb, as though it couldn't move to make even one more mark. At that moment the investigator asked him to sign his name and address for a different purpose. He did so quite easily." Another participant, who said that she could not pick up her hands because they were so tired, immediately picked up her arms effortlessly to adjust her hair. The researcher's conclusion was that "the change of context brought renewed energy."[34] Finding an increase in desire to give may come from choosing a new target for our efforts.

And last, as burnout expert Berkeley psychology professor Christina Maslach emphasizes, "There is now a consistent and strong body of evidence that a lack of social support is linked to burnout."[35] Whether as a clergyperson, teacher, or nurse at work, or a stay-at-home mother enjoying a Mommy and Me program, we are wise to seek out peers to support us.

*Try This: **Chesed** (Compassion) Meditation*

Guided meditation and prayer awaken the desire to give and to do so for an ever-increasing circle of recipients.[36]

http://youtu.be/ Mw4R6VRyRk4

> Sit comfortably and awake. Breathe out tension and breathe in calm.
>
> Bring to mind a person who delights you. See this person in front of you. Now convey the following blessings to him or her with an open heart:
>
> > May you feel at ease.
> >
> > May you live with strength.
> >
> > May you live feeling deeply loved and grateful.
>
> Bring to mind an acquaintance, a familiar stranger, such as the checker at the local grocery store or your mail carrier. Bless this person, after bringing a clear image of him or her before you:
>
> > May you feel at ease.
> >
> > May you live with strength.
> >
> > May you live feeling deeply loved and grateful.
>
> Bring to mind unfamiliar strangers, people near and far who, like you, want to live with safety, strength, and satisfaction; who, like you, desire to safely share a home with their family and celebrate the goodness of their lives. And now reach out compassionately toward each of them and bless them:
>
> > May you feel at ease.
> >
> > May you live with strength.
> >
> > May you live feeling deeply loved and grateful.
>
> Bring to mind someone you love and hear that person bless you:
>
> > May you feel at ease.
> >
> > May you live with strength.
> >
> > May you live feeling deeply loved and grateful.

Before you open your eyes, pause. See yourself radiating love into the world, sending well wishes to all peoples and the whole of creation. Imagine if each person in the world took a moment to radiate such love. Feel the peace. Feel the promise of what could be. Feel the wholeness. Breathe out. Open your eyes.

Tales of Kindness

Because I am a rabbi people often ask me, "How can I become more spiritual?" In many cases, particularly in the context of counseling, I am aware that the person before me is seeking "spirituality" as another form of self-involvement. In response, I often say, "Our most immediate and important spiritual work is how we treat those closest to us—our families, who count on us; our coworkers, with whom we vie for control; our colleagues, with whom we compete. Work on your relationships by seeing the goodness and needs of others, and act generously with concrete actions."

The following is a tale of a Jewish sage who emphasized that spiritual living values prayer and study, but not in a way that is detached from those around you:

> Rabbi Yitzhak Zev Soloveitchik, popularly known as the Brisker Rav, was once studying Jewish law, while his son-in-law was studying in another room. The Brisker's grandchild, his son-in-law's baby, was in her crib in a third room. At some point during their studies, the baby began to cry. The son-in-law continued studying, for he was so immersed in his learning that he was oblivious to everything else. The elder rabbi closed his sacred text, fed the child, and played with her until she fell asleep. Then, on the way back to his room, he stopped to talk to his son-in-law. The Rav instructed the young scholar, "Learn to move in and out of intense concentration. Even Torah study must not block out the sound of a baby crying."[37]

I value greatly the daily discipline of guided meditation and prayer. And yet such spiritual practices are rightly judged by whether they lead toward greater compassion. Popularly attributed to Mahatma Gandhi is the quote "The simplest acts of kindness are by far more powerful than a thousand heads bowing in prayer." And yet even the most generous people I know can feel cranky at times over the many requests made of them. We each need to find a balance between generosity and our own needs. For most of us, the rebalancing moves us toward opening our hearts more. The repeated charge of scripture is to remove the barriers to our insensitivity and self-involvement, often referred to as the circumcising of our heart and ears.[38] Greater inner balance and calm should prompt reaching outward more attentively and less judgmentally. Faith is a context and motivator for compassion, but at the end of the day, actions impact us the most.

Some of the leading sages living in Israel in the second century debated whether study or performing acts of kindness was of greater importance. Rabbi Tarfon stated, "Deed is the priority." Rabbi Akiva rebutted, "Study is more significant." Eventually, they concurred, "Study is more important because study leads to deeds" (*Kiddushin* 40b). Study is the midwife of action, elevating and guiding the work of our hand. The Rabbis also emphasized that although giving is a duty, the giver needs to take into account the dignity of the recipient.[39] Each person is somebody of worth.

⚘ *Try This:* **Writing an Ethical Will**

When I prepare to conduct a funeral, multiple generations share with me their stories and characterizations of their loved one. Rarely do they focus on the possessions the person accumulated. Rather the legacy focuses on character, generosity, and the enduring impact of their values and personality on others.

In that light, there is a practice of writing an ethical will to augment the testament that describes the disbursement of our possessions. You might think of such an ethical will as the writing of one's own eulogy. Putting into writing our life's lessons for the generations after us is an enormous gift of wisdom, identity, and memory making. In an expansive way, the entire book of Deuteronomy is Moses's ethical will to the Israelites. He addresses a new generation with the story of Exodus, a recap of pivotal moments, such as hearing God's address of the Ten Commandments, summarizes many of the laws, cautions the people about potential failures, and closes with a song and a series of blessings. In much shorter form is the precedent of Jacob blessing his twelve sons, in which he speaks of their strengths and weaknesses and his predictions and hopes for them. In the Middle Ages the Jewish community widely practiced the writing of a document to be read by the family after the death of a loved one. Such an ethical will, when used to instill values, is a love letter that is cherished and influences families for generations.

Consider writing an ethical will, a conveyance of what life has taught you. The following sample phrases may help get you started:

> In getting older I learned ...
>
> Some of the happiest moments in my life were ...
>
> What gives my life meaning is ...
>
> As I look back on my life, I am most grateful for ...
>
> May God bless you with ...

The ethical will need be only as long as feels right to you. It is a good exercise to take stock of your own life, whether you give it to others now or reserve the letter for after your own passing. It is wise to keep it with special papers and to review it on a regular basis, as you would your financial will. Some choose to rewrite annually, perhaps before the High Holy Days. Composing such a letter will help you focus on your priorities and how you want to be remembered.[40]

Personal Worth

Hillel, the first-century-BCE Israeli sage, teaches in Pirkei Avot 1:14, "If I am not for myself, who will be for me? And if I am only for myself, what am I? And if not now, when?" In many ways this saying sums up the teaching of this chapter. The place from which compassion emerges is from our own pool of love, gathered from the gracious gifts of others. And yet when a person gives only to please, it can turn into an unhealthy, dependent grabbing for attention. We have a duty to care for our own physical, emotional, and mental health. We grow healthier with the awareness of our distinctive strengths and weaknesses that make up our personal identity and give us self-worth. The Hasidic master the Kotzker Rebbe taught, "If I am I because I am I, and you are you because you are you, then I exist and you exist. But, if I am I because you are you, and you are you because I am I, then I do not exist and you do not exist."[41] Self-identity, in other words, must be self-constructed, rather than given by others.

And yet to see ourselves as interdependent and intertwined with the world is to increase our significance and joy. In the words of contemporary rabbi Rami Shapiro, "Imagining you are apart from the world makes you fearful of the world, placing you in a zero-sum delusion of scarcity that breeds anger, greed, violence, and injustice."[42] "Acting now" when needed is of vital importance to be (and to feel) effective. It is natural to act when it feels convenient for us, but in meeting the needs of others the timetable and frame of reference shift. Once we determine that an action is important, it deserves our full attention. Taking action allows for personal vitality and helps heal the world around us.

Inner and Outer Peace

Toward the close of the *Amidah* prayer, as we move to culminating the daily morning service, we chant, "Grant peace to the world, with happiness and blessing, grace, love, and mercy." The journey of prayer—from body to heart, from head to spirit—culminates with the yearning for a world at peace, marked by safety and inner well-being for all people. Our chants and liturgy are geared to prompt deeds on behalf of God to help materialize peace for the world.

In a concluding hymn of daily prayer, the *Aleinu*, we recite,

> And so we hope in You, *Adonai* our God, we await You, that soon we may behold Your strength revealed in full glory, sweeping away the abominations of the earth, obliterating idols, establishing in the world the sovereignty of the Almighty [*letakken olam bemalkhut Shaddai*]. All flesh will call out Your name—even the wicked will turn toward You.[43]

In the twelfth century, Maimonides stated that the single most important characteristic of God's sovereignty would be an end to the domination of one people over another.[44] Starting in the nineteenth century, the Hebrew phase *tikkun olam*, "repairing the world," became a central expression of Jewish calling and empowerment. The idea is linked to Isaiah's call for Israel to serve as a "light unto the nations" (Isaiah 42:6) by modeling righteousness. In nurturing our own inner peace, there are clear realizations that only when the world is at peace will each of us fully experience peace.

Our hands have power, the ability to effect change. When we use our power on behalf of the stranger, we are affirming our shared humanity. When we use our potential goodness on behalf of the largest sweep of humanity, we act as God's hands. As in the compassion meditation and the sages' guidance on charity, we begin with those closest to us and move outward in concentric circles of care, identifying with each group. The more we expand our sense of "we," the more fully each of us is "me." Our inner wholeness leads us to seeking a greater wholeness in the world around us and gives us enhanced ability to contribute to needed change. Our reward is the satisfaction of giving and the intuitive knowledge that what we do is right. We gain self-worth and the joy of seeing the positive impact that we make on others and that our deeds are a blessing, rippling outward toward healing our world with peace.

CHAPTER SEVEN

INNER PEACE
Balanced from Within

The central message of this book is that we live in a world of many demands, conflicts, and unmet expectations that produce an undertow of anxiety. Yet with the help of resources that have come down to us across the ages—guided meditation, sacred texts, prayer, and service—we can develop our capacity to pause and reflect.

http://youtu.be/
BzTm8GV27tw

In the calm that follows, we find perspective, an ability to evaluate, and approaches to address our logistical and emotional challenges. In time, with a shift toward gratitude, kindness, and leaps of imagination, we can cultivate joyful and holy moments. The body, heart, mind, spirit, and hand are the instruments with which we interpret our reality, shape our identity, and choose our actions. How do we combine these five elements to get from chaos to clarity, frustration to contentment, rushing to reflection, fragmentation to wholeness?

In the description of Shabbat, the seventh day of rest, the biblical text reads, "And God completed the work that God had been doing on the seventh day and rested" (Genesis 2:2). The Rabbis ask, "What was completed *on* the seventh day?" On that day, the sages explain, God observed how all the parts fit together. The Sabbath is set apart to experience a day of harmony, which God called uniquely holy.

To fashion inner peace we survey and strengthen each component—body, heart, mind, spirit, and hand—and for each we are bidden to say, "It is good," just as God did in surveying Creation. When we unite all five components, the sum is mightier than the parts. In Hebrew, the three-letter root of the word for "whole," *shaleim*, is the same as that for "peace," *sha-lom*. To experience inner peace is to feel enlivened and united from within. With inner balance, we craft more realistic expectations, extend ourselves more compassionately, and protect ourselves with necessary boundaries. Inner wholeness offers us the capacity to more readily recover from set-backs and to move forward more effectively.

Experiencing inner wholeness is the opposite of the fragmentation, powerlessness, and hopelessness of depression. If depression is cast as "darkness," then wholeness is marked by light. In those moments when we feel that we are at the right place, with the right people, doing the right actions, we feel that we are "walking in the light." These are moments of delight, marked by place, perspective, and purpose. As if illuminated from within, we experience the gifts of life: choice, connection, and hope. There is a range of brightness of that light, a spectrum of feeling aligned with oneself and the world.

In such moments of alignment we may feel ourselves to be enveloped by a divine light, which holds us, nurtures us, and allows us to blossom. Divine light is hard to describe, because it is not physical or intellectual. Rather, divine light is experienced intuitively as a loving Consciousness that is simultaneously transcendent and embedded in the entirety of Cre-ation. Such an altered state of awareness may emerge rarely, but so palat-ably and significantly that its aftertaste endures powerfully and reshapes our appreciation for what is possible and what matters most.

In the first utterance of the Ten Commandments, "*I am* the Eternal your God," the word *Anokhi* (I am) expresses the totality of Divine Pres-ence.[1] Meditation and prayer guide us to rest in God and to channel God's energy into the world. We are separate neither from our environment nor from the Source of life. When boundaries of identity dissolve, our minds expand, our hearts become more spacious, we are open to the gifts of clarity that come to us as if by grace. To activate God-consciousness is to experience our enormous potential as an illuminating vessel of love in the world. In the expansiveness of silence or the doing of mitzvot (divinely aligned deeds), the divine flow is experienced as nourishing and guiding. We live as an "i" within *Anokhi*, the all-encompassing "I," the enduring eye. The supreme question of wholeness is, *How do I live this moment with a fullness of presence before God's Presence?*

✌ *Try This:* **Walking in the Light**

Breathe out. Relax the muscles in your body.

Breathe out all tension.

Allow yourself to feel safe and surrounded by a gentle light.

Attune to your body. Become aware of how your body parts combine into a united whole, each component contributing to the functioning that allows you to feel physically in balance. Breathe out. Feel gratitude for your body and your health.

http://youtu.be/
G1uGJ_bGsm4

Breathe out. Express gratitude for the world around you. Be aware of how each part of creation operates in tandem and how an integrated earth pulsates with vitality, order, and a yearning for life.

Breathe out. Express praise to God, Source of Creation, for the wonders of creation.

Breathe out. Feel God's light around you.

Breathe out. Identify a recent experience when you felt whole. Where were you? Who were you with? What were you doing? Breathe out while holding the goodness of that moment. See that moment as part of a charm necklace, a stringing together of such moments. See this as a lit necklace around your neck, radiating the light of goodness.

Breathe out. Feel God's presence nurturing you with love. Sit calmly, feeling safe and lovable.

Breathe out. In your mind, see yourself walking. Feel the effortlessness of your motion as you move forward, feeling that all parts of your inner life are in balance.

Breathe out. Feel the light of God strengthening you when needed and offering guidance. Feel humble in the midst of the light. Know that you are an agent of God, tasked to fashion a better world. Breathe out. Feel whole.

Breathe out. Express words of gratitude. Breathe out and savor the delicious light that surrounds you.

Breathe out. Slowly return to this space of wakefulness, aware that you have tasted the sweetness of divine light and with the quiet trust that you will walk forward on illuminated paths. Breathe out and slowly open your eyes.

Change Is Probable

Admittedly there is a gap between the ideal of walking with delight and the reality of our daily experience. Under pressure, we may respond reflexively, resorting to behaviors that often express emotion mindlessly, leading us away from connection and wholeness. Although we seek positive change—whether to live with greater gratitude, patience, and humility or with more attention to the present moment—we are also creatures of habit, and we tend to recoil from the unfamiliar. And yet changes in who we are and how we live are not only possible but probable. With mindfulness and imagination, we may manage that change to prompt exclaiming more often, "It is good!"

When researchers interviewed over nineteen thousand subjects between the ages of sixteen and sixty-eight, most believed that their personality, values, and preferences would change very little in the coming decade, and yet in reviewing the previous decade, they acknowledged that they had changed considerably.[2] This sort of discrepancy appeared regardless of age and did not seem to rest on faulty memory, because the shifts recalled by people matched independent research that had tracked how personality traits had changed with age. Social scientists refer to this phenomenon as "the end of history illusion." People tend to mistakenly see themselves at the watershed of their development. Seeing ourselves as set in our ways reduces anxiety over the unknowns ahead. Often the assertion of continuity is also due to a lack of imagination as to how we might want to change. And yet just as our physical appearance unfolds, so do our beliefs, attitudes, goals, and ways of reacting. Although most of us want to feel accepted just as we are, most of us would also acknowledge that we hope to gain greater wisdom and to grow more whole and joyous. We will change, and we have the power to direct that change. We are as profoundly shaped by where we want to go as by where and with whom we have been. Guided change offers hope. In the words of the nineteenth-century sage Israel Salanter, "The greatest sound in the cosmos is a person changing himself and growing from it."[3]

 Try This: **Looking Back**

Review the past decade and write down six ways that you have changed. After rereading your list, consider how life is filled with surprises, including life-altering events. In reviewing your list, consider which of the changes were consciously made. What did it take to effect those changes?

And now in looking forward, feel empowered, appreciate who you are, and know that you can choose elements of who you will become. Trust the future.

What is one change that you would like to make in the coming year?

What are the excuses that you have made in the past to avoid making that change?

What are the steps that it would take to effect that change?

When will you begin, and how will you recognize your progress?

How will you periodically reward yourself to stay on track?

Tormentors: From Crisis to Purpose

When we look backward, we find that our growth has often emerged from ordeals. Hardships may serve as the impetus for change. An alcoholic usually has to "hit rock bottom," encountering genuine despair, or respond to the intervention of loved ones who point out the nasty results of compulsive behavior, to initiate the arduous, necessary route of recovery, which will demand time and practice to feel owned as a personal choice.

A tragic loss may also prompt acts that ennoble life. Earlier I shared the story of my family member Jordan, who died from undiagnosed diabetes. That bitter loss propelled his parents to marshal their resources to inform and address the growth of diabetes among children through community fundraisers and support for a national effort. Another set of parents who lost their son in a terrorist attack in Israel created a foundation that provides retreats for siblings of terrorist victims.[4] I recently spent time with a lawyer, Gerald Klein, who was dying of lung cancer. He recounted that his greatest professional satisfaction was the nonprofit organization Kids First, which he had created with his wife, who is a therapist. Kids First has helped thousands of people through workshops that cultivate loving relationships between parents and their children after divorce. The logo of the organization shows two separate homes. Before each is a parent, with the words "Still father" for one and "Still mother" for the other. In front of them are a couple of children, with the caption "Still loved." As I spoke with Gerald, he revealed that he had experienced two divorces, one good and one bad. The bad divorce had led to estrangement from his son for two decades, a source of enormous pain. Gerald's volunteer efforts are a moving example of a person who has nobly transformed his own incompleteness into wholeness making for others.

We naturally look to the future with the hope of avoiding pain. In many cases, pain is just destructive and to be exited from as quickly as possible. On the High Holy Days, when Jews traditionally wish each other "a good year," many add the words "and sweet." The Hasidic teaching explains that even though goodness may emerge from pain, we hope to avoid it from the start and experience only the sweet. And yet from a painful situation we may gain a helpful perspective: the humility of knowing that we cannot always control events; the empathic awareness that many who suffer do so in significant part due to circumstances not of their own choosing; a deeper appreciation for our own inner strength and character; and the resolve to redeem something sacred from sorrow by seeking a transcendent good.

Models of Change in the Bible

The Bible offers many examples of communal and personal growth, giving us hope that we too can change for the better. The Israelite bondage and liberation, a central motif, leads to radical transformation. After the Israelites miraculously depart from bondage, they repeatedly complain about life's uncertainties. In the desert, they long for the predictability and the fresh fish and vegetables of their former life, even though they were slaves, treated as property, lacking personal choice or dignity. And yet God charges the Israelites, "You shall be a nation of priests, a holy nation" (Exodus 19:6). This downtrodden people are headed to a promised land with the challenge of communal power and universal concern. From their midst prophets will arise who will demand social justice with words and deeds that will inspire the belief in freedom and responsibility for peoples across time and around the world. Repeatedly the Bible states, "Remember you were slaves in Egypt," as a charge to use that memory as an impetus to help others.

Moses, the exemplar of leadership, begins with self-doubt. He tries to avoid God's call to return to Egypt to wrest freedom for his people (Exodus

3–4). He only agrees once assured that his brother, Aaron, will serve as his spokesman. Eventually, Moses will become a powerful speaker and fashioner of holy community. Deuteronomy, the culmination of the Five Books of Moses, is a series of speeches, blessings, and a lengthy song by this man who formerly described himself as "slow of speech and slow of tongue" (Exodus 4:10). Moses will go on to teach the Ten Commandments, proclaim the *Shema*, and poetically declare, "May my discourse come down as the rain, my speech as the dew, like showers on young growth, like droplets on the grass" (Deuteronomy 32:2). The Jewish sages will identify Moses as Moshe Rabbenu, "Moses our teacher," their highest accolade.

In Genesis, Jacob's name translates as "the circumventer," and in his youth he deceptively acquires the birthright and blessing intended for his firstborn brother, Esau. After twenty-one years of exile and on the eve of reuniting with Esau, Jacob is afraid and alone when he wrestles with an angel. As the sun is rising, Jacob demands a blessing, and the divine figure changes his name to Yisrael, a name with complementary meanings: wrestler with God, straight with God, or prince of God (Genesis 32:25–31). Through struggle, Jacob is transformed from a self-serving deceiver to a forthright man who acts nobly on behalf of God.

The last line of Genesis records Joseph's death as if his life is both the culmination of Genesis and a bridge to the future. There are more verses dedicated to Joseph in the Bible than any other individual until we reach the story of Moses, and in some ways Joseph's transformation is the most extraordinary. In his youth, Joseph is singled out by his father for special affection, and the boy acts with great self-importance. Joseph not only dreams of superiority over his family, he provokes resentment by recounting those dreams to his brothers and father. Joseph's brothers "began to hate him; they could not say a peaceful word to him" (Genesis 37:4). When his father sends the seventeen-year-old Joseph to check up on his shepherd brothers, Joseph goes out to the fields wearing his coat of many colors, a symbol of his father's love that provokes his brothers. His ten brothers want him gone. After considering murder, they sell Joseph into slavery. The Rabbis characterize Joseph as self-involved.[5] And yet the Rabbis will also call Joseph *HaTzaddik*, "the Righteous One."

Elie Wiesel wonders why the Rabbis thought so highly of Joseph. In an essay, Wiesel identifies Joseph's greatness with the gracious forgiveness of his brothers.[6] Soon after his father's death, Joseph reassures his guilt-ridden, cowering brethren, "Do not be afraid. Am I a substitute for God? Although you may have meant to do me harm, God intended it for good, so as to bring about the present result—the survival of many people" (Genesis 50:19–20). Joseph's ability to forgive emerges from a profound inner change. Joseph goes from seeing the world as if in a mirror to peering through a divine window. Joseph goes from self-obsessive to self-effacing, from narcissist to *tzaddik*. Concluding Genesis with the Joseph story is a proclamation: "Radical change is possible!"

In so many ways our personalities seem fixed, whether by nature or nurture or simply by our clinging to the familiar. We may say, "I wish I were the kind of person who could take more risks, who can welcome guests without notice, who can more readily connect with new people, who is more decisive." And yet we do have the capacity to willfully break predictable patterns and perform the unexpected. To effect change consciously takes courage but is necessary to become more effective and whole. As another quotation attributed to Albert Einstein says, "I must be willing to give up what I am in order to become what I will be." To effect change requires the ability to genuinely listen within and to others, whose comments may offer a kind of mirror. We are aided in personal change by inner calm, prayer, inspiring texts, and reflection. We may consciously refashion our behavioral reflexes and worldview by living with increased gratitude, compassion, and justice. Sixteenth-century rabbi Judah Lowe of Prague identified this glorious capacity to alter our usual course of action as evidence of being made in the image of God.

Change is a direction, never a fixed destination. Even after Jacob is renamed Israel the Bible uses both names, as if the patriarch's personality change is incomplete. Still human, he will continue to seesaw temperamentally between a higher self and a more insecure, limited perspective. Nonetheless, his descendants are referred to as *B'nei Yisrael*, "the Children of Israel." Israel's aspiration and achievement to live forthrightly and responsibly dominate our identification with him.

Setting Goals

We can reduce our stress and live with less resentment by gaining control over our own conduct and not taking the behavior of others personally.

And yet we will naturally fall short of such noble achievement as a constant. As I mentioned in chapter 4, to effect change it is important to set both immediate, attainable goals and larger aspirations just out of our reach in order to stretch forward purposefully. Meeting an intermediate goal motivates us to persist. As we have learned with meditation, even when our intention is to focus steadily on breath, thoughts will naturally arise. When they do, we are not to fight the thoughts or chastise ourselves, but simply return to the focus on breath. Likewise, when we neglect to exercise or when we indulge our appetite with an extra slice of pizza, it is not the end of a commitment to get into shape but a predictable lapse. In response, smile humbly and return to the practice, aware of your larger commitment. Changing habits demands steady practice, a realistic goal, and self-forgiveness. The key to transformation is the direction in which we are moving, or as summed up in a Chinese folk saying, "Be not afraid of growing slowly, be afraid only of standing still."

In regard to setting the bar of contentment at an attainable height, I am reminded of Kurt Vonnegut's account of his Uncle Alex, of whom he wrote:

> He was well-read and wise. And his principal complaint about other human beings was they so seldom noticed it when they were happy. So when we were drinking lemonade under an apple tree in the summer, say, and talking lazily about this and that, almost buzzing like honeybees, Uncle Alex would suddenly interrupt the agreeable blather to exclaim, "If this isn't nice, I don't know what is."[7]

Vonnegut states that his uncle made an enduring impact on him and on his sons. They too would regularly pause in the midst of simple pleasures and proclaim, "If this isn't nice, I don't know what is." To serve as an ongoing reminder, I wrote Uncle Alex's exclamation on an index card and taped it on the wall in front of my desk. What I like about the saying is the word "nice." To prompt our appreciation, an event need not be great, let alone the best ever. "Nice" is readily accessible and worthy of our recurring recognition and joy. And yet in daily life, we tend to live with a kind of static in our minds. We replay conversations with a person who upsets us or anticipate fearful scenarios. We live with tension in getting our jobs done well and maintaining smooth, loving relationships with those closest to us. Knowing that life is never perfect is helpful. As in the Creation story, God declared only that it was "good," not "perfect." Understanding this allows us to craft realistic expectations and to thereby more fully appreciate what we do have. Good is good enough to evoke appreciation.

 Try This: **When at Peace**

Jot down, "I feel at peace when ..."; Finish the sentence five times. Reflect on the qualities that give you peace and consider how you can actively increase those moments.

Setting Boundaries and Realistic Expectations

There is an industry of happiness making (and perhaps this book could be catalogued as an entry in that category), yet happiness cannot be achieved directly. As Eleanor Roosevelt observed, "Happiness is not a goal, it's a by-product of a life well lived."[8] We are wise to focus on immediate goals in the context of a larger plan. For instance, a simple act of making a difference today in the happiness of another allows us to find happiness tomorrow too.

Knowledge of our limitations in changing others is also liberating. This is particularly true in dealing with extreme, compulsive behaviors. A person with a personality disorder, for instance, may engage in unprincipled patterns of behavior: grandiosity, manipulation, a disregard for rules or the feelings of others. Beneath such a person's genuine good qualities and talents is often the fear of deep flaws. Working or living with such a person can keep you off-balance, because he or she will ignore or disparage any constructive criticism in order to maintain self-worth. (Such pathological behavior is distinct from authentic self-esteem, where there is a willingness to monitor the reactions and needs of others.) Although healthy people may seek out professional counseling to gain perspective on their own hurtful behavior, narcissists doggedly deny that they have a problem. In the words of psychiatrist M. Scott Peck, a neurotic makes himself crazy; a person with a personality disorder makes everyone else crazy.[9] Being aware of the deeply embedded nature of narcissism reminds us that Joseph's transformation was rare, but possible. For Joseph, prison may have revealed his character as a prism opens up light. However, as the Talmudic Rabbis taught pragmatically, "Do not rely on a miracle" (*Pesachim* 64b). We must form realistic expectations in dealing with others and with our own change too.

Stepping back enables us to identify patterns that range from irritating to hurtful to outright abusive. As meditation enables us to separate who we are from our thoughts, so we may come to know that a person's selfish behavior does not reflect or impact our own self-worth and purpose. Operating with this perspective is easier said than done. When we are threatened by another's manipulative behavior, it is natural to awake in the middle of the night with an adrenaline surge as if in a fight. Hurtful people are best avoided, and yet that is not always a choice. Awareness of their patterns of selfish behavior may facilitate your own boundary making and prompt compassion, contributing toward your own safety and equilibrium.

Although at times we may be dealing with the extreme of a pathological personality, more commonly our daily stresses are due to meeting conflicting needs or unrealistic desires. In planning a wedding, for instance, you cannot invite everyone that you know. When a childhood friend learns that she was not invited, she may feel disappointment and complain to mutual friends. But you do have to draw lines and sometimes say no. Likewise, if you are a physician, you cannot see every patient immediately. You have to know when to refer to an emergency room and when to have your receptionist politely schedule an appointment. When your adult son calls with great upset about how his aunt insulted his spouse, you have to acknowledge bad behavior and try to offer a larger, less personal perspective—even when discussing your own sister. The broader our perspective, the greater our ability to respond compassionately while setting healthy boundaries. In dealing with bad behavior, which abounds, we have the ability to choose to do what is right regardless of what others do. The hard part is learning to pause before responding, so as to react with the wisdom of our higher self. In the words of an unknown author, "Between stimulus and response there is a space. In that space lies our freedom and power to choose our response. In our response lies our growth and our freedom." [10]

Being Trustworthy

Those whom I most admire are trustworthy, consistently matching their deeds with espoused values that express deeply held commitments. In the words of the Talmud, "Any Torah scholar whose inside does not resemble his outside is not really a Torah scholar," analogized to the Holy Ark, which was covered with gold on both the exterior and the interior.[11] We are guided to look beyond charm and first impressions to assess character. As Proverbs 31:30 teaches, "Charm is deceitful and beauty is fleeting, but she who is God-fearing is worthy of praise." "God-fearing" conveys the character qualities of reliability, self-awareness, and honesty—acting as if watched when no other person is present. When Jethro guides his son-in-law Moses to choose judges to assist him, he identifies the necessary qualities of "capability" (*chayil*)[12] and "God-fearing" (*yirei Elohim*) (Exodus 18:21). And yet when Moses chooses the judges, the text states only that he found those who were "capable" (Exodus 18:25). The missing quality of *yirei Elohim* is noted by the twelfth-century Spanish commentator Abraham ibn Ezra, who explains that only God knows who is genuinely God-fearing. There is another possibility: we can judge integrity only after we have worked closely with another person; Moses will know only from experience whether a particular judge warrants trust.

I once heard the Dalai Lama say with his signature giggle to a group of business leaders, "I know very little about business." And then he added, "But what I do know is that acting dishonestly for short-term gains impacts trust, and it is trust that matters in long-term success."[13] Likewise, individuals who consistently rationalize deceptive behavior undermine their relationships. We naturally try to put on our best face in social interactions. And yet the cornerstone of enduring bonds is our sincerity and reliability. As a friend quipped, "The attribute that genuinely matters is sincerity. If I could only learn to fake that, I would have it made."

In integrating our inner life and our outer deeds, we strengthen our friendships and our own self-esteem. When we trust ourselves, we more readily trust others. Most of us, social science research shows, are slightly dishonest. When deciding whether to park in an illegal space to run a quick errand, for instance, we may engage in cost-benefit analysis: the likelihood that we will be caught and the subsequent penalty weighed against how much time we will save. Dan Ariely, the author of *The (Honest) Truth About Dishonesty: How We Lie to Everyone, Especially Ourselves*, shares that most people will hedge the truth when they can do so and still maintain a self-image as a good person. Some people are more prone toward dishonesty than others.[14] Particularly susceptible are those with a greater capacity to tell a good story, thereby conjuring up creative rationalizations. Professor Ariely concludes that the more consistently we act honestly, the more capable we are of maintaining our moral bearings. In seeking to increase our own wholeness, the resolve to act transparently and on principle contributes to feeling whole and effective.

Apologizing and Forgiving

Inevitably we will falter in our consistency, falling short of our ideal. As my mother would say, "We are each two people." That is, we are each steady and erratic, a sober self and, at times, an as-if-inebriated jerk. This switch is particularly pronounced when we are stressed, such as at moments of transition.

Family vacations provide a surprising setting for the flaring of emotions. We invest much enthusiasm in preparation, plus money and time in going away. Expectations are high. But even on vacation, not all goes smoothly. My wife, Linda, and I have traveled widely with our three children. We love being together, but we differ in our priorities. My wife and I tend toward exploration and museums. Our children, even as adults, remind us of the importance of relaxation and play. On a recent trip to the Big Island of Hawaii, we returned to our rented apartment drained from driving on winding roads and some tug-of-war over priorities on a cloudy, windy day. I sat down at the kitchen table in need of escape and took out a chapter of this manuscript. My wife was disappointed that we had not visited a couple of sites on the far side of the island that we had passed along our drive. She interrupted my reverie by reminding me that I had agreed to visit a historic landmark and take a particular Kona coffee plantation tour.

I slammed my fist on the table and exclaimed, "Just give me a break. Enough!" and went to another room with a chapter of *Increasing Wholeness* in hand (now there is irony). Needless to say, I was in trouble. My wife felt hurt and embarrassed by my flare-up. It was only a brief moment, but I needed to make repairs. An apology to my wife an hour later was insufficient. She did not experience her statements as provocative and felt that the tensions we'd experienced throughout the day with the children were due in significant part to the need for more communication. So the next morning I called for a family meeting. I first apologized to my wife in front of our adult children, which she accepted. I then told them that she was wise to suggest a group conversation on how we would spend the upcoming days. We spoke with the recognition that each day was part of a larger canvas of time and that some days would emphasize travel and exploration and on others we would relax on the beach.

I share this story to convey that with all my writing, thinking, and "practice of the pause," I too overreact. I too can bang on the table and only later recognize that I have allowed the inebriation of fatigue and too much Kona coffee to distort my perception. Learning to maintain mutual respect and to get along is an ongoing challenge. Repeatedly, I quote Uncle Alex: "If this isn't nice, I don't know what is." There are so many moments to savor. And yet in the course of a day—any day—there is the rise and fall of emotions. Among the gains of increasing wholeness is being able to more readily make amends and heal once we have acted poorly.

Sacred Text Study: Moses's Temper

When we fail to filter our remarks and temper our responses, the results can be catastrophic, as we learn from Moses's life. His forty-year journey with the Israelites was far more extreme in its physical demands and uncertainty than my family vacation to Hawaii. That journey of the Israelites amplifies the lessons that we need to learn and relearn, including the recognition that dreams may be shattered or the fabric of relationships irreparably torn by a momentary loss of control. Such a warning is dramatically conveyed in the tale of Moses striking the rock. For close to forty years, Moses has led the people through the desert on a journey marked by uncertainty, physical hardship, and repeated complaints. The manna, a kind of honey-dew substance miraculously deposited in camp each night, has provided daily nourishment but does not fully satisfy the imagination. Soon after the death of Miriam, Moses's sister, the Israelites protest,

> We wish that we had died together with our siblings before God! Why did you bring God's congregation to this wilderness? So that we and our livestock should die? Why did you take us out of Egypt and bring us to this terrible place? It is an area where there are no plants, figs, grapes, or pomegranates. There is not even water to drink! (Numbers 20:3–5)

God instructs Moses to take his staff, gather the people, and speak to a rock, from which abundant water will flow. There is a precedent for this situation. Soon after the people left Egypt, there was also a need for water. God directed Moses, "Strike the rock and water will flow." Moses hit the rock and the water emerged (Exodus 17:1–7).

Now, nearly forty years later, God tells Moses, "Order the rock to yield its water." The account continues, "Moses and Aaron assembled the congregation in front of the rock, and he said to them, 'Listen you rebels, shall we get water for you out of this rock?' And Moses raised his hand and struck the rock twice with his rod." Water flows, but God reprimands Moses, "Because you did not trust Me enough to affirm My sanctity in the sight of the Israelite people, therefore you shall not lead this congregation into the land that I have given them." (See Numbers 20:8–12.) The severity of his punishment is commensurate with the enormity of his task.

What was Moses's error? Perhaps it was his failure to have paid close attention to instructions. He relied on past conduct rather than listening closely to God. Leadership on such a lofty level demands attentiveness to the exact needs of each situation. A careful reading finds at least two other faults: Moses asserts his ability to draw out the water, rather than giving credit exclusively to God. He also calls the people "rebels," the only time that he speaks negatively of the people. This cluster of missteps demonstrates that Moses's capacity to lead is greatly diminished. Moses's flawed behavior comes on the heels of his sister's death. Miriam had watched over him as a baby floating down the Nile in the wicker basket and had led the women in triumphant song after crossing the Sea of Reeds to freedom. No doubt, his mourning contributed to his imbalance, impatience, and harsh speech.

When we lose our tempers, it is often fueled by emotions that have simmered under the surface and are not directly connected to the immediate situation. In the throes of upset, we act out exaggerated and uncontrolled emotions. Some selfish or negligent actions warrant anger. Injustice, for instance, deserves righteous indignation. How forcefully we respond shapes our effectiveness and dignity. And yet we who are only human will fall short of ideal behavior. When stressed, we may overreact. Forgiveness is necessary in order to accept our humanity and do better next time. We are wise to monitor ourselves closely and learn to pause mindfully before speaking or acting. Our inner wholeness and effectiveness depend in no small part on self-control. In the words of Proverbs 16:32, "Better to be forbearing than mighty; to have self-control than to conquer a city."

When we feel emotions rising and our body tightening, we need to pay attention. When we pause and breathe deeply, not from the chest alone but from the diaphragm, we begin to gain control. When pausing, we may examine the thought that is upsetting us and monitor the rising emotions.

Among the most common overreactions is to view a specific wrong, like a partner not taking out the garbage in a timely fashion, as an example of an entire pattern of upsetting behavior. We then respond to a specific act with a conclusion that is magnified in content and emotion: "I live with such a slob!"[15] If we can train ourselves to recognize the warning signs of growing anger, to take several deep breaths when we feel our anger rising and pause to gain perspective, we may steady ourselves to act wisely. Such guidance is easier said than done. There are no absolute fixes for conflict, but there are practices to lower the panic, to reduce the adrenaline, to feel more secure and calm. Employing conscious breathing, gratitude, and balancing imagination with reality testing (the essence of cognitive-behavioral therapy) will all increase our steadiness and perspective. We each falter. Even so, I do believe that my efforts to develop conscious pauses and increase inner wholeness, and to humbly offer to make amends, have improved the quality of my relationships and my appreciation for the mystery, duties, and goodness of life.

Mending Ourselves, Mending God

The Jewish mystics describe a shattering of God that left God incomplete too. If God is in need of repair, surely we who are created in the image of God are also broken. The mystics teach that we can make a difference on behalf of God not only in repairing the world and ourselves, but also in mending God.

In sixteenth-century Safed, Israel, Jewish mystics flourished, gathered there in the wake of the Spanish Inquisition. Many of the exiles brought with them a copy of the *Zohar*, the mystical commentary on the Torah. In the *Zohar*, God is manifest as ten *sefirot*, dynamic emanations. These divine qualities mirror the inner attributes of a human being, including intelligence, kindness, self-restraint, and compassion.

Rabbi Isaac Luria, known by the acronym HaAri (also meaning "the lion"), added another layer of divine understanding. After the early death of his father, HaAri moved with his mother from Israel to Egypt, where he lived in his uncle's home. He returned to Israel in his mid-twenties and settled in Safed, where he studied with the great kabbalist Rabbi Moses Cordovero. Luria gathered around him an inner circle of impressive practitioners of Jewish mysticism, questing to understand and experience the presence of the Divine.

Luria augmented the *Zohar's* understanding of Creation with big bang imagery. God is essentially infinite, Luria taught, and initially filled all. To craft a physical world, God withdrew to make a space for Creation. Into this vacuum, God shined divine light and fashioned vessels to hold that light. The divine emanation pulsated with energy and shattered the vessels. Most of the light returned to its divine source, but some of the sparks commingled with the shards of the vessels. With an explosion, history began. The prophetic promise of a messianic era of harmony, Luria taught, would emerge only with the regathering of the holy sparks and the recrafting of the sacred vessels. This story of Creation has immense implications: God, as if broken, depends on people to make the world and God whole again.

For generations of Jews, this Creation account has offered enormous purpose and comfort. Even when they have felt oppressed and politically weak, Jews have believed that with a simple act of kindness or in observing the Sabbath day, they are gathering holy sparks and healing the cosmos. Each mitzvah is a powerful instrument of far-reaching repair. Jewish mysticism honors paradox: God is ultimately infinite and whole and yet manifests as finite and broken; people are limited in years and power, and yet the entire world and God depend on human action. For Jews, a religious life entails sacred acts between a person and God as well as between people. Simple acts of loving-kindness or ritual obedience both meet divine expectations and regather holy sparks.

Luria's imaginative description of origins predated modern physics by hundreds of years. Luria intuited the emergence of the physical world with an explosion. As in modern physics, there is no concept of time, let alone history, or even physical matter or light before the singularity of the big bang. But for Luria, the story of Creation goes beyond a description of how physical reality emerged. For him and later practitioners of Jewish mysticism, the big bang evokes purpose. God depends on us. With simple, accessible acts of goodness, we may reshape the world and even God.

Most of the practices in this book have focused on enhancing inner wholeness by strengthening and integrating our facets of self. And yet our spiritual work encompasses and often begins with how we treat those who are closest to us, whether our spouse, our parents, or a server in a restaurant. We are wise to ask ourselves: Are we able to recognize the humanity of others rather than acting as if they were invisible? Do we perceive the Divine in others? Do we translate that recognition into treating others with dignity? Are we honest with others and with ourselves? Are we able to forgive ourselves for falling short of our potential goodness? And are we willing to hear a divine call of service, even when it goes against our self-interest?

 ## Try This: **A Taste of Wholeness**

Sit and close your eyes, back straight. Breathe out. Relax. See your body as a vessel for a soul. Your soul is consciousness. At the center of your forehead, see a lit candle and watch the smoke rising.

http://youtu.be/
apj-zmHB5KM

Breathe out and allow your soul to rise from the center of your forehead, rising as the smoke. Rising higher and higher. Rising through the stars and higher still until reaching a place of gentle illumination, a kind of cloud of inviting light. This is the collective place of souls.

Breathe out and become aware of the fissures within your soul, become aware of the incompleteness that you sometimes feel.

Breathe out and feel the light of the Divine holding your soul and healing the fissures, allowing you to feel complete.

Breathe out and feel whole. Hold that feeling as you breathe in and out, feeling relaxed, safe, and surrounded by divine light. This is the place of the higher Sabbath, a place of gentle embrace and quiet strength; a place of peace.

In a moment you will begin your descent back into your body. When your soul, your *neshamah*, reaches your body, you will continue to feel peaceful.

Breathe out and begin to descend from the cloud of light, down through the stars, back through the earthly sky, returning to your body.

Breathe out and slowly begin to open your eyes. Continue to feel the taste of wholeness.

Thou Shall Not Avert Thy Gaze

In looking at a broken world, it is natural to look away from the pain, ugliness, and even the unknown. And yet we are whole only when we reach outward with courage. In seeing the beggar on the street, we may choose not to give, but we are called to at least affirm the dignity of the other with a smile or a word of recognition. In seeing the suffering of children on our television screens, we are called to do something, even if only by making a small contribution toward an organization that helps the young or to volunteer to help even one child for one day. Starting with a small act opens the heart to the satisfactions of giving and fans the sparks of goodness into a passion to help others. When giving, we need discernment for self-protection and to avoid callous insularity. Wholeness is always about clarity and balance.

The Bible commands us not to be indifferent (Deuteronomy 22:3). It is inconvenient to notice the needs of others and yet essential to pay attention. In the words of Elie Wiesel, "The opposite of love is not hate, it's indifference. The opposite of art is not ugliness, it's indifference. The opposite of faith is not heresy, it's indifference. And the opposite of life is not death, but indifference between life and death."[16] The challenge of living is to do what is right on behalf of others despite the momentum of self-concern. The deeds of the non-Jews who risked their safety and the well-being of their families to help Jews during World War II challenge us: What would we do for the stranger, simply because it is just? Seeing our "I" before an eternal "eye" and feeling accountable for our actions leads to moral courage and greater wholeness.

As I recognize my own shortcomings, I also acknowledge that no one can tell another person how and when he or she will be most contented. In the words of Joseph Campbell, the author of many books on world mythology, each person must follow his or her "bliss."[17] There are many activities for personal satisfaction and even uplift, including art, dance, music, chess, Sudoku, or aiding others. And yet increasing inner peace relies on both care of self and the recognition of the other, the qualities of self-worth and humility. In law school, my teacher Judge David Nelson said to us, "When you walk into a courtroom, do so with confidence, conveying that you are well prepared, capable, and have something important to say and yet do not hold yourself as superior to others." Cultivating humility is essential to increasing inner joy. We need to know that we are here on earth with precious, limited time and a calling to live as capable students and servants while maintaining our distinctive self-worth and dignity. We naturally prioritize ourselves and a limited number of close family and friends, and yet to increase wholeness we need to expand our commitments in stages toward the widest circles of the world and even the Divine.

 Try This: **Revisiting Obstacles to Our Completeness**

Close your eyes. In your mind's eye, remember the first exercise in this book that guided you to reach into your clothing above your heart. Examine again the object that you withdrew, and become aware of its significance. Become aware of your progress in addressing the problem that it represented.

http://youtu.be/
NoGm1pnBRZQ

Breathe out and reach again into your clothing above your heart and pull out another object that represents a problem. Examine the object and become aware of its significance. Know that you can untie knots within yourself. Know that you can make progress in achieving greater inner wholeness. Become aware of two actions that you will take to address the problem represented by the object. Breathe out. Open your eyes. Feel confident about gaining increased inner peace as you look forward.

The Spirituality of Imagination

The delight of Shabbat hinges on imagination. There is nothing intrinsically more special about a Saturday than a Tuesday. But when we imagine a day of rest and take action to ensure its implementation, Saturday becomes the Sabbath. Rituals are inductions, like hypnosis, to an altered state of awareness. In lighting the Friday night candles to commence Shabbat, a woman closes her eyes and pauses before reciting the blessing: letting go of the week, bringing her family to mind with gratitude, and easing into greater tranquility.

By tasting wholeness even for one day, we have motivation and guidance to craft more such days. What begins with imagination can become a steadfast reality. The leap of spiritual imagination enables us to gain the hope that a string of such days is possible, a coming together that would enable a world that is sublimely peaceful.

At the Passover seder we recite, "In each generation each person is to see him- or herself *as if* he or she went out from Egypt."[18] The retelling of the Exodus story is more than recounting history. In using imagination, our personal memory absorbs collective memory. The ancient story becomes our own, serving as a prompt to consider how from our own ruts we may find redemption. The phrase that prompts imagination is "as if," a spiritual leap conveying immediacy and personalization that is repeatedly used, whether explicitly or implicitly, in sacred Jewish texts.

Whether in looking to the collective past or the significance of an immediate action, imagination may nurture and guide. In regard to the giving of Torah as an ongoing event, the early Rabbis stated, "Each and every year, a person must see him- or herself as if he or she stood at Mount Sinai."[19] To emphasize the importance of your next action, the Talmud states, "Each person must see him- or herself as half innocent or guilty" (*Kiddushin* 40b). Even further upping the ante, Maimonides states that each person should see the entire world as evenly balanced between good and bad deeds, such that the next act that you take will tilt the balance and the entire world's favorable judgment depends on you.[20] Despite such enormous responsibility, we are to live with great joy, as stated in another midrash, dated to the fifth century or earlier: "Each person should desire to see herself as if she were standing beneath the wedding canopy [*chuppah*]—for there is not a day in eternity more joyous."[21]

Spiritual imagination may elicit self-worth and strength. From *Otzer Midrashim*, a collection of early Rabbinic statements: "A person must see him- or herself as if filled to the core with holiness."[22] We are to see ourselves as a vessel for God's divine breath, a vessel that holds the holiness of God. And from an influential guide to Jewish practice, the nineteenth-century *Mishnah Berurah*: "In prayer a person should see himself as if standing in awe before a King ... as if facing *Shechinah* [God's inviting presence], so that the left side of the person is the right side of God." In other words, we are to see ourselves as not only invited to stand before the Ruler of the world, but to see our left side, which for most of us is our weak side, supported by a caring Divine Being.

As with the observance of the Sabbath, we use spiritual imagination to forge an elevated reality. Our life encompasses not only our own limited years, but the peak experiences of an entire people. We are not only flesh and blood, but vessels for God's presence. And when we pray, we are empowered to stand before God, seeing God as welcoming and caring. Imagination is the bridge to actualizing our spiritual potential. Imagination works in tandem with reasoned analysis to create events and deeds that define us and our world. As an Olympic athlete improves performance by visualizing the completion of a gymnastic routine or a three-point shot in basketball, by rehearsing our potential joy and wholeness we become more effective as holy messengers and more fully human. On a more profound level, imagination is a vehicle for inspiration: the ability to see the world through God's eyes and to receive, as if by grace, wisdom.

Moving Toward Wholeness

Although the journey ahead is fraught with uncertainty and potential pain, we gain calm and renewal by seeing our lives as part of a larger whole. As we seek safety and adventure, familiarity and novelty, so a relationship with God entails honoring the paradox of both Presence and Mystery. We cannot control God or our future. Our moods and hopes seesaw, and yet we may learn to shift our spiritual weight closer to the fulcrum, that center point where we find steadiness and calm. More fully present, we live with greater trust in the foundational goodness of life as both a gift and a choice. Optimism is an ongoing act of intuitive artistry. With knowledge of our power to effect change and acceptance of how much is beyond our control, we are more content.

In the words of Rabbi Abraham Joshua Heschel, "Just to be is holy."[23] We may condition ourselves to recognize God's pulsating presence by entering into the expansiveness of silence and into deeds of justice and kindness. Each breath that we take has the potential to anchor us in the moment. Each breath surprises us with life and connects us to all that exists. Sylvia Boorstein, a great teacher of compassion, offers words to relate to each inhalation and exhalation: "May I meet this moment fully; may I meet it as a friend."[24] And in meeting each moment as a friend, we experience inner peace and smile with ease.

The act of silence allows us to open to the joy that we hold within and as a window to wonder. A quiet pause leads to receptivity, an opening to joy. By steadying ourselves with the regularity of a spiritual practice—guided meditation, blessings, and sacred texts—and serving with generosity and integrity, we can consciously cultivate wholeness within, enhance connections outward, and reach upward toward the Divine. Increasing wholeness draws forth the delight of life.

✎ *Try This:* **Infused by Light**

The psalmist wrote, "In Your light we shall see light" (Psalm 36:10), and the nineteenth-century Russian Hasidic master Rabbi Aaron Karlin explained that God's light is within each of us, a light that we may awaken and attune to the divine light that surrounds us.[25] This closing meditation is intended to enable you to engage the divine light from within yourself as a sustainable awareness for increasing vitality and wholeness.

> For a week, start your day with twenty to thirty minutes of meditation. Toward the end of your sit, pause and see a ball of light at the center of your lower abdomen. Feel the light expanding and filling your whole body. Taste the light and feel a quiet joy. Experience your mind as a still pond lit by a gentle light. See the light surrounding you, holding you, allowing you to feel safe and valuable. See yourself as radiant, expressing love to those near and far, toward those known and unknown. Breathe out and slowly open your eyes. When you do, hold on to the experience of wholeness with delight, aware of the divine light that always flows through you and that holds you tenderly.

To deepen your meditation skill, consider the resources of group practice and instruction offered at a meditation retreat center and an extended series of sitting and walking meditations over several days, a week, or even longer.[26] The gains of meditation are cumulative. At its best, the combination of meditation, blessings, and sacred texts simultaneously offers deeper awareness of the mystery of our interior and greater inner access. In the words of the contemporary Sufi teacher Kabir Helminski:

Anyone who has probed the inner life, who has sat in silence long enough to experience the stillness of the mind behind its apparent noise, is faced with a mystery. Apart from all the outer attractions of life in the world, there exists at the center of human consciousness something quite satisfying and beautiful in itself, a beauty without features. The mystery is not so much that these two dimensions exist—an outer world and the mystery of the inner world—but that we are suspended between them, as a space in which both worlds meet ... as if the human being is the meeting point, the threshold between two worlds.[27]

 Try This: **A Final Blessing**

The *Amidah* prayer contains the threefold priestly blessing taken from Numbers 6:24–26:

> May God bless you and protect you.
> May the light of God's face be upon you and
>   deal graciously with you.
> May God turn God's face to you and place
>   upon you peace.[28]

During the time of the Temple, the priests would pronounce these biblical priestly words each day for those gathered in the courtyard of the Holy Temple.

Once the Temple was destroyed, the role of the priests as active mediators between God and the people disappeared. Yet the words of blessing persisted. Clergy in synagogues and churches invoke them on behalf of their congregations. In traditional Jewish practice, parents use this formula to bless each of their children as part of the Friday night table rituals. In synagogues during holy days, descendants of the priests, *kohanim*, place their prayer shawls over their heads and, following the prompt of the prayer leader, chant them in a haunting tone word by word. The traditional custom is for congregants to avoid looking at the priests during this act of blessing, either by turning away or by placing prayer shawls over their heads and over those of their children. In this mystery-laden ritual, the priests begin with an introductory blessing acknowledging that they are going to bless the people with love.

These three short blessings summarize the quest for inner peace. Each word is purposeful and multifaceted in meaning. The words that follow also contain elements of traditional commentary, which I offer as a blessing for you. I encourage you to use the link provided to hear the blessing spoken over you.

Breathe out. Feel deep calm as the following blessings are bestowed on you:

http://youtu.be/ IpluyTWqtik

Yevarekhekha Adonai veyishmerekha——"May God bless you and protect you" by providing physical and emotional well-being. May God bless you with possessions and protect those possessions from both thieves and from corrupting you.

Ya'eir Adonai panav eilekha vichuneka—"May the light of God's face be upon you and deal graciously with you," strengthening your intellect and intuition, and may you use all your God-given talents to illuminate those around you.

Yisa Adonai panav eilekha veyaseim lekha shalom—"May God turn God's face to you and place upon you peace." May you know that God loves you and turns toward you compassionately. Embraced by the Divine Presence, may you taste inner peace, combining all your facets into wholeness and holiness. May you walk forward in God's light with delight. Amen.

CRAFTING A PRACTICE

Throughout this book you were offered many "try this" opportunities. The goal of the exercises was to expand your awareness and increase your wholeness. Now that you have completed the book, pause to consider which of the experiences made an impact on how you see yourself or the world and which of the exercises—such as a specific guided meditation, blessing exercise, or journal reflection—is worth repeating on a regular basis. Change is a product of altering habits. What habit of daily spiritual practice do you currently have, and what might you add from the menu items that you have tasted in this book?

The Sabbath

The Sabbath is a vital resource for renewal and growth, a time to imaginatively experience our sought ideal of wholeness, calm, and spaciousness within. I encourage you to consider creating space for Sabbath, or pondering any elements you may want to add to or subtract from your current Sabbath practice as you consider how to continue on your journey to inner wholeness.

Among the Ten Commandments, the Sabbath is the only ritual. It is the fourth commandment, coming between those that deal exclusively with God and the commands that focus on our relationship with others. The Sabbath is the bridge between the Divine and our social lives, integrating the various dimensions of our inner and outer lives. Observing the Sabbath as a day of refraining from creation is to experience the world one day a week as if it were already whole. Such an experience opens possibilities of a future in which each day would manifest festivity and harmony. Experiencing the Sabbath entails imagination, coupled with the self-discipline to demarcate such a day of rest. To experience our lives and the world as if whole one day a week is to deepen the awareness of what is precious and possible, personally and universally.

A friend tells the story of traveling on an intercity bus at night. The elderly passenger next to him turned on the overhead light to read as the bus pulled out of the station. For the next forty-five minutes he intently read a small book in Hebrew. When he closed the book, my friend asked his neighbor about his reading, which led to questions about his religious life. My friend asked, "So what does the Sabbath mean to you?"

The man turned to face him and with eyes beaming with joy said, "The Sabbath? It is paradise."

My poet friend decided then that although he might not practice the Sabbath in a fully traditional mode, he would make it a priority to set aside one day a week from work and to engage with others in Sabbath rest, and he did.

My friend's story reminded me of another tale, which I heard from the late Rabbi Shlomo Carlebach. A father, deeply upset by his teenage son's disregard for the rules of the Sabbath, took him to a venerated rabbi. After a short private meeting, the young man emerged and thereafter observed the holy day with great ardor. "What did the rabbi say to you?" many asked, but he would never answer. Only when quite old did he reveal what had occurred.

"I walked into the rabbi's study anticipating that he would berate me as others had done. Instead with kind eyes he gestured for me to take a seat opposite him. He took my hand gently in his, and his eyes slowly filled with tears. Looking into mine, he said, 'Shabbos' [Yiddish for "the Sabbath"]. A hot tear fell onto my hand and singed the skin. I decided then and there that I would honor and love the Sabbath too."

The Sabbath in the Jewish tradition is often described as a queen or bride—an anthropomorphism that conveys the weekly meeting as one of much anticipated union and love.

The traditional observance of the Sabbath is carefully regulated, enabling clarity of expectations and constancy of practice. Rabbi Abraham Joshua Heschel described the Sabbath as "a palace in time." Just as a building has a detailed blueprint, so there are many fine lines drawn to craft the holy structure of a day set apart, providing freedom not to tend to an errand when there is a clear commitment to a structure of rest. And yet within the structure there is choice as to how to use the time in satisfying ways. Deciding ahead of time the contours of your chosen Sabbath and then engaging in both self-restraint and celebration will create spaciousness in your inner self and in your practice of the Sabbath.

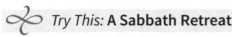 *Try This:* **A Sabbath Retreat**

Give yourself a full day of Sabbath retreat. Experience it as if you were a passenger on a cruise ship by preparing your meals in advance and refraining from commerce. Begin with the setting of the sun, and provide yourself a fine meal with wine and candlelight in the evening. Unplug from the technology that places demands on you during the week. Arrange to share meals with friends. Seek out a communal worship and study service that meets your spiritual inclinations. In the afternoon, consider an Epsom salt bath, a nap, reading, or playing with your family. Simply enjoy the harmony of the present and the beauty of world. Wait for three stars to appear before you exit this time of being that is set apart from the doing of the work week.

Incremental Change

Our increase in wholeness is incremental. To grow in a balanced and enduring way requires the constancy of small acts. There are no shortcuts or quick fixes to enlightenment. And yet the path of inner growth is inviting, enjoyable, and deeply satisfying. As you complete this book, may you find that you have gained from our time together. May you feel motivated to engage in a regularity of practice to attain greater ease, integration, strength, spiritual uplift, and full-bodied groundedness.

May you close this book as if parting from a friend.

ACKNOWLEDGMENTS

Five years ago I offered a class on "Increasing Wholeness" with an emphasis on guided imagery. It was well attended and deeply satisfying to teach, prompting me to offer the class again, this time with a camera crew from Chapman University. I sensed that if I was to write a book on this material, the guided imagery needed to be heard rather than only read. I did not yet know how such recordings could be integrated with the written word. Erica Taylor, a congregant and friend, was my key motivator and editorial guide in offering those classes and turning them into this book. Erica introduced me to Jeff Swimmer, the professor at Dodge College of Film and Media Arts, who arranged for students to film my classes. Erica also reviewed my many written drafts, offered insightful critiques, sent me related articles, and reassured me repeatedly that this project was worthy of persistence.

Marla Nathan transcribed the videos of my classes, offering me a first draft. I presented that material in a seminar to congregants. My gratitude to Beth Elster for hosting that six-part gathering, which included the homemade chocolates of Barbara King, and to my students whose written critiques moved the process forward, including Susan Seely, Jay and Sheila Witzling, Drs. Harris and Jan Shultz, Nancy Raymon, Ellen Nise, and Howard Mirowitz. I turned to others to react to the second draft, among them Professor Julia Lupton, Rabbi K'vod Wieder, Sylvia Bar, Jean Kravitz, and Dr. Ray Lederman. The third draft was honed by the insight and encouragement of Professor Ron Wolfson and Rabbis Uzi Weingarten, Chuck Simon, and Bradley Shavit Artson.

The recordings that are embedded in this book were videotaped and uploaded by congregants Sheila Witzling and Andrea Alfi, with the technical support of Michael Rosenthal.

Stuart M. Matlins, publisher of Jewish Lights Publishing, read the fourth draft and offered to publish it. I have written two previous books for Jewish Lights and have found Stuart a brilliant guide and a trusted friend in crafting and distributing a book. My editor, Alys Yablon Wylen, took that fourth draft and with great skill and sensitivity sculpted away material, enhancing the message that I sought to convey. Emily Wichland and Rachel Shields of Jewish Lights masterfully guided the editing of the final draft.

The members of my synagogue staff offered their encouragement and guidance. I want to thank Sandy Klein, Lisa Heller, Barbara Sherman, Helene Coulter, James Shipp, Debbie Hebron, Ana Cottle, and Cantor Marcia Tilchin.

I am grateful to my *chavrutot*, study companions, who have kept my text learning insight-making and nourishing: Rabbis Bradley Shavit Artson, Gersh Zylberman, and Shuey Eliezrie.

In all that I do, I am motivated and grounded by the constancy of love of my wife, Linda, and of our children, Joey, Jon, and Anna.

I am indeed blessed in so many ways, so many are my privileges, including your reading these words.

Finally, a prayer of *Shehecheyanu* thanksgiving: Praised are You, Ever Present One, who has given me life, sustained me, and allowed me to reach this moment.

In Recognition of Thirty-Six Who Are My Foundation

In Jewish folk tradition thirty-six is the number of righteous who sustain the world. The following thirty-six, from among scores of valued teachers and friends, have distinctly provided the supports and wisdom that hold up my worldview:

My parents, Heddy and Arthur Spitz, who loved me unconditionally and modeled the choice of life in the shadow of sorrow

Bradley Shavit Artson, my *chavrutah* (study companion), whose enthusiastic learning and insight have stretched me creatively and soulfully

David Cooper, who showed me that Jews meditate and who exemplified meditative listening

Elliot Dorff of American Jewish University, who giggles like a guru and approaches ethical issues with deep learning, steady analysis, and empathy

Zev Falk, professor of law at Hebrew University, whose curiosity, friendship, erudition, and piety elevated me

Paul Mendes Flohr of Hebrew University, who was the first professor to mentor me

Marielle Fuller and Colette Aboulker-Muskat, artists of wakeful dreaming

Simon Greenberg, a giant of character, who grew taller with the years

Marilyn Harran of Chapman University, for her dedication to justice and instilling compassion in a new generation

David Hartman, who exemplified losing sleep over ideas and wakefully building a community of learners

Margie Jones, who taught me to dance to "the Blues" and to pronounce "w"

Bernie King, who taught me that when I preach I am talking first and foremost to myself

Ray Lederman, whose steadfast friendship has shown me the value of constancy

David Lieber, for his effective leadership both institutionally and with the crafting of the Torah commentary *Etz Hayim*, and his accessible mentoring

Stuart M. Matlins, my publisher, whose talent and commitment to the power of books has expanded my horizons

Peter Pitzele, who introduced me to Bibliodrama and who shares his inner life as a fount of poetry, creativity, and possibility

David Rebibo, principal of Phoenix Hebrew Academy, who with his wife, Odette, introduced me to the beauty of a traditional Shabbat and sacred text

Jack Riemer, whose curiosity, erudition, and preaching inform my teaching of Torah

Zalman Schachter-Shalomi, for his Rebbe craft, embracing the immediacy of God and modelling the yearning and tools for spiritual experience

Huston Smith, who showed me the wisdom of many faiths and true spiritual character

Michael Steingart, for his passion for music and unbridled performances

Abe Twerski, whose friendship and melding of Torah and human insight nourish my soul

Moshe Tutnauer, my childhood rabbi in Phoenix, who lived with a prophetic passion for ideas and ideals

Mark Weiss, my cousin, who has cared for me as a younger brother

Richard (Ricky) Weiss, who introduced this country boy to the vices and virtues of the big city

Elie Wiesel, who put into words so much that my parents could not articulate, while exemplifying wisdom, warmth, and humility

My siblings, Mark, Livia, Helene, and Joe, whose ongoing care for each other and for me shows that our parents did a great job and offered a solid foundation for life

My children, Joey, Jon, and Anna, whose vitality and love for Linda, each other, and me are life's greatest reward

My beloved wife, Linda, whose companionship and wisdom ground, elevate, and embrace me

NOTES

Introduction

1. Yissocher Frand, "Rabbi Frand on *Parshas Kedoshim*," *Torah.org*, accessed December 20, 2014, www.torah.org/learning/ravfrand/5757/kedoshim. html. Also attributed to Rabbi Menachem Mendel Morgenstern of Kotzk; see Pinchas Allouche, "Re-defining Religion," *Algemeiner*, August 15, 2011, www.algemeiner.com/2011/08/15/re-defining-religion/.

2. Alcoholic Anonymous, *The Big Book*, 4th ed. (New York: Alcoholics Anonymous World Services, 2001), 77.

3. I owe my introduction to Colette Aboulker-Muscat to Eve Ilsen, a student of Colette's and a master practitioner of guided imagery in her own right. During a nine-month sabbatical in Jerusalem, I spent Thursday mornings in a small group experiencing original guided imageries composed and conducted by Colette. On Saturday nights, Collette hosted a salon during which she also often led imageries (participants had to be at least twenty-six years old). She was among the most colorful personalities I have ever encountered. She was raised in Algeria in an aristocratic family that traced its roots back to King David. When her father, a head and neck surgeon, departed to World War I with the French troops, he insisted that a young Collette keep her mouth covered so that she would protect her developing vocal cords to better foster her singing voice. The one exemption he offered was the ability to speak on Shabbat. For over two years she sat silently, listening to adult conversation and developing her imagination. She went on to become the psychologist in charge of the mental patients at the military hospital in Algiers, the largest in North Africa. After the war she moved to Paris and studied with Robert DeSoille, the first to write on the therapeutic value of guided imagery. In 1954 she moved to Jerusalem, where her work drew a broad range of participants, including secular artists and ultra-Orthodox yeshiva students. She offered prescriptions of imageries for everything from weight loss ("see yourself as a noodle coming through the pressing machine") to anxiety. People made appointments to gain her wisdom—only one question per visit. In her apartment decorated with oil paintings of her regal family and artifacts of their wealth, such as colorful hand-carved wooden window decorations, she sat in beautiful clothes with every one of her white hairs in place. She conveyed self-importance along with penetrating insight. Her technique of guided imagery was based on "shock" (stated with her thick

French accent), arising from a quick inner response to a surprising image. The series of images often presented a journey. To hear the images that arose for others due to Colette's prompts, usually shared between guided imageries, was to get to know other people quite intimately.

4. I owe my introduction to Marielle Fuller to Rebbetzin Stella Eliezrie. Stella had learned of Marielle's work in an *LA Times* article that focused on an AIDS clinic in Laguna Beach and its oldest volunteer. I went to meet Marielle, curious about her as a person. I ended up spending two years—separated by my year of sabbatical in Jerusalem—experiencing one hour a week of guided imagery with her. Marielle, a daughter of a French-Canadian physician and life-long avid reader, had gained an introduction to imagery by reading Robert DeSoille in French. In the early 1970s she volunteered at UCLA Medical Center and began to do guided imageries with psychiatric patients. Although she lacked formal training or an advanced academic degree, the head of the department saw that she had a distinctive skill and asked her to teach it to the residents. She did so as part of a weekly seminar for close to twenty years. Marielle's technique relied on leading a participant on an inner journey often encountering guides: a wizard, a witch, a jester, an angel. The journey included surprises, such as opening a series of packages or opening a set of doors. Marielle was a religious Catholic and in her final months saw herself as bestowing blessings on those who had died tragically and needed aid in transition. She was a remarkably kind and perceptive soul.

5. Described by Malcolm Gladwell in several places, including *What the Dog Saw, and Other Adventures* (New York: Little, Brown, 2009), 432.

Chapter One

1. The verse can also be translated as "and stay there," the chosen interpretation of Rashi.

2. Rabbi Menachem Mendel of Kotzk, cited by Aharon Yaakov Greenberg in *Iturei Torah*, vol. 3 (Tel Aviv: Yavneh Press, 1985), 199.

3. *Shemot Rabbah* 24:1.

4. *Pesikta deRav Kahana* 12, edited in Israel as early as the fifth century CE.

5. In the Zohar, *nefesh* is animation, *ruach* is hardly used, and *neshamah* is the Divine spark or breath that allows for connection to the Divine. After the sixteenth century, *neshamah* is also used to refer to analytic mind, including the faculties of observation, measurement, formula making, verification, and intention (shared by Dr. Menachem Kallus). Only in more contemporary times is *ruach* identified with emotion (and moral discernment). See Isaiah Tishby, *Mishnat HaZohar* (Hebrew) (Jerusalem: Mosad Bialik, 1981) vol. 2, 11–19). My use of terms for *soul* emerges from Zalman Schachter-Shalomi, *Gate to the Heart: A Manual of Contemplative Jewish Practice* (Boulder, CO: Albion-Andalus Books, 2013), 7–13.

6. Pharaoh identifies Joseph with *ruach Elohim* (the spirit of God) (Genesis 41:38), and the crafters of the Holy Ark are said to possess *ruach chochmah* (a spirit of wisdom) (Exodus 28:3).

7. The *Zohar* uses the acronym *naran* to encapsulate soul as *nefesh, ruach,* and *neshamah.*

8. Baal Shem Tov, quoted in Yitzhak Buxbaum, *The Light and Fire of the Baal Shem Tov* (New York: Continuum, 2005), 200.

9. Widely attributed to Chinese Zen master Linji Yixuan (d. 866).

10. Alan Lew, with Sherril Jaffe, *One God Clapping: The Spiritual Path of a Zen Rabbi* (Woodstock, VT: Jewish Lights, 2001).

11. Alan Lew, "After Twenty Minutes of Yoga," *Volt: A Magazine of the Arts,* Sonoma State University, vol. 15 (2010), 93.

12. See Michael Polanyi, *Personal Knowledge: Towards Post-Critical Philosophy* (Chicago: University of Chicago Press, 1974), 56.

13. "Amazing Uses for Epsom Salt," on Dr. Mehmet Oz's official website, April 9, 2014, www.doctoroz.com/slideshow/epsom-salt-uses.

Chapter Two

1. Sherril Jaffe, private conversation in 2012; she attributed the idea to poet Robert Creely.

2. Simon Greenberg, private conversation.

3. Elie Kaplan Spitz, *Does the Soul Survive? A Jewish Journey to Belief in the Afterlife, Past Lives, and Living with Purpose,* 2nd ed. (Woodstock, VT: Jewish Lights, 2015).

4. Stated by a Hindu teacher at the Parliament of World Religions (2009); also attributed to Walter Van Miller, Jr., in *A Canticle for Leibowitz,* third section, "Fiat Voluntas Tua."

5. William Blake, quoted by Algernon Charles Swinburne in *William Blake: A Critical Essay* (Charleston, SC: Nabu Press, 2010), 210.

6. Abraham Joshua Heschel, *Who Is Man?* (Stanford, CA: Stanford University Press, 1965), 38–39.

7. Martin Buber, *Die chassidischen Bücher* (Berlin: Schocken, 1927), 157, cited in *The Torah: A Modern Commentary,* ed. W. Gunther Plaut (New York: Union of American Hebrew Congregations, 1981), 24.

8. "Rashi" is an acronym for Rabbi Shlomo Yitzhaki (France, 1040–1106).

9. Louis I. Newman, "The Maggid's Shoe Laces," *The Hasidic Anthology: Tales and Teachings of the Hasidim* (Northvale, NJ: Jason Aronson, 1987), 29–30.

10. Herbert Benson and Miriam Z. Klipper, *The Relaxation Response* (New York: HarperCollins, 1975).

11. *Shulchan Arukh, Orach Chayim* 93:1.

12. An insight of Rabbi Zalman Schachter-Shalomi, conveyed in private conversation.

13. *Yoma* 85a, citing Genesis 7:22; see also Maimonides, *Mishneh Torah*, "The Laws of Shabbat," 2:19; *Shulchan Arukh*, *Orach Chayim* 330:5.

14. Three of the final Hebrew syllables of that line contain a dot (called a *mapeek*) in the letter *hey*, indicating a breathier exhalation and the link between God and breath.

15. Lists of such blessings are contained in prayer books such as Jules Harlow, *Siddur Sim Shalom: A Prayerbook for Shabbat, Festivals and Weekdays* (New York: Rabbinical Assembly, 1989).

16. Cited by Daniel Kahneman in *Thinking, Fast and Slow* (New York: Farrar, Straus and Giroux, 2011), 226.

17. Exodus 21:10, which states that a husband must provide his wife with food, clothing, and *ona'ah* (widely understand as sexual pleasure, although some interpret as oil/ointment or shelter). According to Jewish law, husband and wife are entitled to sexual satisfaction (*Mishnah*, *Ketubot* 5:6–7).

18. See Esther Perel's "The Secret to Desire in a Long-Term Relationship," video, 19:10, from a TED Talk in February 2013, www.ted.com/talks/esther_perel_the_secret_to_desire_in_a_long_term_relationship.html. She also teaches that infidelity has less to do with the desire for sex and is more about self-exploration.

19. Ethan Kross, et al., "Social Rejection Shares Somatosensory Representations with Physical Pain," *Proceedings of the National Academy of Sciences* 108, no. 15 (April 2011): 6270–6275.

20. Edward E. Smith, quoted in "Suffering from a 'Broken Heart'," *Neurology Diagnostics*, last modified July 26, 2011, www.neurodiagnosticdevices.com/suffering-from-a-broken-heart.htm.

Chapter Three

1. Abraham Joshua Heschel, *Man's Quest for God: Studies in Prayer and Symbolism* (New York: Scribner, 1966), xiv.

2. Alfred Adler, as cited by Bryce Nelson in "Why Are Earliest Memories So Fragmentary and Elusive?" *New York Times*, December 7, 1982, www.nytimes.com/1982/12/07/science/why-are-earliest-memories-so-fragmentary-and-elusive.html.

3. *Seder Hayom* (Venice, 1599), cited in by Macy Nulman in "Modeh Ani," *The Encyclopedia of Jewish Prayer* (Northvale, NJ: Aronson Press, 1993), 251–252.

4. The phrase appears close to ninety times in Hebrew scripture and is the focus of a book by Rabbi Harold S. Kushner, *Conquering Fear: Living Boldly in an Uncertain World* (New York: Anchor, 2010).

5. See Louis Ginzberg, *The Legends of the Jews* (Philadelphia: Jewish Publication Society, 1937), 286–287; *Sefer ha-Yashar*, *Va'era*; *Pirkei d'Rebbe Eliezer* 32.

6. Attributed to Mark Twain in *Reader's Digest*, April 1934. See Fred Shapiro, "Quotes Uncovered: Twain or Not Twain," Freakonomics, April 25, 2011, http://freakonomics.com/2011/04/25/quotes-uncovered-twain-or-not-twain/.

7. Eleanor Roosevelt, *You Learn by Living* (Louisville, KY: Westminster John Knox, 1960), 29–30.

8. Pesach Krauss, *Why Me? Coping with Grief, Loss and Change* (New York: Bantam Books, 1988), 162.

9. The three paragraphs of the *Shema* prayer are taken from Deuteronomy 6:4–9; 11:13–21; and Numbers 15:37–41.

10. I learned this from Cantor Susan Deutsch as "the healing hand," now further developed in her book *The Healing Hand: Five Discussions to Have with the Dying Who Are Living* (Mission Viejo, CA: Handutch Press, 2014). The steps of saying goodbye to a loved one are well presented in palliative physician Ira Byock's *The Four Things That Matter Most: A Book About Living,* 10th anniv. ed. (New York: Atria Books, 2014).

11. Paul Tillich, *The Eternal Now* (New York: Scribner, 1963), quoted in Byock, *The Four Things That Matter Most*, 35.

12. Adin Steinsaltz, *The Thirteen Petalled Rose* (New York: Basic Books, 2006), 131–132.

Chapter Four

1. Eliezer Steinman, "The Dancing Jews," *Chabad*, February 11, 2002, www.chabad.org/library/article_cdo/aid/36751/jewish/The-Dancing-Jews.htm.

2. Huston Smith, *The World's Religions*, 50th anniv. ed. (New York: HarperCollins, 2008).

3. Sarah Macdonald, *Holy Cow: An Indian Adventure* (New York: Broadway Books, 2004).

4. Rabbi Jonathan Omer-Man's visit with the Dalai Lama is documented in Rodger Kamenetz's book, *The Jew in the Lotus: A Poet's Rediscovery of Jewish Identity in Buddhist India* (New York: HarperOne, 1994).

5. Harold S. Kushner, *When Bad Things Happen to Good People*, 2nd ed. (New York: Schocken, 2004).

6. Expressed by Rabbi Kushner in personal conversation (2009).

7. Erich Fromm, *The Forgotten Language: An Introduction to the Understanding of Dreams, Fairy Tales and Myths* (New York: Grove Press, 1951), 108. See also *The Art of Loving*, cent. ed. (New York: Continuum, 2008).

8. Joseph Campbell, *A Joseph Campbell Companion: Reflections on the Art of Living* (San Anselmo, CA: Joseph Campbell Foundation, 2011), ebook.

9. Elizabeth Spelke, interview by Natalie Angier, "Insights from the Youngest Minds," *New York Times*, April 30, 2012, www.nytimes.com/2012/05/01/science/insights-in-human-knowledge-from-the-minds-of-babes.html.

10. I owe this exercise to Jacob Weisberg, author of *Does Anybody Listen? Does Anybody Care?* (Englewood, CO: Medical Group Management Association, 1994).

11. Even the shapes and sounds of the three Hebrew letters that constitute the word *Shema* (שמע) convey a message about the nature of listening. Observe that the base of the three letters of *shema* are each relatively flat, in contrast to the letters for "look," *re'ah* (ראה), which are upright as if on the move.

12. Aryeh Kaplan, *Jewish Meditation: A Practical Guide* (NY: Schocken, 1985).

13. Kahneman, *Thinking, Fast and Slow*, 367.

14. Ibid., 373.

15. This is a homiletic based on the similarity of letters, rather than grounded in the actual roots of the two words.

16. Abraham Flexner, as cited by Abraham Joshua Heschel in *God in Search of Man: A Philosophy of Judaism* (New York: Farrer, Straus and Giroux, 1976), 57.

17. Ibid., 47.

18. In context, Reik had asked his mentor whether he should pursue a career in psychoanalysis and this was Freud's reply. Freud goes on to say, "In the important decisions of personal life, we should be governed, I think, by the deep inner needs of our nature." From Theodor Reik, *Listening with the Third Ear: The Inner Experience of a Psychoanalyst* (New York: Farrer, Straus and Giroux, 1948), vii.

Chapter Five

1. Gary A. Klein, *Sources of Power: How People Make Decisions* (Cambridge, MA: MIT Press, 1999), quoted in Kahenman, *Thinking, Fast and Slow*.

2. Herbert Simon, "What Is an Explanation of Behavior?" *Psychological Science* 3, no. 3 (May 1992): 150–161, quoted in Kahenman, *Thinking, Fast and Slow*.

3. Kahneman, *Thinking, Fast and Slow*, 237.

4. Ibid., 241.

5. Ibid., 368–370.

6. Albert Einstein, quoted in William Hermanns, *Einstein and the Poet: In Search of the Cosmic Man* (Brookline Village, MA: Branden Press, 1983), 173.

7. Ibid., 16.

8. A fine book on the neurology of creativity that points to the operation of intuitive pathways of the brain for surprising combinations of ideas is Jonah Lehrer's *Imagine: How Creativity Works* (Boston: Houghton Mifflin Harcourt, 2012).

9. Some quotes of Jung's relevant to the divine mind: "For it is not that 'God' is a myth, but that myth is the revelation of a divine life in man.... The word of God comes to us, and we have no way of distinguishing whether and to

what extent it is different from God.... We cannot explain an inspiration. Our chief feeling about it is that it is the not the result of ratiocinations, but that it came to us from elsewhere.... If therefore we speak of 'God' as an 'archetype,' we are saying nothing about His real nature but are letting it be known that 'God' already has a place in that part of our psyche which is preexistent to consciousness and that He therefore cannot be considered an invention of consciousness." Carl Gustav Jung, "Late Thoughts," *Selected Writings* (New York: Book of the Month Club, 1997), 542, 549.

10. Elizabeth Lloyd Mayer, *Extraordinary Knowing: Science, Skepticism, and the Inexplicable Powers of the Human Mind* (New York: Bantam Books, 2007).

11. These are called "priming experiments," such as subjects shown the word "assassin" in a rapid fashion so that they did not consciously note the word, but when tested a week later could fill in the blanks for "A - - A - - IN" more readily than subjects not shown the full word the week before. Endel Tulving, Daniel L. Schacter, and H. A. Stark, "Priming Effects in Word-Fragment Completion Are Independent of Recognition Memory," *Journal of Experimental Psychology, Learning, Memory, and Cognition* 8, no. 4 (July 1982): 336–342.

12. This research began with Lloyd H. Silverman of New York University in 1982. See Lloyd H. Silverman, "'Mommy and I Are One': Implicatations for Psychotherapy," *American Psychologist* 40, no. 12 (1985): 1296–1308. See also J. R. Palmatier and P. H. Bornstein, "The Effects of Subliminal Stimulation of Symbiotic Merging Fantasies on Behavior Treatment of Smokers," *Journal of Nervous and Mental Disease* 168, no. 12 (December 1980): 715–720.

13. Daniel Goleman, *Social Intelligence: The New Science of Human Relationships* (New York: Bantam Books, 2006), 42–43.

14. See Mayer, *Extraordinary Knowing*, chapter 11, fn. 25, citing sources as Dean I. Radin, *Entangled Minds: Extrasensory Experiences in a Quantum Reality* (New York: Simon & Schuster, 2006) and Alex Sabell, C. Clarke, and P. Fenwick, "Inter-Subject EEG Correlations at a Distance—The Transferred Potential," *Proceedings of the 44th Annual Convention of the Parapsychological Association* (New York, 2001), 419–422.

15. Philo, *On the Migration of Abraham* 32–5, in *Selected Writings: Philo of Alexandria*, ed. Hans Lewy (New York: Dover, 2004), 73.

16. Albert Einstein, prologue to Max Planck, *Where Is Science Going?* (New York: W.W. Norton, 1933), 10.

17. In my retelling, I substitute some female characters for male. I first heard this story from Rabbi David Wolpe. See David Wolpe, *Teaching Your Children About God* (New York: Henry Holt, 1993), 28.

18. Rabbi Abraham Isaac Kook, *Orot HaKodesh*, 1:262.

19. "Maybe the burning bush wasn't a miracle, but a test. God wanted to find out if Moses could see mystery in something as ordinary as a little bush on fire. For Moses had to watch the flames long enough to realize that the branches were not being consumed and that something awesome was happening. Once God saw that Moses could pay attention, God spoke to him." Lawrence Kushner, *The Book of Miracles: A Young Person's Guide to Jewish Spiritual Awareness* (Woodstock, VT: Jewish Lights, 1987), 7–8.

20. The middle thirteen blessings of the *Amidah* prayer are as follows: (1–2) acknowledging our human capacity for discernment and God's willingness to forgive; (3) asking for forgiveness; (4) acknowledging God's power to redeem from bondage; (5–6) asking for physical healing and abundance; (7) gathering the dispersed of the people of Israel; (8) rewarding the righteous; (9) restoring judges; (10) punishing the arrogant; (11) restoring Jerusalem as a Jewish center; (12) fostering a messianic era, marked by universal harmony; (13) responding to our collective pleas.

21. Marla E. Eisenberg, et al., "Correlations Between Family Meals and Pyschological Well-Being Among Adolescents," *Pediatric Adolescent Medicine* 158, no. 8 (2004): 792–176, http://archpedi.jamanetwork.com/article.aspx?articleid=485781; Sharon Jayson, "Each Family Dinner Adds Up to Benefits for Adolescents," *USA Today*, March 24, 2013, www.usatoday.com/story/news/nation/2013/03/24/family-dinner-adolescent-benefits/2010731/.

22. Dov Ber of Mezeritch (also known as the Maggid of Mezeritch), *Likkutim Yekarim* 2a.

23. See Heschel, *God in Search of Man*, 148. Regarding knowing God, he writes, "Maimonides does not offer a speculative proof for the existence of God. He states that the source of our knowledge of God is the inner eye, 'the eye of the heart,' a medieval name for intuition." Heschel adds more from Maimonides in the corresponding footnote: "'Forms devoid of matter cannot be perceived by the eyes of the body, but only by the eye of the heart. In the same way we know the Lord of the universe without physical vision.' *Mishneh Torah*, 'The Laws of the Basic Principles of the Torah,' 4:7. See the Duties of the Heart, 2:55; The chosen ones are endowed with an 'inner eye which sees things as they really are' (*Yehudah HaLevi, Kuzari* IV, 3); see Ibn Ezra, Commentary on Exodus 7:89."

24. Daniel C. Matt, *God and the Big Bang: Discovering Harmony Between Science and Spirituality* (Woodstock, VT: Jewish Lights, 1996), 14–15.

Chapter Six

1. Abraham Joshua Heschel's emphasis on God's care is centrally conveyed in *God in Search of Man*.

2. Stephanie L. Brown, et al., "Providing Social Support May Be More Beneficial Than Receiving It: Results from a Prospective Study of Mortality,"

Psychological Science 14, no. 4 (July 2003): 320–327; Marc A. Musick, A. Regula Herzog, and James S. House, "Volunteering and Mortality Among Older Adults: Findings from a National Sample," *Journal of Gerontology: Social Sciences* 54, no. 3 (May 1999): S173–S180.

3. Peggy A. Thoits and Lyndi N. Hewitt, "Volunteer Work and Well-being," *Journal of Health and Social Behavior* 42, no. 2 (June 2001): 115–131.

4. William T. Harbaugh, Ulrich Mayr, and Daniel R. Burghart, "Neural Responses to Taxation and Voluntary Giving Reveal Motives for Charitable Donations," *Science* 316, no. 5831 (June 2007): 1622–1625; Jorge Moll, et al., "Human Fronto-Mesolimbic Networks Guide Decisions About Charitable Donations," *Proceedings of the National Academy of Sciences* 103, no. 42 (October 2006): 15623–15628.

5. Adam M. Grant, *Give and Take: A Revolutionary Approach to Success* (New York: Viking, 2013).

6. Ibid., 4–5.

7. Ibid., 6–7.

8. Bill Gates, "Creative Capitalism," (speech, World Economic Forum, Davos, Switzerland, January 24, 2008), www.gatesfoundation.org/media-center/speeches/2008/01/bill-gates-2008-world-economic-forum.

9. Robert Homant, "Risky Altruism as a Predictor of Criminal Victimization," *Criminal Justice and Behavior* 37, no. 11 (November 2010), 1195–1216.

10. Adam M. Grant and David M. Mayer, "Good Soldiers and Good Actors: Prosocial and Impression Management Motives as Interactive Predictors of Affiliative Citizenship Behaviors," *Journal of Applied Psychology* 94, no. 4 (July 2009): 900–912.

11. First published in 1833, but when republished in 1842 the alterations in the way of excision and addition were very extensive. The quotation here is from the 1842 version.

12. The juxtaposition of the Moses' story with Homer and Tennyson's "Lotus Eaters" and the teaching of Rabbi Moshe Halfon of Djerba came to my attention from a chain of 2013 sermons: Rabbi Mishael Zion of Jerusalem, which was then developed by Rabbi Jack Riemer of Boca Raton, Florida. Rabbi Zion attributes this quotation to Halfon's small book *Darkei Moshe*. See Mishael Zion, "Moses in Djerba: The Island of the Lotus Eaters," *Text and the City*, December 18, 2013, http://textandcity.blogspot.com/2013/12/moses-in-djerba-island-of-lotus-eaters.html.

13. From Maimonides, *Mishneh Torah*, "The Laws of *Tzedakah*," 10:7–14. Organized from the most to least honorable way to give charity: 8. Investing in a poor person in a manner that they can become self-sufficient; 7. Giving to the poor without knowledge of the recipient and without allowing the recipient to know your identity; 6. Giving to the poor with knowledge of the

recipient but without allowing the recipient to know your identity; 5. Giving to the poor without knowledge of the recipient but allowing the recipient to know your identity; 4. Giving to the poor without or before being asked; 3. Giving to the poor after being asked; 2. Giving to the poor happily but inadequately; 1. Giving to the poor unwillingly.

14. Rabbi Abraham Isaac Kook, *Orot HaKodesh*, 3:324.

15. Similarly, "You surely open your hand and provide for all those in need" (Psalm 145:16).

16. *Ketubot* 50a; *Arakhin* 28a; Maimonides, *Mishneh Torah*, "Laws Concerning Gifts for the Poor," 7:5.

17. Maimonides, "Laws Concerning Gifts for the Poor," 7:2; similarly see *Vayikra Rabbah* 34:9.

18. *Ketubot* 50a, as interpreted by Tosafot; also see Maimonides, "Laws Concerning Gifts for the Poor," 7:5.

19. Moshe Leib of Sasov, quoted in Martin Buber, *Tales of the Hasidim: The Later Masters*, vol. 2, trans. Olga Marx (New York: Schocken, 1947), 85.

20. *Vayikra Rabbah* 34:9. Upholding the presumption of trust, when Rabbi Elazar (second century, Israel) learned of deception by beggars, he would say, "Come let us be grateful for the cheaters. For if not for them, we [who ignore requests] would sin every day" (*Ketubot* 67a–68a).

21. *Vayikra Rabbah* 34:9.

22. *Bava Batra* 9a; Jerusalem Talmud, *Pe'ah* 8:7; *Vayikra Rabbah* 34:14. As codified, see Maimonides, "Laws Concerning Gifts for the Poor," 7:6; Tur, *Yoreh De'ah* 251; *Shulchan Arukh, Yoreh De'ah* 251:10.

23. *Bava Batra* 10b; *Avodah Zarah* 17b, specifically citing first- to second-century Israeli rabbi Hananyah ben Teradyon as an exemplar of integrity and communal concern; Maimonides, "Laws Concerning Gifts for the Poor," 10:8 and 9:1; Tur, *Yoreh De'ah* 256; *Shulchan Arukh* 256:1; Rashi to *Pesachim* 49b.

24. Jerusalem Talmud, *Pe'ah* 8:8 [3:33a]; *Vayikra Rabbah* 34:1.

25. The Lubavitcher Rebbe, Menachem Mendel Schneerson, encouraged the daily giving of change into a charity box to cultivate the habit of giving. See Joseph Telushkin, *Rebbe: The Life and Teachings of Menachem M. Schneerson, the Most Influential Rabbi in Modern History* (New York: Harperwave, 2014), 74.

26. This chapter ends with the command of wearing *tzitzit* as a reminder that God brought the people of Israel out of Egypt (Numbers 15:37–41).

27. "'Open, you shall open your hand to him' (Deuteronomy 15:7–8). Now, I would have known only about the poor of your own town. From where is it derived for the poor of another town? The verse states, 'open, you shall open'—in all cases. 'Give, you shall give' (Deuteronomy 15:10)" (*Bava Metzia* 31b).

28. Paraphrase of a saying in Louis Jacob, *The Jewish Religion: A Companion* (Oxford: Oxford University Press, 1995), 71.

29. Vicki S. Helgeson and Hiedi L. Fritz, "The Implications of Unmitigated Agency and Unmitigated Communion for Domains of Problem Behavior," *Journal of Personality* 68, no. 6 (December 2000): 1031–1057. In a survey, college students who were selfless were found to decline in their grades during the semester due to "missing classes and failing to study because they were attending to friends' problems."

30. Grant, *Give and Take*, 114.

31. Ibid., 206.

32. Yehonatan Turner, et al., "The Effect of Adding a Patient's Photograph to the Radiographic Examination," (Study presented at the Annual Meeting of the Radiological Society of North America, Chicago, IL, February 18, 2008).

33. Grant, *Give and Take*, 162–165. Citing, among others, his own work with the university callers: Adam M. Grant, et al., "Impact and the Art of Motivation Maintenance: The Effects of Contact with Beneficiaries on Persistence Behavior," *Organizational Behavior and Human Decision Processes* 103, no. 1 (May 2007): 53–67.

34. Description of the research of Anitra Karsten in *Mindfulness* by Ellen J. Langer (Reading, MA: Addison-Wesley, 1989), 136.

35. C. Maslach, W. B. Schaufeli, and M. P. Leiter, "Job Burnout," *Annual Reviews* 52 (2001), 397–422, quoted in Grant, *Give and Take*, 177.

36. Sylvia Boorstein, self-described as a student of the mind and a master practitioner of *metta* (compassion) meditation, inspired this meditation. In Buddhist practice, *metta* meditation seeks to awaken loving-kindness. Sylvia Boorstein is a founder of the Buddhist Spirit Rock Meditation Center in Marin County, California, and an active teacher in the Jewish community.

37. This story is also attributed to the founder of Chabad Hasidism, Rabbi Shneur Zalman of Liadi, and his son, the Mitteler Rebbe, Dovber Schneuri. See Telushkin, *Rebbe*, 93.

38. See Leviticus 26:41; Deuteronomy 10:16; Jeremiah 4:4, 6:10, 9:26; Ezekiel 44:7; Acts 7:51.

39. Maimonides, "Laws Concerning Gifts for the Poor," 10:7–14; "One who performs acts of *tzedakah* in secret is greater than Moses, our teacher" (*Bava Batra* 9b).

40. For examples of ethical wills and further practical guidance on writing your own, see Jack Riemer and Nathaniel Stampfer, eds., *Ethical Wills and How to Prepare Them: A Guide to Sharing Your Values from Generation to Generation* (Woodstock, VT: Jewish Lights, 2015).

41. As quoted in Martin Buber, "Comparing One to Another," *Tales of the Hasidim*, 283.

42. Rami Shapiro, *Ethics of the Sages:* Pirkei Avot—*Annotated and Explained* (Woodstock, VT: Jewish Lights, 2006), 14.

43. Translation from Edward Feld, ed., *Mahzor Lev Shalem: Rosh Hashanah and Yom Kippur,* (New York: Rabbinical Assembly, 2010), 25.

44. *Mahzor Lev Shalem* cites Maimonides and explains that the phrase *l'takkein olam* signifies "to repair the world" as partners with God in achieving an epoch of peace and righteousness. *Mahzor Lev Shalem,* 25.

Chapter Seven

1. Wayne Dosick, *The Real Name of God: Embracing the Full Essence of the Divine* (Rochester, VT: Inner Traditions, 2012). Dosick explores *Anokhi* as the name for and relationship with God that is most relevant for our time.

2. Jordi Quoidback, Timothy D. Wilson, and Daniel T. Gilbert, "The End of History Illusion," *Science* 339 no. 6115 (January 2013), 96–98. See also John Tierney, "Why You Won't Be the Person You Expect to Be," *New York Times,* January 3, 2013, www.nytimes.com/2013/01/04/science/study-in-science-shows-end-of-history-illusion.html.

3. Israel Salanter, quoted by Alan Morinis in *Everyday Holiness* (Boston: Trumpeter, 2007), 37.

4. The Kobi Mandell Foundation, www.kobymandell.org.

5. Rashi commenting on the word *na'ar,* "lad" (Genesis 37:2): "For he would do the things a lad does such as arranging his hair, fixing his eyes so as to appear handsome."

6. Elie Wiesel, "Joseph or the Education of a *Tzaddik,*" *Messengers of God: Biblical Portraits and Legends* (New York: Random House, 1976), 139–169.

7. Kurt Vonnegut, *A Man Without a Country* (New York: Seven Stories Press, 2005), 132.

8. Eleanor Roosevelt, *You Learn by Living,* 95.

9. M. Scott Peck, *The Road Less Travelled: A New Psychology of Love, Traditional Values and Spiritual Growth* (London: Rider Books, 1988), 38.

10. This quote gained much recognition after its citation by Stephen R. Covey in *Seven Habits of Highly Effective People* (New York: Free Press, 1989), ix, where it was attributed to Viktor Frankl. Others have followed Covey's lead and cited Frankl's *Man's Search for Meaning* (New York: Beacon Press, 2006), where, however, these words do not appear.

11. *Yoma* 72b, citing as proof text the description of the Holy Ark at Exodus 25:11. The Hebrew expression for the same inside and outside is *betokho kevaro.*

12. *Chayil* is widely translated by commentators as "capable," but there are other interpretations: "resourceful" (Hirsch); "possessing leadership qualities" (Ramban); "possessing status" (Rashbam); "possessing wealth" (Rashi, *Mekhilta*).

13. Lunch meeting at University of California, Irvine, April 2004.

14. Dan Ariely, *The (Honest) Truth About Dishonesty: How We Lie to Everyone, Especially Ourselves* (New York: Harper Perennial, 2013).

15. Aaron Beck, *Love Is Never Enough: How Couples Can Overcome Misunderstandings, Resolve Conflicts, and Solve Relationship Problems Through Cognitive Therapy* (New York: Harper Perennial, 1989). Beck says a common problem for couples is that actions are treated as a symbol of other behaviors that get clustered, magnified, and labeled, rather than addressed as specific negative deeds.

16. Elie Wiesel, interview by Alvin P. Sanoff, "One Must Not Forget," *US News & World Report*, October 27, 1986, 68.

17. "The way to find out about your happiness is to keep your mind on those moments when you feel most happy, when you really are happy—not excited, not just thrilled, but deeply happy. This requires a little bit of self-analysis. What is it that makes you happy? Stay with it, no matter what people tell you. This is what I call 'following your bliss.'" Joseph Campbell, with Bill Moyers, *The Power of Myth* (New York: Doubleday, 1988), 193.

18. Italics mine. Originally found in *Mishnah, Pesachim* 10.

19. *Otzar Midrashim*, a collection of 200 midrashim collected by Julius Eisenstein and published in 1915; quote found in the fifth section, *Perek Arakim*.

20. "It is necessary that every one, throughout the year, should regard himself as if he were half innocent and half guilty; and should regard the whole of humanity as half innocent and half guilty. If then he commits one more sin, he presses down the scale of guilt against himself and the whole world and causes its destruction. If he fulfills one commandment, he turns the scale of merit in his favor and in that of the whole world, and brings salvation and deliverance to all his fellow creatures and to himself, as it is said, 'The righteous person is the foundation of the world' (Proverbs 10:25); that is to say, that he who acts justly presses down the scale of merit in favor of the world and saves it" (Maimonides, *Mishneh Torah*, "The Laws of Repentance," 4:4). Likewise the mystical text the *Zohar*, a century after Maimonides, states, "One must always see himself as if the whole world depended on him"; *Zohar*, second section, *Ra'ayah Mi'hemna*.

21 Salomon Buber, *Midrash Tanchuma*, (Jerusalem: Makor, 1976).

22. Literally, "as if holiness abides in his guts." Julius Eisenstein's 1915 *Otzer Midrashim*, fifth section, *Perek L'olam*.

23. Abraham Joshua Heschel, *A Passion for Truth* (Woodstock, VT: Jewish Lights, 1995), 249.

24. Words conveyed in 2009 at a retreat at Spirit Rock, the Buddhist center in Marin, CA.

25. Aaron of Karlin, quoted by Heschel in *God in Search of Man*, 143. Heschel comments, "There is a divine light in every soul, it is dormant and eclipsed

by the follies of the world. We must awaken this light, then the upper light will come upon us."

26. Some retreat centers to consider: Isabella Freedman Jewish Retreat Center of Falls Village, CT, particularly the annual weeklong retreat of Elat Chayyim; and Vipassana Buddhist Insight Meditation Society Center of Barre, MA, and Spirit Rock in Marin County, CA.

27. Kabir Helminski, *The Knowing Heart: A Sufi Path of Transformation* (Boston: Shambala, 1999), 69.

28. My translation of the three phrases leans toward the literal Hebrew, which concisely contain three, five, and seven words.

SUGGESTIONS FOR FURTHER READING

Comparative Religion

Armstong, Karen. *A History of God: The 4,000 Year Quest of Judaism, Christianity and Islam*. New York: Ballantine, 1994.

Prothero, Stephen. *God Is Not One: The Eight Rival Religions That Run the World—and Why Their Differences Matter*. New York: HarperCollins, 2010.

Smith, Huston. *The World's Religions*. 50th anniv. ed. New York: HarperCollins, 2008.

Meditation Practice

Benson, Herbert, and Miriam Z. Klipper. *The Relaxation Response*. Rev. ed. New York: HarperCollins, 2001.

Brotman, Edith R. *Mussar Yoga: Blending an Ancient Jewish Spiritual Practice with Yoga to Transform Body and Soul*. Woodstock, VT: Jewish Lights, 2014.

Cooper, David A. *A Heart of Stillness: A Complete Guide to Learning the Art of Meditation*. Woodstock, VT: SkyLight Paths, 1999.

Glick, Yoel. *Living the Life of Jewish Meditation: A Comprehensive Guide to Practice and Experience*. Woodstock, VT: Jewish Lights, 2014.

Hanh, Thich Nhat. *Peace Is Every Step: The Path of Mindfulness in Everyday Life*. New York: Bantam, 1991.

Kaplan, Aryeh. *Jewish Meditation: A Practical Guide*. New York: Schocken, 1985.

Lew, Alan. *Be Still and Get Going: A Jewish Meditation Practice for Real Life*. New York: Little, Brown, 2005.

Paranormal Phenomena

Mayer, Elizabeth Lloyd. *Extraordinary Knowing: Science, Skepticism, and the Inexplicable Powers of the Human Mind*. New York: Bantam Books, 2007.

Spitz, Elie Kaplan. *Does the Soul Survive? A Jewish Journey to Belief in the Afterlife, Past Lives and Living with Purpose*. 2nd ed. Woodstock, VT: Jewish Lights, 2015.

Psychology

Beck, Aaron T. *Love Is Never Enough: How Couples Can Overcome Misunderstandings, Resolve Conflicts, and Solve Relationship Problems Through Cognitive Therapy*. New York: Harper Perennial, 1989.

Brooks, David. *The Social Animal: The Hidden Sources of Love, Character, and Achievement*. New York: Random House, 2011.

Cialdini, Robert B. *Influence: The Psychology of Persuasion*. Rev. ed. New York: HarperCollins, 2010.

Fromm, Erich. *The Art of Loving*. Centennial ed. New York: Continuum, 2008.

Goleman, Daniel. *Social Intelligence: The New Science of Human Relationships*. New York: Bantam Books, 2006.

Grant, Adam. *Give and Take: A Revolutionary Approach to Success*. New York: Viking, 2013.

Kahneman, Daniel. *Thinking, Fast and Slow*. New York: Farrar, Straus and Giroux, 2011.

Sacred Text and Commentary

Buber, Martin. *Tales of the Hasidim: The Later Masters*. Translated by Olga Marx. New York: Schocken, 1947.

Cohen, Norman J. *The Way Into Torah*. Woodstock, VT: Jewish Lights, 2004.

Feld, Edward, ed. *Mahzor Lev Shalem: Rosh Hashanah and Yom Kippur*. New York: Rabbinical Assembly, 2010.

Kaplan, Aryeh. *The Living Torah*. New York: Maznaim, 1981.

Lieber, David, ed. *Etz Hayim: Torah and Commentary*. Philadelphia: Jewish Publication Society, 2001.

Luzzatto, Moshe Chaim. *The Path of the Just*. Translated by Yosef Liebler. Torah Classics Library. New York: Feldheim, 2010.

Maimonides, Moses. *The Guide for the Perplexed*. Translated and with commentary by Shlomo Pines. 2 vols. Chicago: University of Chicago Press, 1974.

Milgrom, Jacob. *Leviticus: A Book of Rituals and Ethics*. Minneapolis, MN: Fortress Press, 2004.

Steinsaltz, Adin. *The Thirteen Petalled Rose: A Discourse in the Essence of Jewish Existence and Belief*. Translated by Yehuda Hanegbi. New York: Basic Books, 2006.

Spiritual Biography

Buxbaum, Yitzhak. *The Light and Fire of the Baal Shem Tov*. New York: Continuum, 2005.

Green, Arthur. *The Tormented Master: The Life and Spiritual Quest of Rabbi Nahman of Bratslav*. Woodstock, VT: Jewish Lights, 1992.

Goldman, Ari L. *The Late Starters Orchestra*. Chapel Hill, NC: Algonquin Books, 2014.

Heschel, Abraham Joshua. *A Passion for Truth*. Woodstock, VT: Jewish Lights, 1995.

Lew, Alan, and Sherril Jaffe. *One God Clapping: The Spiritual Path of a Zen Rabbi*. Woodstock, VT: Jewish Lights, 2001.

Riemer, Jack, and Nathaniel Stampfer, eds. *Ethical Wills and How to Prepare Them: A Guide to Sharing Your Values from Generation to Generation*. Woodstock, VT: Jewish Lights, 2015.

Spiritual Guidance

Byock, Ira. *The Four Things That Matter Most: A Book About Living*. 10th anniv. ed. New York: Atria Books, 2014.

Deutsch, Sue Knight. *The Healing Hand: Five Discussions to Have with the Dying Who Are Living*. Mission Viejo, CA: Handutch Press, 2014.

Krauss, Pesach, and Morrie Goldfischer. *Why Me? Coping with Grief, Loss and Change*. New York: Bantam Books, 1990.

Peck, M. Scott. *The Road Less Travelled: A New Psychology of Love, Traditional Values, and Spiritual Growth*. 25th anniv. ed. London: Rider Books, 2012.

Peltz, Lawrence A. *The Mindful Path to Addiction Recovery: A Practical Guide to Regaining Control over Your Life*. Boston: Shambhala, 2013.

Spitz, Elie Kaplan. *Healing from Despair: Choosing Wholeness in a Broken World*. Woodstock, VT: Jewish Lights, 2008.

Twerski, Abraham J. *Happiness and the Human Spirit: The Spirituality of Becoming the Best You Can Be*. Woodstock, VT: Jewish Lights, 2007.

Theology

Artson, Bradley Shavit. *God of Becoming and Relationship: The Dynamic Nature of Process Theology*. Woodstock, VT: Jewish Lights, 2013.

Dosick, Wayne. *The Real Name of God: Embracing the Full Essence of the Divine*. Rochester, VT: Inner Traditions, 2012.

Feinstein, Edward. *The Chutzpah Imperative: Empowering Today's Jews for a Life That Matters*. Woodstock, VT: Jewish Lights, 2014.

Heschel, Abraham Joshua. *God in Search of Man: A Philosophy of Judaism*. New York: Farrar, Straus and Giroux, 1976.

———. *Man's Quest for God: Studies in Prayer and Symbolism*. New York: MacMillan Publishing, 1954.

———. *Who Is Man?* Stanford, CA: Stanford University Press, 1965.

Kushner, Harold S. *When Bad Things Happen to Good People*. 2nd ed. New York: Schocken, 2004.

———. *Who Needs God*. New York: Simon & Schuster, 2002.

Matt, Daniel C. *God and the Big Bang: Discovering Harmony Between Science and Spirituality*. Woodstock, VT: Jewish Lights, 1996.

INDEX OF PRACTICES

Bible Study / Midrash

Passing Life's Tests: Spiritual Reflections on the Trial of Abraham, the Binding of Isaac *By Rabbi Bradley Shavit Artson, DHL*
Invites us to use this powerful tale as a tool for our own soul wrestling, to confront our existential sacrifices and enable us to face—and surmount—life's tests.
6 x 9, 176 pp, Quality PB, 978-1-58023-631-7 **$18.99**

Speaking Torah: Spiritual Teachings from around the Maggid's Table—in Two Volumes *By Arthur Green, with Ebn Leader, Ariel Evan Mayse and Or N. Rose*
The most powerful Hasidic teachings made accessible—from some of the world's preeminent authorities on Jewish thought and spirituality.
Volume 1—6 x 9, 512 pp, HC, 978-1-58023-668-3 **$34.99**
Volume 2—6 x 9, 448 pp, HC, 978-1-58023-694-2 **$34.99**

A Partner in Holiness: Deepening Mindfulness, Practicing Compassion and Enriching Our Lives through the Wisdom of R. Levi Yitzhak of Berdichev's *Kedushat Levi*
By Rabbi Jonathan P. Slater, DMin; Foreword by Arthur Green; Preface by Rabby Nancy Flam
Contemporary mindfulness and classical Hasidic spirituality are brought together to inspire a satisfying spiritual life of practice.
Volume 1— 6 x 9, 336 pp, HC, 978-1-58023-794-9 **$35.00**
Volume 2— 6 x 9, 288 pp, HC, 978-1-58023-795-6 **$35.00**

The Genesis of Leadership: What the Bible Teaches Us about Vision, Values and Leading Change *By Rabbi Nathan Laufer; Foreword by Senator Joseph I. Lieberman*
6 x 9, 288 pp, Quality PB, 978-1-58023-352-1 **$18.99**

Hineini in Our Lives
Learning How to Respond to Others through 14 Biblical Texts and Personal Stories
By Dr. Norman J. Cohen 6 x 9, 240 pp, Quality PB, 978-1-58023-274-6 **$18.99**

Masking and Unmasking Ourselves: Interpreting Biblical Texts on Clothing & Identity *By Dr. Norman J. Cohen* 6 x 9, 224 pp, HC, 978-1-58023-461-0 **$24.99**

The Messiah and the Jews: Three Thousand Years of Tradition, Belief and Hope
By Rabbi Elaine Rose Glickman; Foreword by Rabbi Neil Gillman, PhD
Preface by Rabbi Judith Z. Abrams, PhD 6 x 9, 192 pp, Quality PB, 978-1-58023-690-4 **$16.99**

The Modern Men's Torah Commentary: New Insights from Jewish Men on the 54 Weekly Torah Portions *Edited by Rabbi Jeffrey K. Salkin*
6 x 9, 368 pp, HC, 978-1-58023-395-8 **$24.99**

Moses and the Journey to Leadership: Timeless Lessons of Effective Management from the Bible and Today's Leaders *By Dr. Norman J. Cohen*
6 x 9, 240 pp, Quality PB, 978-1-58023-351-4 **$18.99**; HC, 978-1-58023-227-2 **$21.99**

The Other Talmud—The *Yerushalmi*: Unlocking the Secrets of *The Talmud of Israel* for Judaism Today *By Rabbi Judith Z. Abrams, PhD*
6 x 9, 256 pp, HC, 978-1-58023-463-4 **$24.99**

Sage Tales: Wisdom and Wonder from the Rabbis of the Talmud
By Rabbi Burton L. Visotzky
6 x 9, 256 pp, Quality PB, 978-1-58023-791-8 **$19.99**; HC, 978-1-58023-456-6 **$24.99**

The Torah Revolution: Fourteen Truths That Changed the World
By Rabbi Reuven Hammer, PhD 6 x 9, 240 pp, Quality PB, 978-1-58023-789-5 **$18.99**
HC, 978-1-58023-457-3 **$24.99**

The Wisdom of Judaism: An Introduction to the Values of the Talmud
By Rabbi Dov Peretz Elkins 6 x 9, 192 pp, Quality PB, 978-1-58023-327-9 **$16.99**

Or phone, fax, mail or email to: JEWISH LIGHTS Publishing
Sunset Farm Offices, Route 4 • P.O. Box 237 • Woodstock, Vermont 05091
Tel: (802) 457-4000 • Fax: (802) 457-4004 • www.jewishlights.com
Credit card orders: (800) 962-4544 (8:30AM–5:30PM EST Monday–Friday)
Generous discounts on quantity orders. SATISFACTION GUARANTEED. Prices subject to change.

Congregation Resources

New Membership & Financial Alternatives for the American Synagogue
From Traditional Dues to Fair Share to Gifts from the Heart
By Rabbi Kerry M. Olitzky and Rabbi Avi S. Olitzky; Foreword by Dr. Ron Wolfson
Afterword by Rabbi Dan Judson
Practice values-driven ways to make changes to open wide the synagogue doors to many.
6 x 9, 208 pp, Quality PB, 978-1-58023-820-5 **$19.99**

Relational Judaism: Using the Power of Relationships to Transform the Jewish Community
By Dr. Ron Wolfson How to transform the model of twentieth-century Jewish institutions into twenty-first-century relational communities offering meaning and purpose, belonging and blessing.
6 x 9, 288 pp, HC, 978-1-58023-666-9 **$24.99**

The Spirituality of Welcoming: How to Transform Your Congregation into a Sacred Community
By Dr. Ron Wolfson
Shows crucial hospitality is for congregational survival and dives into the practicalities of cultivating openness. 6 x 9, 224 pp, Quality PB, 978-1-58023-244-9 **$19.99**

Jewish Megatrends: Charting the Course of the American Jewish Future
By Rabbi Sidney Schwarz; Foreword by Ambassador Stuart E. Eizenstat
Visionary solutions for a community ripe for transformational change—from fourteen leading innovators of Jewish life. 6 x 9, 288 pp, HC, 978-1-58023-667-6 **$24.99**

Building a Successful Volunteer Culture: Finding Meaning in Service in the Jewish Community
By Rabbi Charles Simon; Foreword by Shelley Lindauer; Preface by Dr. Ron Wolfson
6 x 9, 192 pp, Quality PB, 978-1-58023-408-5 **$16.99**

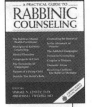

The Case for Jewish Peoplehood: Can We Be One?
By Dr. Erica Brown and Dr. Misha Galperin; Foreword by Rabbi Joseph Telushkin
6 x 9, 224 pp, HC, 978-1-58023-401-6 **$21.99**

Empowered Judaism: What Independent Minyanim Can Teach Us about Building Vibrant Jewish Communities
By Rabbi Elie Kaunfer; Foreword by Prof. Jonathan D. Sarna
6 x 9, 224 pp, Quality PB, 978-1-58023-412-2 **$18.99**

Inspired Jewish Leadership: Practical Approaches to Building Strong Communities
By Dr. Erica Brown 6 x 9, 256 pp, HC, 978-1-58023-361-3 **$27.99**

Judaism and Health: A Handbook of Practical, Professional and Scholarly Resources
Edited by Jeff Levin, PhD, MPH, and Michele F. Prince, LCSW, MAJCS
Foreword by Rabbi Elliot N. Dorff, PhD
6 x 9, 448 pp, HC, 978-1-58023-714-7 **$50.00**

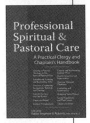

Jewish Pastoral Care, 2nd Edition: A Practical Handbook from Traditional & Contemporary Sources
Edited by Rabbi Dayle A. Friedman, MSW, MA, BCC
6 x 9, 528 pp, Quality PB, 978-1-58023-427-6 **$40.00**

A Practical Guide to Rabbinic Counseling
Edited by Rabbi Yisrael N. Levitz, PhD, and Rabbi Abraham J. Twerski, MD
6 x 9, 432 pp, HC, 978-1-58023-562-4 **$40.00**

Professional Spiritual & Pastoral Care: A Practical Clergy and Chaplain's Handbook
Edited by Rabbi Stephen B. Roberts, MBA, MHL, BCJC
6 x 9, 480 pp, HC, 978-1-59473-312-3 **$50.00***

Reimagining Leadership in Jewish Organizations: Ten Practical Lessons to Help You Implement Change and Achieve Your Goals
By Dr. Misha Galperin 6 x 9, 192 pp, Quality PB, 978-1-58023-492-4 **$16.99**

Rethinking Synagogues: A New Vocabulary for Congregational Life
By Rabbi Lawrence A. Hoffman, PhD 6 x 9, 240 pp, Quality PB, 978-1-58023-248-7 **$19.99**

Revolution of Jewish Spirit: How to Revive *Ruakh* in Your Spiritual Life, Transform Your Synagogue & Inspire Your Jewish Community
By Rabbi Baruch HaLevi, DMin, and Ellen Frankel, LCSW; Foreword by Dr. Ron Wolfson
6 x 9, 224 pp, Quality PB, 978-1-58023-625-6 **$19.99**

*A book from SkyLight Paths, Jewish Lights' sister imprint

Social Justice

Where Justice Dwells
A Hands-On Guide to Doing Social Justice in Your Jewish Community
By Rabbi Jill Jacobs; Foreword by Rabbi David Saperstein
Provides ways to envision and act on your own ideals of social justice.
7 x 9, 288 pp, Quality PB, 978-1-58023-453-5 **$24.99**

There Shall Be No Needy
Pursuing Social Justice through Jewish Law and Tradition
By Rabbi Jill Jacobs; Foreword by Rabbi Elliot N. Dorff, PhD; Preface by Simon Greer
Confronts the most pressing issues of twenty-first-century America from a deeply Jewish perspective. 6 x 9, 288 pp, Quality PB, 978-1-58023-425-2 **$16.99**
There Shall Be No Needy Teacher's Guide 8½ x 11, 56 pp, PB, 978-1-58023-429-0 **$8.99**

Conscience
The Duty to Obey and the Duty to Disobey
By Rabbi Harold M. Schulweis (z"l)
Examines the idea of conscience and the role conscience plays in our relationships to government, law, ethics, religion, human nature, God—and to each other.
6 x 9, 160 pp, Quality PB, 978-1-58023-419-1 **$16.99**; HC, 978-1-58023-375-0 **$19.99**

Judaism and Justice: The Jewish Passion to Repair the World
By Rabbi Sidney Schwarz; Foreword by Ruth Messinger
6 x 9, 352 pp, Quality PB, 978-1-58023-353-8 **$19.99**

Spirituality / Women's Interest

Embracing the Divine Feminine: Finding God through the Ecstasy of Physical Love—The Song of Songs Annotated & Explained
Annotation and Translation by Rabbi Rami Shapiro; Foreword by Rev. Cynthia Bourgeault, PhD
Restores the Song of Songs' eroticism and interprets it as a celebration of the love between the Divine Feminine and the contemporary spiritual seeker.
5½ x 8½, 176 pp, Quality PB, 978-1-59473-575-2 **$16.99***

The Women's Haftarah Commentary
New Insights from Women Rabbis on the 54 Weekly Haftarah Portions, the 5 Megillot & Special Shabbatot
Edited by Rabbi Elyse Goldstein
Illuminates the historical significance of female portrayals in the Haftarah and the Five Megillot. 6 x 9, 560 pp, Quality PB, 978-1-58023-371-2 **$19.99**

The Women's Torah Commentary
New Insights from Women Rabbis on the 54 Weekly Torah Portions
Edited by Rabbi Elyse Goldstein
Over fifty women rabbis offer inspiring insights on the Torah, in a week-by-week format.
6 x 9, 496 pp, Quality PB, 978-1-58023-370-5 **$19.99**; HC, 978-1-58023-076-6 **$34.95**

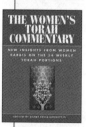

The Divine Feminine in Biblical Wisdom Literature
Selections Annotated & Explained
Translation & Annotation by Rabbi Rami Shapiro; Foreword by Rev. Cynthia Bourgeault, PhD
5½ x 8½, 240 pp, Quality PB, 978-1-59473-109-9 **$18.99***

New Jewish Feminism: Probing the Past, Forging the Future
Edited by Rabbi Elyse Goldstein; Foreword by Anita Diamant
6 x 9, 480 pp, HC, 978-1-58023-359-0 **$24.99**

The Quotable Jewish Woman
Wisdom, Inspiration & Humor from the Mind & Heart
Edited by Elaine Bernstein Partnow
6 x 9, 496 pp, Quality PB, 978-1-58023-236-4 **$19.99**

*A book from SkyLight Paths, Jewish Lights' sister imprint

Ecology / Environment

A Wild Faith: Jewish Ways into Wilderness, Wilderness Ways into Judaism
By Rabbi Mike Comins; Foreword by Nigel Savage
6 x 9, 240 pp, Quality PB, 978-1-58023-316-3 **$18.99**

Ecology & the Jewish Spirit: Where Nature & the Sacred Meet
Edited by Ellen Bernstein 6 x 9, 288 pp, Quality PB, 978-1-58023-082-7 **$18.99**

Torah of the Earth: Exploring 4,000 Years of Ecology in Jewish Thought
Vol. 1: Biblical Israel & Rabbinic Judaism; Vol. 2: Zionism & Eco-Judaism
Edited by Rabbi Arthur Waskow Vol. 1: 6 x 9, 272 pp, Quality PB, 978-1-58023-086-5 **$19.95**
Vol. 2: 6 x 9, 336 pp, Quality PB, 978-1-58023-087-2 **$19.95**

The Way Into Judaism and the Environment *By Jeremy Benstein, PhD*
6 x 9, 288 pp, Quality PB, 978-1-58023-368-2 **$18.99**; HC, 978-1-58023-268-5 **$24.99**

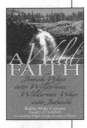

Graphic Novels / Graphic History

The Adventures of Rabbi Harvey: A Graphic Novel of Jewish Wisdom and Wit in the
Wild West *By Steve Sheinkin*
6 x 9, 144 pp, Full-color illus., Quality PB, 978-1-58023-310-1 **$16.99**

Rabbi Harvey Rides Again: A Graphic Novel of Jewish Folktales Let Loose in the
Wild West *By Steve Sheinkin*
6 x 9, 144 pp, Full-color illus., Quality PB, 978-1-58023-347-7 **$16.99**

Rabbi Harvey vs. the Wisdom Kid: A Graphic Novel of Dueling Jewish Folktales in
the Wild West *By Steve Sheinkin*
6 x 9, 144 pp, Full-color illus., Quality PB, 978-1-58023-422-1 **$16.99**

The Story of the Jews: A 4,000-Year Adventure—A Graphic History Book
By Stan Mack 6 x 9, 304 pp, Illus., Quality PB, 978-1-58023-155-8 **$18.99**

Grief / Healing

Facing Illness, Finding God: How Judaism Can Help You and Caregivers Cope
When Body or Spirit Fails *By Rabbi Joseph B. Meszler*
6 x 9, 208 pp, Quality PB, 978-1-58023-423-8 **$16.99**

Grief in Our Seasons: A Mourner's Kaddish Companion *By Rabbi Kerry M. Olitzky*
4½ x 6½, 448 pp, Quality PB, 978-1-879045-55-2 **$18.99**

Healing and the Jewish Imagination: Spiritual and Practical Perspectives on
Judaism and Health *Edited by Rabbi William Cutter, PhD*
6 x 9, 240 pp, Quality PB, 978-1-58023-373-6 **$19.99**

Healing from Despair: Choosing Wholeness in a Broken World
By Rabbi Elie Kaplan Spitz with Erica Shapiro Taylor; Foreword by Abraham J. Twerski, MD
5½ x 8½, 208 pp, Quality PB, 978-1-58023-436-8 **$16.99**

Healing of Soul, Healing of Body: Spiritual Leaders Unfold the Strength & Solace
in Psalms *Edited by Rabbi Simkha Y. Weintraub, LCSW*
6 x 9, 128 pp, 2-color illus. text, Quality PB, 978-1-879045-31-6 **$16.99**

Judaism and Health: A Handbook of Practical, Professional and Scholarly Resources
Edited by Jeff Levin, PhD, MPH, and Michele F. Prince, LCSW, MAJCS
Foreword by Rabbi Elliot N. Dorff, PhD 6 x 9, 448 pp, HC, 978-1-58023-714-7 **$50.00**

Midrash & Medicine: Healing Body and Soul in the Jewish Interpretive Tradition
Edited by Rabbi William Cutter, PhD; Foreword by Michele F. Prince, LCSW, MAJCS
6 x 9, 352 pp, Quality PB, 978-1-58023-484-9 **$21.99**

Mourning & Mitzvah, 2nd Edition: A Guided Journal for Walking the Mourner's
Path through Grief to Healing *By Rabbi Anne Brener, LCSW*
7½ x 9, 304 pp, Quality PB, 978-1-58023-113-8 **$19.99**

Tears of Sorrow, Seeds of Hope, 2nd Edition: A Jewish Spiritual Companion
for Infertility and Pregnancy Loss *By Rabbi Nina Beth Cardin*
6 x 9, 208 pp, Quality PB, 978-1-58023-233-3 **$18.99**

A Time to Mourn, a Time to Comfort, 2nd Edition
A Guide to Jewish Bereavement *By Dr. Ron Wolfson; Foreword by Rabbi David J. Wolpe*
7 x 9, 384 pp, Quality PB, 978-1-58023-253-1 **$21.99**

When a Grandparent Dies: A Kid's Own Remembering Workbook for Dealing
with Shiva and the Year Beyond *By Nechama Liss-Levinson, PhD*
8 x 10, 48 pp, 2-color text, HC, 978-1-879045-44-6 **$15.95** *For ages 7–13*

Theology / Philosophy / The Way Into... Series

The Way Into... series offers an accessible and highly usable "guided tour" of the Jewish faith, people, history and beliefs—in total, an introduction to Judaism that will enable you to understand and interact with the sacred texts of the Jewish tradition. Each volume is written by a leading contemporary scholar and teacher, and explores one key aspect of Judaism. The Way Into... series enables all readers to achieve a real sense of Jewish cultural literacy through guided study.

The Way Into Encountering God in Judaism
By Rabbi Neil Gillman, PhD
For everyone who wants to understand how Jews have encountered God throughout history and today.
6 x 9, 240 pp, Quality PB, 978-1-58023-199-2 **$18.99**; HC, 978-1-58023-025-4 **$21.95**
Also Available: **The Jewish Approach to God:** A Brief Introduction for Christians
By Rabbi Neil Gillman, PhD
5½ x 8½, 192 pp, Quality PB, 978-1-58023-190-9 **$16.95**

The Way Into Jewish Mystical Tradition
By Rabbi Lawrence Kushner
Allows readers to interact directly with the sacred mystical texts of the Jewish tradition. An accessible introduction to the concepts of Jewish mysticism, their religious and spiritual significance, and how they relate to life today.
6 x 9, 224 pp, Quality PB, 978-1-58023-200-5 **$18.99**

The Way Into Jewish Prayer
By Rabbi Lawrence A. Hoffman, PhD
Opens the door to 3,000 years of Jewish prayer, making anyone feel at home in the Jewish way of communicating with God.
6 x 9, 208 pp, Quality PB, 978-1-58023-201-2 **$18.99**

The Way Into Jewish Prayer Teacher's Guide
By Rabbi Jennifer Ossakow Goldsmith
8½ x 11, 42 pp, PB, 978-1-58023-345-3 **$8.99**
Download a free copy at www.jewishlights.com.

The Way Into Judaism and the Environment
By Jeremy Benstein, PhD
Explores the ways in which Judaism contributes to contemporary social-environmental issues, the extent to which Judaism is part of the problem and how it can be part of the solution.
6 x 9, 288 pp, Quality PB, 978-1-58023-368-2 **$18.99**; HC, 978-1-58023-268-5 **$24.99**

The Way Into *Tikkun Olam* (Repairing the World)
By Rabbi Elliot N. Dorff, PhD
An accessible introduction to the Jewish concept of the individual's responsibility to care for others and repair the world.
6 x 9, 304 pp, Quality PB, 978-1-58023-328-6 **$18.99**

The Way Into Torah
By Rabbi Norman J. Cohen, PhD
Helps guide you in the exploration of the origins and development of Torah, explains why it should be studied and how to do it.
6 x 9, 176 pp, Quality PB, 978-1-58023-198-5 **$16.99**

The Way Into the Varieties of Jewishness
By Sylvia Barack Fishman, PhD
Explores the religious and historical understanding of what it has meant to be Jewish from ancient times to the present controversy over "Who is a Jew?"
6 x 9, 288 pp, Quality PB, 978-1-58023-367-5 **$18.99**; HC, 978-1-58023-030-8 **$24.99**

Theology / Philosophy

Does the Soul Survive? 2nd Edition: A Jewish Journey to Belief in Afterlife, Past Lives & Living with Purpose *By Rabbi Elie Kaplan Spitz; Foreword by Brian L. Weiss, MD* A skeptic turned believer recounts his quest to uncover the Jewish tradition's answers about what happens to our souls after death.
6 x 9, 288 pp, Quality PB, 978-1-58023-818-2 **$18.99**

God of Becoming and Relationship: The Dynamic Nature of Process Theology *By Rabbi Bradley Shavit Artson, DHL* Explains how Process Theology breaks us free from the strictures of ancient Greek and medieval European philosophy. 6 x 9, 208 pp, HC, 978-1-58023-713-0 **$24.99**

God of Becoming and Relationship Study Guide
8½ x 11, 53 pp, PB, 978-1-58023-825-0 **$9.99**

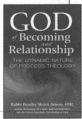

The Way of Man: According to Hasidic Teaching
By Martin Buber; New Translation and Introduction by Rabbi Bernard H. Mehlman and Dr. Gabriel E. Padawer; Foreword by Paul Mendes-Flohr
An accessible and engaging new translation of Buber's classic work—*available as an eBook only.* eBook, 978-1-58023-601-0 Digital List Price **$14.99**

Believing and Its Tensions: A Personal Conversation about God, Torah, Suffering and Death in Jewish Thought *By Rabbi Neil Gillman, PhD*
5½ x 8½, 144 pp, HC, 978-1-58023-669-0 **$19.99**

The Death of Death: Resurrection and Immortality in Jewish Thought
By Rabbi Neil Gillman, PhD 6 x 9, 336 pp, Quality PB, 978-1-58023-081-0 **$19.99**

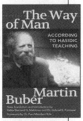

From Defender to Critic: The Search for a New Jewish Self
By Dr. David Hartman (z"l) 6 x 9, 336 pp, HC, 978-1-58023-515-0 **$35.00**

The God Who Hates Lies: Confronting & Rethinking Jewish Tradition
By Dr. David Hartman (z"l) with Charlie Buckholtz 6 x 9, 208 pp, Quality PB, 978-1-58023-790-1 **$19.99**

A Heart of Many Rooms: Celebrating the Many Voices within Judaism
By Dr. David Hartman (z"l) 6 x 9, 352 pp, Quality PB, 978-1-58023-156-5 **$19.95**

Jewish Theology in Our Time: A New Generation Explores the Foundations and Future of Jewish Belief *Edited by Rabbi Elliot J. Cosgrove, PhD; Foreword by Rabbi David J. Wolpe; Preface by Rabbi Carole B. Balin, PhD*
6 x 9, 240 pp, Quality PB, 978-1-58023-630-0 **$19.99**; HC, 978-1-58023-413-9 **$24.99**

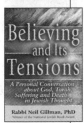

Maimonides—Essential Teachings on Jewish Faith & Ethics: The Book of Knowledge & the Thirteen Principles of Faith—Annotated & Explained
Translation and Annotation by Rabbi Marc D. Angel, PhD
5½ x 8½, 224 pp, Quality PB, 978-1-59473-311-6 **$18.99***

Our Religious Brains: What Cognitive Science Reveals about Belief, Morality, Community and Our Relationship with God
By Rabbi Ralph D. Mecklenburger; Foreword by Dr. Howard Kelfer; Preface by Dr. Neil Gillman
6 x 9, 224 pp, HC, 978-1-58023-508-2 **$24.99**

Your Word Is Fire: The Hasidic Masters on Contemplative Prayer
Edited and translated by Rabbi Arthur Green, PhD, and Barry W. Holtz
6 x 9, 160 pp, Quality PB, 978-1-879045-25-5 **$16.99**

God, Faith & Identity from the Ashes
Reflections of Children and Grandchildren of Holocaust Survivors
Almost ninety contributors from sixteen countries inform, challenge and inspire people of all backgrounds. *Edited by Menachem Z. Rosensaft; Prologue by Elie Wiesel*
6 x 9, 352 pp, HC, 978-1-58023-805-2 **$25.00**

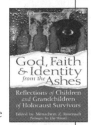

I Am Jewish
Personal Reflections Inspired by the Last Words of Daniel Pearl
Almost 150 Jews—both famous and not—from all walks of life, from all around the world, write about many aspects of their Judaism.
Edited by Judea and Ruth Pearl 6 x 9, 304 pp, Deluxe PB w/ flaps, 978-1-58023-259-3 **$19.99**
Download a free copy of the *I Am Jewish Teacher's Guide* at www.jewishlights.com.

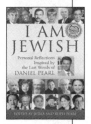

*A book from SkyLight Paths, Jewish Lights' sister imprint

Spirituality / Prayer

Davening: A Guide to Meaningful Jewish Prayer
By Rabbi Zalman Schachter-Shalomi (z"l) with Joel Segel; Foreword by Rabbi Lawrence Kushner
A fresh approach to prayer for all who wish to appreciate the power of prayer's poetry, song and ritual, and to join the age-old conversation that Jews have had with God. 6 x 9, 240 pp, Quality PB, 978-1-58023-627-0 **$18.99**

Jewish Men Pray: Words of Yearning, Praise, Petition, Gratitude and Wonder from Traditional and Contemporary Sources
Edited by Rabbi Kerry M. Olitzky and Stuart M. Matlins; Foreword by Rabbi Bradley Shavit Artson, DHL
A celebration of Jewish men's voices in prayer—to strengthen, heal, comfort, and inspire—from the ancient world up to our own day.
5 x 7¼, 400 pp, HC, 978-1-58023-628-7 **$19.99**

Making Prayer Real: Leading Jewish Spiritual Voices on Why Prayer Is Difficult and What to Do about It *By Rabbi Mike Comins* 6 x 9, 320 pp, Quality PB, 978-1-58023-417-7 **$18.99**

Witnesses to the One: The Spiritual History of the *Sh'ma*
By Rabbi Joseph B. Meszler; Foreword by Rabbi Elyse Goldstein
6 x 9, 176 pp, Quality PB, 978-1-58023-400-9 **$16.99**; HC, 978-1-58023-309-5 **$19.99**

My People's Prayer Book Series: Traditional Prayers, Modern Commentaries *Edited by Rabbi Lawrence A. Hoffman, PhD*
Provides diverse and exciting commentary to the traditional liturgy. Will help you find new wisdom in Jewish prayer, and bring liturgy into your life. Each book includes Hebrew text, modern translations and commentaries from all perspectives of the Jewish world.

Vol. 1—The *Sh'ma* and Its Blessings
  7 x 10, 168 pp, HC, 978-1-879045-79-8 **$29.99**
Vol. 2—The *Amidah* 7 x 10, 240 pp, HC, 978-1-879045-80-4 **$29.99**
Vol. 3—*P'sukei D'zimrah* (Morning Psalms)
  7 x 10, 240 pp, HC, 978-1-879045-81-1 **$29.99**
Vol. 4—*Seder K'riat Hatorah* (The Torah Service)
  7 x 10, 264 pp, HC, 978-1-879045-82-8 **$29.99**
Vol. 5—*Birkhot Hashachar* (Morning Blessings)
  7 x 10, 240 pp, HC, 978-1-879045-83-5 **$29.99**
Vol. 6—*Tachanun* and Concluding Prayers
  7 x 10, 240 pp, HC, 978-1-879045-84-2 **$24.95**
Vol. 7—Shabbat at Home 7 x 10, 240 pp, HC, 978-1-879045-85-9 **$29.99**
Vol. 8—*Kabbalat Shabbat* (Welcoming Shabbat in the Synagogue)
  7 x 10, 240 pp, HC, 978-1-58023-121-3 **$24.99**
Vol. 9—Welcoming the Night: *Minchah* and *Ma'ariv* (Afternoon and
  Evening Prayer) 7 x 10, 272 pp, HC, 978-1-58023-262-3 **$24.99**
Vol. 10—Shabbat Morning: *Shacharit* and *Musaf* (Morning and
  Additional Services) 7 x 10, 240 pp, HC, 978-1-58023-240-1 **$29.99**

Spirituality / Lawrence Kushner

I'm God; You're Not: Observations on Organized Religion & Other Disguises of the Ego
  6 x 9, 256 pp, Quality PB, 978-1-58023-513-6 **$18.99**; HC, 978-1-58023-441-2 **$21.99**
The Book of Letters: A Mystical Hebrew Alphabet
  Popular HC Edition, 6 x 9, 80 pp, 2-color text, 978-1-879045-00-2 **$24.95**
  Collector's Limited Edition, 9 x 12, 80 pp, gold-foil-embossed pages, w/ limited-edition silkscreened print, 978-1-879045-04-0 **$349.00**
The Book of Miracles: A Young Person's Guide to Jewish Spiritual Awareness
  6 x 9, 96 pp, 2-color illus., HC, 978-1-879045-78-1 **$16.95** *For ages 9–13*
God Was in This Place & I, i Did Not Know: Finding Self, Spirituality and Ultimate Meaning 6 x 9, 192 pp, Quality PB, 978-1-879045-33-0 **$18.99**
Honey from the Rock: An Introduction to Jewish Mysticism
  6 x 9, 176 pp, Quality PB, 978-1-58023-073-5 **$18.99**
Invisible Lines of Connection: Sacred Stories of the Ordinary
  5½ x 8½, 160 pp, Quality PB, 978-1-879045-98-9 **$16.99**
The Way Into Jewish Mystical Tradition
  6 x 9, 224 pp, Quality PB, 978-1-58023-200-5 **$18.99**

Inspiration

The Chutzpah Imperative: Empowering Today's Jews for a Life That Matters By Rabbi Edward Feinstein; Foreword by Rabbi Laura Geller
A new view of chutzpah as Jewish self-empowerment to be God's partner and repair the world. Reveals Judaism's ancient message, its deepest purpose and most precious treasures. 6 x 9, 192 pp, HC, 978-1-58023-792-5 **$21.99**

Judaism's Ten Best Ideas: A Brief Guide for Seekers
By Rabbi Arthur Green, PhD A highly accessible introduction to Judaism's greatest contributions to civilization, drawing on Jewish mystical tradition and the author's experience. 4½ x 6½, 112 pp, Quality PB, 978-1-58023-803-8 **$9.99**

Into the Fullness of the Void: A Spiritual Autobiography By Dov Elbaum
One of Israel's leading cultural figures provides insights and guidance for all of us. 6 x 9, 304 pp, Quality PB, 978-1-58023-715-4 **$18.99**

The Bridge to Forgiveness: Stories and Prayers for Finding God and Restoring Wholeness
By Rabbi Karyn D. Kedar 6 x 9, 176 pp, Quality PB, 978-1-58023-451-1 **$16.99**

The Empty Chair: Finding Hope and Joy—Timeless Wisdom from a Hasidic Master, Rebbe Nachman of Breslov Adapted by Moshe Mykoff and the Breslov Research Institute
4 x 6, 128 pp, Deluxe PB w/ flaps, 978-1-879045-67-5 **$9.99**

The Gentle Weapon: Prayers for Everyday and Not-So-Everyday Moments— Timeless Wisdom from the Teachings of the Hasidic Master Rebbe Nachman of Breslov Adapted by Moshe Mykoff and S. C. Mizrahi, together with the Breslov Research Institute
4 x 6, 144 pp, Deluxe PB w/ flaps, 978-1-58023-022-3 **$9.99**

God Whispers: Stories of the Soul, Lessons of the Heart By Rabbi Karyn D. Kedar
6 x 9, 176 pp, Quality PB, 978-1-58023-088-9 **$16.99**

God's To-Do List: 103 Ways to Be an Angel and Do God's Work on Earth
By Dr. Ron Wolfson 6 x 9, 144 pp, Quality PB, 978-1-58023-301-9 **$16.99**

Happiness and the Human Spirit: The Spirituality of Becoming the Best You Can Be
By Rabbi Abraham J. Twerski, MD
6 x 9, 176 pp, Quality PB, 978-1-58023-404-7 **$16.99**; HC, 978-1-58023-343-9 **$19.99**

Life's Daily Blessings: Inspiring Reflections on Gratitude and Joy for Every Day, Based on Jewish Wisdom By Rabbi Kerry M. Olitzky 4½ x 6½, 368 pp, Quality PB, 978-1-58023-396-5 **$16.99**

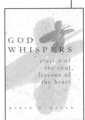

Restful Reflections: Nighttime Inspiration to Calm the Soul, Based on Jewish Wisdom
By Rabbi Kerry M. Olitzky and Rabbi Lori Forman-Jacobi
4½ x 6½, 448 pp, Quality PB, 978-1-58023-091-9 **$16.99**

Sacred Intentions: Morning Inspiration to Strengthen the Spirit, Based on Jewish Wisdom
By Rabbi Kerry M. Olitzky and Rabbi Lori Forman-Jacobi
4½ x 6½, 448 pp, Quality PB, 978-1-58023-061-2 **$16.99**

Saying No and Letting Go: Jewish Wisdom on Making Room for What Matters Most
By Rabbi Edwin Goldberg, DHL; Foreword by Rabbi Naomi Levy
6 x 9, 192 pp, Quality PB, 978-1-58023-670-6 **$16.99**

The Seven Questions You're Asked in Heaven: Reviewing and Renewing Your Life on Earth By Dr. Ron Wolfson 6 x 9, 176 pp, Quality PB, 978-1-58023-407-8 **$16.99**

Kabbalah / Mysticism

Ehyeh: A Kabbalah for Tomorrow
By Rabbi Arthur Green, PhD 6 x 9, 224 pp, Quality PB, 978-1-58023-213-5 **$18.99**

The Gift of Kabbalah: Discovering the Secrets of Heaven, Renewing Your Life on Earth
By Tamar Frankiel, PhD 6 x 9, 256 pp, Quality PB, 978-1-58023-141-1 **$18.99**

Jewish Mysticism and the Spiritual Life: Classical Texts, Contemporary Reflections Edited by Dr. Lawrence Fine, Dr. Eitan Fishbane and Rabbi Or N. Rose
6 x 9, 256 pp, Quality PB, 978-1-58023-719-2 **$18.99**

Seek My Face: A Jewish Mystical Theology By Rabbi Arthur Green, PhD
6 x 9, 304 pp, Quality PB, 978-1-58023-130-5 **$19.95**

Zohar: Annotated & Explained Translation & Annotation by Dr. Daniel C. Matt
Foreword by Andrew Harvey 5½ x 8½, 176 pp, Quality PB, 978-1-893361-51-5 **$18.99**
(A book from SkyLight Paths, Jewish Lights' sister imprint)

See also *The Way Into Jewish Mystical Tradition* in The Way Into... Series

Spirituality

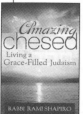

Amazing Chesed: Living a Grace-Filled Judaism
By Rabbi Rami Shapiro Drawing from ancient and contemporary, traditional and non-traditional Jewish wisdom, reclaims the idea of grace in Judaism.
6 x 9, 176 pp, Quality PB, 978-1-58023-624-9 **$16.99**

Jewish with Feeling: A Guide to Meaningful Jewish Practice
By Rabbi Zalman Schachter-Shalomi (z"l) with Joel Segel
Takes off from basic questions like "Why be Jewish?" and whether the word *God* still speaks to us today and lays out a vision for a whole-person Judaism.
5½ x 8½, 288 pp, Quality PB, 978-1-58023-691-1 **$19.99**

Perennial Wisdom for the Spiritually Independent: Sacred Teachings—Annotated & Explained *Annotation by Rabbi Rami Shapiro; Foreword by Richard Rohr*
Weaves sacred texts and teachings from the world's major religions into a coherent exploration of the five core questions at the heart of every religion's search.
5½ x 8½, 336 pp, Quality PB, 978-1-59473-515-8 **$16.99***

A Book of Life: Embracing Judaism as a Spiritual Practice
By Rabbi Michael Strassfeld 6 x 9, 544 pp, Quality PB, 978-1-58023-247-0 **$24.99**

Bringing the Psalms to Life: How to Understand and Use the Book of Psalms
By Rabbi Daniel F. Polish, PhD 6 x 9, 208 pp, Quality PB, 978-1-58023-157-2 **$18.99**

Does the Soul Survive? 2nd Edition: A Jewish Journey to Belief in Afterlife, Past Lives & Living with Purpose *By Rabbi Elie Kaplan Spitz; Foreword by Brian L. Weiss, MD*
6 x 9, 288 pp, Quality PB, 978-1-58023-818-2 **$18.99**

Entering the Temple of Dreams: Jewish Prayers, Movements and Meditations for the End of the Day *By Tamar Frankiel, PhD, and Judy Greenfeld*
7 x 10, 192 pp, illus., Quality PB, 978-1-58023-079-7 **$16.95**

First Steps to a New Jewish Spirit: Reb Zalman's Guide to Recapturing the Intimacy & Ecstasy in Your Relationship with God *By Rabbi Zalman Schachter-Shalomi (z"l) with Donald Gropman*
6 x 9, 144 pp, Quality PB, 978-1-58023-182-4 **$16.95**

Foundations of Sephardic Spirituality: The Inner Life of Jews of the Ottoman Empire
By Rabbi Marc D. Angel, PhD 6 x 9, 224 pp, Quality PB, 978-1-58023-341-5 **$18.99**

God & the Big Bang: Discovering Harmony between Science & Spirituality
By Dr. Daniel C. Matt 6 x 9, 216 pp, Quality PB, 978-1-879045-89-7 **$18.99**

God in Our Relationships: Spirituality between People from the Teachings of Martin Buber
By Rabbi Dennis S. Ross 5½ x 8½, 160 pp, Quality PB, 978-1-58023-147-3 **$16.95**

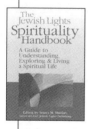

The God Upgrade: Finding Your 21st-Century Spirituality in Judaism's 5,000-Year-Old Tradition *By Rabbi Jamie Korngold; Foreword by Rabbi Harold M. Schulweis*
6 x 9, 176 pp, Quality PB, 978-1-58023-443-6 **$15.99**

The Jewish Lights Spirituality Handbook: A Guide to Understanding, Exploring & Living a Spiritual Life *Edited by Stuart M. Matlins*
6 x 9, 456 pp, Quality PB, 978-1-58023-093-3 **$19.99**

Judaism, Physics and God: Searching for Sacred Metaphors in a Post-Einstein World
By Rabbi David W. Nelson
6 x 9, 352 pp, Quality PB, inc. reader's discussion guide, 978-1-58023-306-4 **$18.99**
HC, 352 pp, 978-1-58023-252-4 **$24.99**

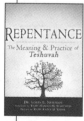

Repentance: The Meaning and Practice of Teshuvah
By Dr. Louis E. Newman; Foreword by Rabbi Harold M. Schulweis; Preface by Rabbi Karyn D. Kedar
6 x 9, 256 pp, HC, 978-1-58023-426-9 **$24.99**; Quality PB, 978-1-58023-718-5 **$18.99**

The Sabbath Soul: Mystical Reflections on the Transformative Power of Holy Time
Selection, Translation and Commentary by Eitan Fishbane, PhD
6 x 9, 208 pp, Quality PB, 978-1-58023-459-7 **$18.99**

Tanya, the Masterpiece of Hasidic Wisdom: Selections Annotated & Explained
Translation & Annotation by Rabbi Rami Shapiro; Foreword by Rabbi Zalman Schachter-Shalomi (z"l)
5½ x 8½, 240 pp, Quality PB, 978-1-59473-275-1 **$18.99***

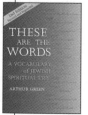

These Are the Words, 2nd Edition: A Vocabulary of Jewish Spiritual Life
By Rabbi Arthur Green, PhD 6 x 9, 320 pp, Quality PB, 978-1-58023-494-8 **$19.99**

*A book from SkyLight Paths, Jewish Lights' sister imprint

Meditation / Yoga

Increasing Wholeness: Jewish Wisdom & Guided Meditations to Strengthen & Calm Body, Heart, Mind & Spirit
By Rabbi Elie Kaplan Spitz Combines Jewish tradition, contemporary psychology and world spiritual writings with practical contemplative exercises to guide you to see the familiar in fresh new ways.
6 x 9, 208 pp, Quality PB, 978-1-58023-823-6 **$19.99**

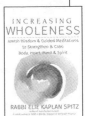

Living the Life of Jewish Meditation: A Comprehensive Guide to Practice and Experience *By Rabbi Yoel Glick*
Combines the knowledge of Judaism with the spiritual practice of Yoga to lead you to an encounter with your true self. Includes nineteen different meditations.
6 x 9, 272 pp, Quality PB, 978-1-58023-802-1 **$18.99**

Mussar **Yoga:** Blending an Ancient Jewish Spiritual Practice with Yoga to Transform Body and Soul
By Edith R. Brotman, PhD, RYT-500; Foreword by Alan Morinis
A clear and easy-to-use introduction to an embodied spiritual practice for anyone seeking profound and lasting self-transformation.
7 x 9, 224 pp, 40+ b/w photos, Quality PB, 978-1-58023-784-0 **$18.99**

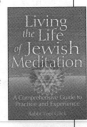

The Magic of Hebrew Chant: Healing the Spirit, Transforming the Mind, Deepening Love *By Rabbi Shefa Gold; Foreword by Sylvia Boorstein*
Introduces this transformative spiritual practice as a way to unlock the power of sacred texts and make prayer and meditation the delight of your life. Includes musical notations. 6 x 9, 352 pp, Quality PB, 978-1-58023-671-3 **$24.99**

The Magic of Hebrew Chant Companion—The Big Book of Musical Notations and Incantations 8½ x 11, 154 pp, PB, 978-1-58023-722-2 **$19.99**

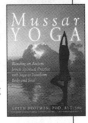

Aleph-Bet Yoga: Embodying the Hebrew Letters for Physical and Spiritual Well-Being
By Steven A. Rapp; Foreword by Tamar Frankiel, PhD, and Judy Greenfeld; Preface by Hart Lazer
7 x 10, 128 pp, b/w photos, Quality PB, Lay-flat binding, 978-1-58023-162-6 **$16.95**

Discovering Jewish Meditation, 2nd Edition
Instruction & Guidance for Learning an Ancient Spiritual Practice
By Nan Fink Gefen, PhD 6 x 9, 208 pp, Quality PB, 978-1-58023-462-7 **$16.99**

The Handbook of Jewish Meditation Practices
A Guide for Enriching the Sabbath and Other Days of Your Life
By Rabbi David A. Cooper 6 x 9, 208 pp, Quality PB, 978-1-58023-102-2 **$16.95**

Jewish Meditation Practices for Everyday Life: Awakening Your Heart, Connecting with God *By Rabbi Jeff Roth* 6 x 9, 224 pp, Quality PB, 978-1-58023-397-2 **$18.99**

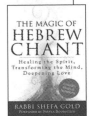

Ritual / Sacred Practices

God in Your Body: Kabbalah, Mindfulness and Embodied Spiritual Practice
By Jay Michaelson 6 x 9, 272 pp, Quality PB, 978-1-58023-304-0 **$18.99**

Jewish Ritual: A Brief Introduction for Christians
By Rabbi Kerry M. Olitzky and Rabbi Daniel Judson
5½ x 8½, 144 pp, Quality PB, 978-1-58023-210-4 **$14.99**

The Rituals & Practices of a Jewish Life: A Handbook for Personal Spiritual Renewal
Edited by Rabbi Kerry M. Olitzky and Rabbi Daniel Judson
6 x 9, 272 pp, Illus., Quality PB, 978-1-58023-169-5 **$18.95**

The Sacred Art of Lovingkindness: Preparing to Practice
By Rabbi Rami Shapiro 5½ x 8½, 176 pp, Quality PB, 978-1-59473-151-8 **$16.99***

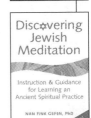

Mystery & Detective Fiction

Criminal Kabbalah: An Intriguing Anthology of Jewish Mystery & Detective Fiction
Edited by Lawrence W. Raphael; Foreword by Laurie R. King
6 x 9, 256 pp, Quality PB, 978-1-58023-109-1 **$16.95**

Mystery Midrash: An Anthology of Jewish Mystery & Detective Fiction
Edited by Lawrence W. Raphael; Preface by Joel Siegel
6 x 9, 304 pp, Quality PB, 978-1-58023-055-1 **$16.95**

*A book from SkyLight Paths, Jewish Lights' sister imprint

About Jewish Lights

People of all faiths and backgrounds yearn for books that attract, engage, educate, and spiritually inspire.

Our principal goal is to stimulate thought and help all people learn about who the Jewish People are, where they come from, and what the future can be made to hold. While people of our diverse Jewish heritage are the primary audience, our books speak to people in the Christian world as well and will broaden their understanding of Judaism and the roots of their own faith.

We bring to you authors who are at the forefront of spiritual thought and experience. While each has something different to say, they all say it in a voice that you can hear.

Our books are designed to welcome you and then to engage, stimulate, and inspire. We judge our success not only by whether or not our books are beautiful and commercially successful, but by whether or not they make a difference in your life.

For your information and convenience, at the back of this book we have provided a list of other Jewish Lights books you might find interesting and useful. They cover all the categories of your life:

Bar/Bat Mitzvah	Life Cycle
Bible Study / Midrash	Meditation
Children's Books	Men's Interest
Congregation Resources	Parenting
Current Events / History	Prayer / Ritual / Sacred Practice
Ecology / Environment	Social Justice
Fiction: Mystery, Science Fiction	Spirituality
Grief / Healing	Theology / Philosophy
Holidays / Holy Days	Travel
Inspiration	Twelve Steps
Kabbalah / Mysticism / Enneagram	Women's Interest

Stuart M. Matlins, Publisher